INDIAN WRITING in ENGLISH

VOLUME – I

Edited by

RAMA KUNDU

ATLANTIC
PUBLISHERS & DISTRIBUTORS

Published by
ATLANTIC PUBLISHERS AND DISTRIBUTORS
B-2, Vishal Enclave, Opp. Rajouri Garden, New Delhi-27
Phones : 5413460, 5429987, 5466842

Sales Office
4215/1, Ansari Road, Darya Ganj, New Delhi-02
Phones : 3273880, 3285873, 3280451
Fax : 91-11-3285873
web : www.atlanticbooks.com
e-mail : info@atlanticbooks.com

ISBN 81-269-0205-1 (Vol. I)
ISBN 81-269-0206-X (Set)

Typeset at
APD Computer Graphics, Delhi
Printed in India at
Nice Printing Press, Delhi

Introduction

Indian English writing is a vast arena today. With new trends emerging, new talents making their mark, new creative and critical branches sprouting in various directions, as well as with the thematic varieties, technical experiments, and linguistic innovations—it is now 'God's plenty.' The extraordinary richness and variety of Indian writing today, indeed, pose a challenging task for any critic or anthologist in the area, since it has become next to impossible to give any comprehensive view or idea of this fast-growing literature in its totality within the compass of a single volume.

Still it remains the critic's responsibility as well as pleasure to 'find' the new authors and texts side by side with the older and already canonized ones. As Robert Kroetsch, the Canadian author, says, 'We want the critic to find us out'—our Indian authors today also should legitimately expect the perceptive-responsive critic to 'find' them out. It is especially needed in the present case since the Indian writers in English are still engaged in the process of writing from outside the mainstream, and, therefore, are in serious need of the right critical attention and understanding.

It is precisely this situation that has been kept in view in compiling the present anthology of a bunch of critical essays on a cross-section of Indian fiction, poetry and drama in English. Quite a number of the texts discussed in this volume have been written in recent years, whereas a few earlier texts—M.R. Anand's, for example—have also been included in order to help the reader to view the spectrum in a total perspective. The critical range of this volume includes Mulk Raj Anand, Khushwant Singh, Ruth Jhabvala, Anita Desai, Manju Kapur,

Amitav Ghosh in fiction, A.K. Ramanujan, Nissim Ezekiel, Kamala Das in poetry and Girish Karnad's *Tuglaq* and *Hayavadana* in drama.

Chaman Nahal had claimed, "There is a future for Commonwealth literature only when we respect our native identities. And there is a future for it when we allow native brands of English, more dialectical and plastic than the queen's English, to develop." Whereas Chaman Nahal's well-known contention holds good for Indian English writing in general, it particularly helps us to understand the specific problems and challenges that the pioneers and early generations of writers had to grapple with—the tough task they had set themselves of reconciling the demands of a double heritage, and of moulding a new literature out of a fructifying tension between the indigenous and the foreign, the old and the new. It appears that by the 1980s Indian writers have already reached a new turn; they have already outgrown the anxieties and compulsions of the era of aggressive/self-conscious cultural nationalism and are now presently engaged in an interesting creative process of forging a unique tie between post-colonialism and post-modernism. This is particularly evident in the writings of Amitav Ghosh, Arundhati Roy, Githa Hariharan, *et al.* The articles constituting the present volume allow us a glimpse into both these trends in a brief way.

Ashok Kumar Bachchan, in his article on Mulk Raj Anand's experiment with the language in his early novels, probes the novelist's original ways of handling with the challenge of Indianizing English. As Raja Rao had said in his 'Foreword' to *Kanthapura*, "We are all instinctively bilingual, many of us writing in our own language and English. *We cannot write like the English. We should not. We cannot write only as Indians* [emphasis added]. We have grown to look at the large world as part of us. Our method of expression, therefore, has to be a dialect which will some day prove to be as distinctive and colourful as the Irish or the American." Dr Bachchan shows with adequate illustrations as to how Anand tries to devise this new idiom in his early works.

Khushwant Singh's *Train to Pakistan* is one of the canonised books on the theme of Partition, the publication of which had justly won instant fame for its author. It captures a particularly traumatic moment of our national history, which has left an indelible scar on the psyche of at least a generation of writers and readers. Still Mr Singh does not lose his taste for the comical side of things, and Mallikarjun Patil brings out this element of mellowed humour in the novel, which, he finds, adds a softening touch to the grim reality of the contemporary history as depicted in the story.

However, by 1999, Khushwant Singh appears to have already come a long way from the village of Mano Majra, and the 'train' that had started from Mano Majra has apparently taken him toward a different direction. Or is it possible that the latent carnival element of the earlier phase only progressively surfaces in the writings of old age? *The Company of Women* (1999), according to the authorial admission, is composed of 'figments' of the 'senile fantasies' of an octogenarian; though the author claims to have achieved celebration of sex, many find the book to have sadly failed to justify the claim. Basavaraj Naikar, however, carefully examines the controversial work by Singh in order to show that in spite of the preponderance of so-called pornographic elements, the novel also symptomatises certain basic patterns of human behaviour and way of the world.

Marie Fernandes's paper offers an interesting comparative study between two texts selected across the gulf of two different continents and centuries: Bronte's *Jane Eyre* and Jhabvala's *Heat and Dust*. In her subtle and penetrative study of the two novels, the critic establishes the points of their correspondence at various levels and thus helps the reader to see both the novels in perspective; she also examines the premises of feminism and imperialism as used by the respective authors in dealing with their female protagonists *vis-á-vis* the Byronic hero figure.

Journey has been an archetypal motif in literature across space and time, and it has been an old tradition in Europe to regard India as a trope around which the motif of journey comes to operate. Usha Rani, in her article on two novels of Anita Desai, analyses the novelist's use of the old motif and trope in a new way. The critic focuses on the journeying protagonists of the two novels, who come over from Europe to India and brings out the core of sadness in their experiences—their bewilderment at never reaching the 'home' they looked for, as India proves but an ambiguous 'Ithaca' at best.

Suman Jana, on the other hand, examines Desai's *Journey to Ithaca* as a quest-novel, in which India finally emerges to be a religious 'space,' capable of offering some positive messages in spite of all its ambiguities.

Journey to Ithaca sticks out from the rest of Desai's novels—both in subject and treatment. In the subsequent novel *Fasting, Feasting* (1999) she returns to her accustomed mode. In his critique of the novel, M.Q. Khan underscores the author's sensitive and insightful treatment of the suffering of a simple self-sacrificing woman trapped by her own family into a barren life. In an exquisitely lucid way, the critic brings out the uniqueness of the novel in Desai's canon and shows as to how in this particular work Desai tries to transcend all her earlier limitations and presents a 'simple' human situation in the most simple way.

Asha Choubey, again, makes a comparative study of *Fasting, Feasting* with another novel of the 1990s, *i.e.*, Manju Kapur's *Difficult Daughters* (1997). The critic perceptively underscores the respective ways of the two authors to explode the myth of motherhood. She highlights the problematization of mother-daughter relationship which is, indeed, a major emergent preoccupation with the feminist writers over the world, and carefully probes the down-to-earth de-romanticised portraiture of the mother-daughter relationship in these two recent novels by two women writers. The critic's scholarship places her analysis on a solid theoretical foundation.

Sobha Chattopadhyay's paper on Amitav Ghosh is particularly enlightening as she, in her exquisitely perceptive and scholarly way, has taken her discussion forward to the difficulty of 'framing' Indian English writing of the 1990s which she rightly defines as a post-modernist phase of post-colonial novel in India. Sobha analyses, interprets and problematizes the post-modern post-colonial novel in India with reference to Amitav Ghosh's *The Calcutta Chromosome* (1996) and shows how Ghosh freely sweeps across the 'shadow lines' between realism and fantasy.

Mallikarjun Patil's lucid paper on Nissim Ezekiel serves as a general introduction to, and useful overview of Nissim Ezekiel's poetry. It is simultaneously informative, perceptive and analytical.

Qamar Talat examines Ezekiel's poetry from the perspective of Ezekiel's poetic response *vis-á-vis* the contemporary Indian social-political scenario.

Suka Joshua makes an excellent scholarly exploration into Ezekiel's poetry in order to define the poet's concept of 'Poesy.' The critic underscores Ezekiel's preference for a balance between freedom and discipline, between experimentations and conventional styles: he also probes Ezekiel's ideas like 'the dancing minute,' 'the spacious hour,' the 'calculated couplet,' *et al.*, with illuminating illustrations to make the point. Joshua also compares Ezekiel and Ramanujan with reference to their respective approaches to the subject of 'Poesy.'

N. Sharada Iyer offers a sensitive analysis of the texture of Ramanujan's poetry, and catches the nostalgia for the home left behind by the expatriate who appears to be torn between the contrary pulls of his old and new homes, and of modernity and tradition.

Santosh Chakrabarti examines Kamala Das's poetry from her own premise—the feminist stance of a 'hurt' woman. The critic makes an exhaustive study of this psychic wound as it recurs in the poems as subject, mood, image and expression; he also notes the boldness of the poet in frankly articulating tabooed feelings and desires.

Anurag Chauhan presents a lucid and detailed comparison between Shaw's *The Apple Cart* and Karnad's *Tuglaq* with particular reference to the thematic similarity of the two plays as also their respective treatment of specific historical-political situations and philosophical-visionary ideas regarding statesmanship.

A very rich paper is Mohit K. Ray's study of Karnad's *Hayavadana*. Ray approaches the play from the angle of Karnad's use of source-texts, folk form and ritual in *Hayavadana*. In this erudite essay which is yet written with extraordinary lucidity, Ray places Karnad in the emerging trend of avant-garde drama across the post-colonial world, and shows as to how Karnad assimilates in his play the Western dramatic convention, the tradition of Indian classical drama, and the rich heritage of Indian folk forms in order to create a rich array of significances in the modern context.

A word of apology about the format. Uniformity of format should have been desirable. Some of the papers were in the standard format of *MLA Handbook*, 3rd edition, but it was not possible for obvious reasons to re-format the rest.

I thank all the contributors for their scholarly papers. I am particularly grateful to my learned colleagues, Professor Sobha Chattopadhyay and Santosh Chakrabarti for kindly responding to my invitation to contribute a paper and thus enriching the collection. I am also grateful to Professor M.Q. Khan, a renowned senior scholar, for allowing me to include his paper.

I acknowledge my deep gratitude to Professor Mohit K. Ray for permitting me to print his valuable paper on Karnad, which was presented in the International Conference on World

Drama, held in Estonia in September 2001. I am also indebted to him for unstinted scholarly help and advice in editing this volume.

Last, but not the least, is my pleasurable duty to acknowledge my thanks to Dr K.R. Gupta, Managing Director of Atlantic Publishers and Distributors, for inviting me to edit the volume, while shouldering all the drudgeries of the job himself—from collecting the papers to seeing the book through the press and all the details in between.

RAMA KUNDU
Editor

CONTENTS

1

Indian Nuances of Anand's English: An Examination of His Early Novels

ASHOK KUMAR BACHCHAN

Mulk Raj Anand adopts English as the medium of his artistic expression and nourishes it to proper growth, in his own way. He applies various methods, techniques and devices to impart an Indian identity to his English as an untiring experimenter. T.D. Brunton reflects on the tendencies and possibilities of the Indianization of English:

> When a novel first reached India in the late 18th and 19th century, it must have seemed quite strange, even to those few educated Indians who could read English [...]. The strength and maturity of much Indian writing in English are beyond dispute, and it ought not to be necessary at this stage to ask such questions whether an Indian can write in English. But amidst much bold creativity, there still lingers a sterile tradition which blights even major talents [...]. The tradition I refer to is that of Indianness. It is still frequently assumed that a novel in English by an Indian author can only be justified if it is Indian in some peculiar and essential fashion. Thus novels come to be valued not so much upon their power as fiction, as upon their content of this national quintessence.[1]

There are many reasons for justifying the peculiarities of Indo-English novels *viz.* peculiar Indian speech-habits, social conditions, traditional values, ethical and theological concepts which distinguish and identify Indian life. At a moment of sudden pain an Indian (except the Christians who live here) never cries 'Christ, o, Christ!' but 'Ram, He Ram' or 'Ya Allah' or 'Wahe Guru', etc. There would be nothing more absurd than to depict Indian peasants, labours and outcastes in the standard British diction and phraseology. In Anand's pre-Independence novels, *i.e.* the novels of the first phase, characters with all their social, personal, economic, political and religious problems and linguistic habits seem to be moving and breathing with us. He wrote *Untouchable* (1935), *Coolie* (1936), *Two Leaves And A Bud* (1937), *The Village* (1938), *Across The Black Waters* (1938) and *The Sword and the Sickle* (1940). The last novel of this phase is *The Big Heart* (1945). He is so alive to Indian consciousness, Indian sensibility and to the problem of exploitation of the poor by the rich that the entire locale of Indian life is recreated before the reader.

Dr M.R. Anand's characters grow on the Indian soil and imbibe the Indian culture in all its rusticity as well as refinement. We may for convenience categorise Anand's use of Indianism in the following groups: (I) Use of popular Indian idioms and phrases, (II) Indian terms of abuse, expletives, swear-words, distorted Indian words and sentences, and distorted English words, (III) Indian imagery, symbols, similes and metaphors, (IV) Dialogues transliterated from the vernacular and (V) Reflection of the social, political, religious, moral and cultural aspects of Indian life.

POPULAR INDIAN IDIOMS AND PHRASES

Dr Anand uses a number of transliterated Indian idioms and phrases in his early novels in order to impart an Indian flavour to his English. These idioms and phrases catch the rhythm and tone of the vernacular speech most of the time. They also match with Indian culture and Indian sensibility which distinguish Indian English from American, Australian or African English. For example, most of the invocational phrases mentioned below are chanted by Indians, either at moments of excitement or while they take bath or when they go to bed at night or get up in the morning:

(a) *Ram, Ram Sri, Hari Narayan; Sri Krishna* (*U.* 65),[2] (b) *Hey Hanuman Jodha* (*U.* 65), (c) *Om, Shanti Deva* (*U.* 65), (d) *Kali Mai* (*U.* 65), (e) *Arti, Arti* (*U.* 68), (f) *Sri Ram Chandra Ki Jai* (*U.* 68), (g) *Alakh, Alakh* (*U.* 80), (h) *Bham Bham Bhole Nath* (*U.* 80), (i) *Krishnaji Maharaja* (*U.* 155), (j) *Jai Deva* (*U.* 35), (k) *Ya Allah* (*U.* 196), (1) *Ishwar, Ishwar Parmeshwar* (*TLB.* 84). It is supposed that the various names of gods and goddesses may relieve one of cares and anxieties and bring peace and prosperity. *Mahatma Gandhi ki jai* (*U.* 151), *Hindu Mussulman ki jai* and *Mahatma Gandhi ki jai, Harijan ki jai* (*U.* 167), *Mahatmaji ki jai* (*U.* 167) were some popular slogans during the Freedom struggle in India.

There are some peculiarly Indian 'ji' formations to depict a formal respect, such as *Punditji* (*U.* 32), *babuji* (*U.* 90), *mianji* (*U.* 48), *Sadhuji* (*U.* 80), *Mahatmaji* (*U.* 157), *Krishnaji* (*U.* 155), *Bhaiji* (*U.* 156), *Yogiji* (*C.* 155), *Havildarji* (*U.* 18), *Lallaji* (*C.* 35), *Hakimji* (*U.* 90). These interjections impart a special Indian colour to Anand's language.

A number of Indian phrases are used to describe Indian characters, situations, beliefs and are not very different from their counterparts in the vernacular. They function differently, sometimes as common invocations or address and sometimes as noun, adjective, verb or adverb. They also throw light on Indian customs and manners, and sometimes they become symbolic of their poverty: *mud-walled houses* (*U.* 11), *leather-worker's son* (*U.* 12), *egg-shaped face* (*U.* 43), *low-caste boys* (*U.* 45), *henna-dyed beards* (*U.* 47), *betel-leaf shop* (*U.* 47), *remnant seller's stall* (*U.* 63), *maize-flour bread* (*U.* 86), *a little breath-left* (*U.* 91), *tailor-master's son* (*U.* 126), *bandmaster's sons* (*U.* 126), *become a nawab* (*U.* 131), *turned-up moustache* (*U.* 136), *cast off trousers* (*U.* 146), *smoke-scented evening* (*U.* 160), *grass-cutter's wife* (*U.* 146), *Angrezi Sarkar* (*TLB.* 3), *two-horned yama* (*TLB.* 3), *Ram, Ram brother* (*TLB.* 36), *no consideration for anyone's mother or sister* (*TLB*. 42), *Salaam Huzoor* (*TLB*. 49), *cow-dung cakes* (*TLB*. 76), *lifting joined hands* (*TLB*. 148), *open-air kitchen* (*TLB*. 152), *The Congress wallahs* (*TLB*. 212), *a springtime of her beauty* (*TLB*. 214), *Hai Ma Hai* (*TLB*. 259), *gazelle-eyed courtesans* (*TLB*. 264), *burning with fever* (*TLB*. 79), *La hol billah!* (*TBH*. 78), *wah Guru!* (*TBH*. 26), *the cow-dust hour* (*TBH*. 172), *eyed the young girls* (*TV*. 55), *to be a lion's son* (*TV*. 221), *deeds worthy of forefathers* (*TV*. 222), *struck by the hand of fate* (*ATBW*. 197), *talking openly to girls* (*ATBW*. 84), *the sepoy heart* (*ATBW*. 231), *grovel in the dust with joined hands* and *the mainspring of convention* (*TV*. 223).

Thakur Guru Prasad[3] takes no notice of the above mentioned phrases which help in presenting intimately the various aspects of Indian life in a language approximated to the vernacular. They not only impart special Indian flavour to Anand's English but also gives English its Indian domicile. There are some typical Indian forms of address such as: *the mother of my daughter; the mother of Leila; Ram, Ram, brother,* etc. In the conservative Indian society, a person does not mention the name of his wife; so he addresses her as mother of someone (name of his son or daughter).

The following determiners have been borrowed from regional languages: *leather-worker's son, egg-shaped face, low-caste boys, high class men, tailor-master's son* and *grass-cutter's wife.* We encounter some such phrases as are rendered from Punjabi or Hindustani expressions: *a little breath left, become a nawab, Angrezi Sarkar* (British government), *the Congress wallahs* (the members of the Congress party), *a springtime of* [...] *beauty* (age of charming youth), *cry* [...] *eyes out* (weep bitterly), *the cow-dust hour* (twilight), *the owner of my house* (husband), *to be a lion's son* (to be brave), *deeds worthy of forefathers* (noble deeds), *talking openly to girls* (to be shameless in Indian context) and *the sepoy heart* (hard heart).

Indian ways or manners of obeisance are indicated by such phrases as *lifting joined hands, raised hands to forehead* and *grovel in the dust with joined hands.* These phrases show how poor people from low-castes paid respects to socially superior beings.

There are some idioms, proverbs and superstitions which have been transliterated from the original Punjabi, Hindi and Urdu languages to create an Indian atmosphere or to suggest the Indian background of the concerned characters such as: (a) *to teach* [...] *the lesson* (*U.* 109), (b) *A straw in the beard of a thief* (*U.* 117), *guilty conscience,* (c) *Gold teeth in the mouth of a thief* (*U.* 117), *prosperity of an evil-doer,* (d) *not see* [...] *face again* (*U.* 132, excessive hatred), (e) *Mouth watered* (*U.* 86, an intense gustatory sensuousness), (f) *Men with abiding purpose cherish neither hatred nor love* (*TLB.* 173), (g) *to eat ashes* (*TBH.* 122, to suffer), (h) *A single plea will not burst the oven!* (*TBH.* 116, a single person cannot change the order of life), (i) *Even the loin-cloth of a running thief is good enough* (*TBH.* 118, something is better than nothing), (j) *the chicken at home is equal to lentils* (*THB.* 91, devaluating a familiar thing or familiarity breeds contempt), (k) *iron cuts iron* (*TBH.* 147, like cures like), (l) *a well-fed man needs religion* (*TBH.* 155), (m) *A crow tried to strut like a peacock* (*TBH.* 168), (n) *What can a dog know of the taste of butter* (*TBH.* 199), (o) *running with the hare and hunting with the hounds* (*TBH.* 202, hypocrite), (p) *The camels are being swept away, the ants say they float* (*TBH.* 211), (q) *Never believe a barber or a brahmin* (*TLB.* 8), (r) *Warm the hand* (*TLB.* 111, to bribe), (s) *If wishes could rain, cowherds would be kings* (*TLB.* 169), (t) *to bring a piece of iron home on Monday was the sure harbinger of an impending tragedy* (*TLB.* 116, superstition), (u) *If the frog makes water on your hand, you will get leprosy* (*TLB.* 110, superstition), (v) *throw away the turban off* [...] *head* (*C* 252, disparaging act), (w) *Cut nose* (*TV.* 39, to insult) and (x) *to cut the throat of* (*ATBW.* 246, to slay). The idioms, phrases and proverbs mentioned above are functional and not a useless embellishment of the language by Anand They reveal characters and situations and also catch the spirit of Indian life.

INDIAN TERMS OF ABUSE, EXPLETIVES, SWEAR-WORDS, DISTORTED INDIAN AS WELL AS ENGLISH WORDS AND SENTENCES

Anand' s novels are littered with terms of abuse, expletives or curses, swear-words and with so many Indian and English words and sentences in their distorted form. The dialect of central Punjab which influences Anand's English so much and which is the mother-tongue of many of his characters is full of such expressions. They reveal the nature, the status and the social condition of the characters who use them. Commonly, the illiterate, unsophisticated and peevish characters abundantly use these items of Indianism. The following catalogue contains:

(a) Terms of Abuse

Lover of your mother (*U.* 12), *Son of a pig* (*U.* 15), *betichod* (*TBH.* 180), *Bitch! Prostitute wanton* (*U.* 28), *Eater of dung and drinker of urine* (*U.* 29), *You swine* (*U.* 53), *Cock-eyed son of a bow-legged scorpion!* (*U.* 53), *Dirty dog! son of a bitch! offspring of a pig* (*U.* 53), *son of a dog!* (*U.* 55), *vay, eater of your masters, may the vessel of your lie never float in the sea of existence, may you perish and die* (*U.* 80), *O bey brother-in-law* (*U.* 102), *oh, illegally begotten* (*U.* 102), *shut up bitch* (*U.* 103), *The wife of a hundred husbands* (*TLB.* 168), *the daughter of a shameless mother* (*TLB.* 168), *Owls!* (*TBH.* 39), *Rape mothers!* (*TBH.* 214), *rape-sister* (*TBH.* 214), *the bitch goddess machine!* (*TBH.* 216), *vultures* (*TBH.* 227), *bahinchod!* (*C.* 200).

The most remarkable point about these expletives and abuses is that their number decreases from novel to novel. As Anand gains in maturity and experience, he avoids using them or confines them to a very limited number. But whenever they are used, they are never out of the context. People from Punjab—it is a fact—get up with them, live for the whole day with them and also go to bed with them.

(b) Indian words and phrases and Indianized English words or distorted English expressions

Untouchable. *Jemadar* (14), *goras* (12), *Baksheesh* (15), *Sahib* (14), *bania* (23), *izzat* (15), *maidan* (24), *Hai Hai* (29), *Pundit* (30), *jalebis* (31), *kheer* (31), *kara parshad* (31), *Han* (34), *Acha* (40), *Puff-puffing* (36, onomatopoeia), *burra babu* (42), *Tan-Nana-Nan Tan* (47, onomatopoeia), *biris* (47), *bazaar* (49), *rasgulas, gulabjamans* and *ladus* (51, Indian sweetmeats), *Lat sahib* (55), *Laften Gornor* (55), *Kalijug* (55), *Nahin* (55), *langar* (98), *chapatis* (86), *Hakim* (90), *dawaikhana* (90), *dakdar* (90), *Bhangi* (92, sweeper), *chandal* (92), *sarkar* (92), *tamasha* (69, show), *ghats* (99), *handi* (93), *yar* (109), *sahibhood* (113), *Mehrbani* (120), *Nawab* (131), *jao* (138), *chamars* (147), *girja ghar* (142), *avtar* (153), *Dilli* (154), *Kothi* (154, edifice), *vilayat* (154), *swadharma* (155), *Sarkari Adalat* (156), *panchayat* (156, local court), *puggareed* (160, with puggaree on head), *pandal* (160), *ksatriya, vaishya, sudras* (164), *swadeshi* (168), *maya* (170, illusion), *nirvana* (170, redemption), *Nawan jug* (272, New or Naween becomes Nawan in Punjabi), *Karma* (172), *oh Maharaj! Maharaj* (130), *Salaam babuji* (42), *twice-born* (19), *kala admi zamin par hangne wala* (21-22), *I have only one life to live* (51), *Don't know what the world is coming to* (54), *You sweepers have lifted your head to the sky nowadays* (81), *Is this your father's house that you come and rest here?* (80), *Tum udas* (137), *Sur ka bacha* (139), *Kute ka bacha* (139), *Ither Ither*! (147), *mem sahib* (148, English woman), *take a ploughman from the plough, wash off his dirt,* and *he is fit to rule a kingdom* (172), *Salad* (95) and *The Babu's sons were babu's sons* (125).

Two Leaves and a Bud. *Seth* (3), *Chowkidar* (3, guard), *mai bap* (4), *Parbat* (11), *Sayce* (33), *Pukka kothi* (34, brick-built edifice), *angrezi log* (34), *basti* (34, village), *Kismet* (37, luck), *budmash* (42, stupid), *bacho* (47, save yourself), *Gurkha* (49), *Mistri* (58), *the khansamah* (53), *Shaitan* (65, Devil), *Ping-Pong* (a Punjabi game, 94), *darji* (94, tailor), *swargbash* (107, death), *daftar* (109, office), *motucar* (111, motor-car), *chaprasi* (111, peon), *nazrana* (111, gift), *Hum hum Ho Hum* (145), *Purdah* (148, curtain), *dai* (171, midwife), *charpai* (166, cot), *thup* (154, *dhup* or incense becomes 'thub' in Punjabi), *Ashshtant* (171, assistant), *Sabha* (210, meeting), *Fakir* (210), *Railgaries* (211), *Zoolm* (213), *Zalim* (214, tyrant), *a ginn or a bhut* (246, evil spirits), *Shikaries* (252, hunters), *Kheddah* (252, trap for elephants), *dhotied* (268, wearing dhoti), *Flat-nosed gurkha woman* (51), *Acha hai* (56), *Koi hai* (60), *pahlwan* (62, wrestler), *gymkhana* (61), *Ja! Ja! chala ja* (115), *Hosh karo* (193, come to senses), *By the oath of God* (197, by God), *Khabardar! Chalo! Jao!* (206, Be warned, go away), *Satis* (57, women burnt on the pyre of their husbands).

The Big Heart. *goonda* (173), *kalal khana* (119, ale house), *ohe buk nahin, bastard* (209), *ohe chup kar!* (111, be silent), *That is the true talk* (191, that's the matter), *Hut duray, duray* (145), *puris* (54, loaves fried in ghee), *Injan* (59, Engine), *dacoos* (155), *hookah* (172), *Bombai* (173, Bombay), *Maulvis and Pundits* (210), *Coal-black face* (20), *remorseless wheel of Jagannath* (88), *I wish I could take your fever myself* (175), *I beg you stop this kind of talk, ohe brothers* (210), *oh putar* (109, oh son).

Coolie. *Mochi* (299, cobbler), *May be live child* (152), *tortoise speed* (154), *langotis* (238, loin-clothes), *Jaldi chalo* (211, Hurry up).

Anand uses these very words, idioms, phrases, proverbs, expletives, swear-words, Anglicized Hindi, Urdu or Punjabi sentences, words and epithets over and over again in his novels. They become familiar not only to the Indian readers but also to the readers abroad. The number of these items decreases by and by in successive novels. As enumerated, there are only rare examples of distorted English words such as *fashun, motucar* and *injan* as they are as naturally used by the Indian speakers of the rank of Rakha, Lakha, Gulabo, Narayan, Ralia and many like them, as an Englishman uses Hindi words like *Coi hai, tum udas, kute ka bacha,* etc. Therefore, Meenakshi Mukherjee's[4] objection to their use does not carry conviction.

INDIAN IMAGERY, SYMBOLS, SIMILES AND METAPHORS

Mulk Raj Anand makes use of Indian images, symbols, similes and metaphors which have a definite bearing upon the social, cultural, religious and situational facts of Indian life such as (a) steaming earthen saucepan, tumblerful of tea (*U.* 16, symbol of stark poverty), (b) sacred thread twisted around their left ear (*U.* 20, a religious rite of the Brahmins), (c) brahminee bull (*U.* 60, an ox is offered in the memory of someone dead in India), (d) beating their breasts in mourning for the dead (*U.* 77), (e) Smoke-bottomed handi (*U.* 93, symbolizes poverty of the person who uses it), (f) a tall girl with a face as brown as ripe wheat and hair as black as the rain clouds (*U.* 97, simile for describing a beautiful girl), (g) Baba pese de (*U.* 150, a slogan of Indian beggars), (h) fierce-looking red-cheeked Pathans (*U.* 152), (i) Clean-shaven head (*U.* 159, Indian sanyasis do shave their heads and sometimes Hindus get their heads shaved as a symbol of mourning for a dead relative), (j) two-bricks—with-a-space-in between fireplace (*U.* 16, showing poverty of the outcastes), (k) The betel-leaf seller threw some water over it (nicked coin given by Bakha) [...]. Then he flung a red-lamp cigarette at Bakha, as a butcher might throw a bone to an insistent dog sniffing round the corner of his shop (*U.* 48, an image of humiliation of the low castes), (l) The swarms of crows, which blackened the sky like the harbingers of famine and which are now spreading over the countryside with droves of vultures around them, spell the surest disaster (*TBH.* 18, an ominous symbol of destruction), (m) And he could hear the dead mourning under the feet of the woman, whom he soon recognized as the goddess Kali, for her tongue was bulging out red, and her eyes were like two sharp glint discs shining like diamonds from the coal-black face (*TBH*, an image of Kali, a symbol of destruction for the devils), (n) suspended by the tuft-knot over the edge of the burning ground in the hands of Yama (*TBH.* 38, Yama is the symbol of death), (o) Oh, he was such a noble creature—much nobler than all those lotus! (*TBH.* 227,

Lotus is a simile of beauty and grandeur), (p) O God, Let the earth open up and swallow me! otherwise they will destroy me, the vultures who are sitting (*TBH*, 227, Janki refers here to Sita who was swallowed up by the earth after being abandoned by Lord Rama. It is a typical mythological Indian symbol), (q) Come ni, Leila, come vay, Budhu (*TBH*. 35, 'ni' and 'vay' are specially Punjabi forms of address or suffix to effect Punjabi tone), (r) A distance of three days and three nights (*TLB*. 36, an Indian way of expressing distance), (s) eyes like long beans, great big noses like fried dumplings [...] twisted faces bursting with skin diseases like rotten melons (*TBH*. 66, Indian similes), (t) come and buy, come and buy! (*TBH*, 70 a slogan of stall keepers in a fair to attract the buyers), (u) he stepped back without showing his posterior (*TLB*. 133, an Indian court manner observed in Mughal darbars), (v) what can we do, Huzoor? You are our mai-bap, Huzoor (*TLB*. 200 a faithful presentation of low-caste people), (w) I fall at your feet (*TV*, 55, a Punjabi way of greeting an elder), (x) they were struck by the hand of Fate (*ATBW*. 197, an Indian way of expression for 'people with ill-luck'), (y) Behold, the brother-in-law thought to take his hand to his head and salaamed the Germans [...] he abused the Angrez sahibs and made a sign as if he meant to cut the throat of the whole Angrezi race (*ATBW*. 246), (z) backboneless creatures who would abjectly catch hold of the feet of a policeman and grovel in the dust with joined hands [...] (*TSTS*. 279, a symbolical picture of the humility of the low-caste people).

DIALOGUES TRANSLITERATED FROM THE VERNACULAR (PUNJABI, HINDI OR URDU)

Dr Anand transliterates many Punjabi, Urdu and Hindi clauses, sentences and expressions to make his dialogues appear natural and appropriate for the concerned characters. Very much like Charles Dickens and the Russian novelists, he reaches the core of his characters' hearts and the inmost recesses of their minds and succeeds in giving voice to their thoughts, emotions and feelings. Anand's characters belong to the lower sections of

Indian society and that in their day-to-day life they do not converse in English. Since they are illiterate, unsophisticated, they cannot speak even their own regional language correctly. They use many distorted English words and they are also made to use numerous words, idioms and phrases from their colloquial language in their transliterated forms. The dialogues of Anand's early novels may be divided into three categories:

(i) An illiterate rustic talking to another person of his or her class

Anand's novels of the first phase are literally crowded with illiterate characters. He wields their speech in such a way that not only their intonation but their joys and fears, agonies and rancour, love and hatred are properly voiced. The whole characteristics of the class of characters are reflected through their dialogues so much so that they appear natural and animated.

Bakha touches a Hindu by chance in the market and the latter hurls a torrent of abuses on the former in *Untouchable*:

> Dirty dog! son of a bitch! offspring of a pig! keep to the side of the road, the low caste vermin! why don't you call you swine and announce your approach! Do you know you have touched me and defiled me, cock-eyed son of a bow-legged scorpion! Now I will have to go and take a bath to purify myself. And it was a new dhoti and a shirt I put on this morning! (52-53).

The speaker's contempt towards a low-caste boy like Bakha is well recorded in this dialogue. It reveals the vulgarity of his language and his orthodoxy. Anand does not want to strain himself to Indianize the borrowed language; he rather wants to reflect an actual social condition in a touch and defile Indian society and succeeds in doing so.

In *Untouchable,* an illiterate housewife showers curses and abuses on Bakha who happens to sit on the wooden platform of her house to rest for a while in a colloquial Indian language rather than English:

> Vay, eater of your masters, may the vessel of your life never float in the sea of existence. May you perish and die! you have defiled my house! Go! Get up, get up! Eater of your masters! why don't you shout if you wanted food? Is this your father's house that you come and rest here (80).

In *The Big Heart,* the characters like Murlidhar, Karmo Devi and Ralia use a similar language to express themselves. Karmo Devi beseeches her step-son, Ananta:

> Han, son, it is all for you; only for you. So don't be hard on your old mother. I have cried my eyes out for years waiting for your bride. You don't know what it will mean to me. The women of the brotherhood will come to beat the drum, and there will be the bridal party [...] oh then shall the Gods bless us and your bride will come home and fall at your feet (26).

There are numerous such examples of phrases and expressions in *The Big Heart.*

In *Coolie,* we come across a series of dialogues spoken by illiterate people which have in them the element of vulgarity and distortion of the standard British English. Anand records the plight of exploited coolies and the inhuman behaviour of the privileged-class people. Chimta Sahib, an illiterate foreman chides Hari who seeks re-employment in the former's factory:

> You think bloody fool, that you go away 'when you like' and come back when you like and get the same pay all the time? The 'burra sahib' has ordered me not to take any coolies back who have once left. He does not want old and used men. I am doing you a favour 'bahinchod' (199-200).

Piari Jan addresses Ratan, the wrestler in *Coolie*:

> 'Aao,' welcome, Pahalwanji. 'where have you kept yourself hidden so long?' 'My eyes have gone blind looking at the way along which you were to come to grace my house' (214).

The above expression cannot be rendered in its true spirit in standard English. The Hindi word 'Aao' translated into 'come' and the expressions 'where have you kept yourself hidden so long' and 'My eyes have gone blind [...] to grace my house'; if changed a little, may distort Piari Jan's Indian character.

Gangu and Narayan, the two poor coolies at Macpherson Tea Estate in *Two Leaves and a Bud*, talk to each other:

> 'Ram, Ram brother' said Narayan, an emaciated little man, as he came up with a hookah in his hand, bare except a loin-cloth.
>
> 'Ram, Ram' said Gangu with a smile. 'Have you come from afar?' asked Narayan, 'A distance of three days and three nights,' said Gangu [...] (112).

The address 'Ram, Ram brother' and the expression 'A distance of three days and three nights' convey the illiteracy of the persons conversing. That they are utterly poor is reflected through the images of 'hookah' and 'loin-cloth.'

(ii) An uneducated person talking to an educated or urban character

When an illiterate person talks to an educated person we discover utter humility and minimum distortion of the language in dialogues. Such characters as Sauda and Mohan in *Coolie*, Ananta, Puran Singh and Janki in *The Big Heart* are more or less educated and therefore use a sophisticated language with only a few colloquial expressions. We rarely come across the terms of abuse, swear-words or curses in them. Sauda incites coolies against the tyranny of the owners of the factory:

> You are human beings. Have you forgotten your notion of izzat? Would you let anyone throw the turbans off your head? (252).

The hybrid term 'notion of izzat' and the expression 'throw away the turbans off your head' reveal the Indian identity of the speaker. He seems to be talking in a colloquial language.

Puran Singh Bhagat in *The Big Heart* speaks a language similar to that used by the characters of R.K. Narayan. He proves to be a true mouthpiece of Anand through his following utterance:

> All the world is in a whirl in which men and women are devastating each other, while delirium burns the cities and villages of *Hindustan.* I tell you there is hope for our land except in Revolution. But that requires devotion and thought. Perhaps it will be achieved through *Uncle Viroo's belief in Karma*; if not by reciting the verses of Karma. "Sow good seeds and you will reap good deeds"—only I believe you get your reward here on earth and not in heaven (62).

Anand's English characters are shown anglicizing Indian sentences and words. Reggie Hunt, the worst exploiter of the poor coolies on Macpherson Tea Estate addresses the revolting coolies:

> 'Hosh Karo! Hosh Karo! Have you no sense! Donkeys? [...] I will shoot you all,' Reggie roared [...]. 'Because, Sahib none of our wives, sisters and mothers are safe,' someone ventured from the back of the crowd.
>
> 'Dare you utter a sound and I will shoot you dead,' he snarled[7] (193-94).

(iii) An educated person conversing with educated persons

Dialogues among educated persons, though rare in the novels of the first phase, are less racy and impressive because we find the rhythm of vernacular speech missing in them. Images, life-styles of speakers, and the specific references bear testimony to the Indian background of these dialogues. The dialogues delivered by the poet and Mahatma Gandhi in *Untouchable,* by the Count in *The Sword and the Sickle,* the conversation between Ananta and his beloved, Janki, in *The Big Heart,* and the talk between Comrade Joshi and Lala Murlidhar in the same novel are good examples of such dialogues. Lala Murlidhar neglects his clan out of pride and later on he has to placate them by all means. He asks forgiveness from his clan:

> Listen brothers, I have put my turban at the feet of all of you, save this ceremony. *I have sinned.* I have erred. You can beat my old head with your shoes. But let us have this betrothal [...]. *A crow tried to strut like a peacock* but seeing

> his feet wept and cried. That is my condition. Forgive me (162).

Anand wants to introduce Indian rites and rituals, ceremonies and customs and at the sametime wins the curiosity of the readers both Indian and foreign. Therefore, it is natural that dialogues of educated characters in these novels are less impressive than those of the illiterate and rustic ones.

(v) Reflection of the social, political, religious, moral and cultural aspect of Indian life.

Anand considers art as a means to some end in itself. As a true reformist-humanist, he wants to bring about a radical change in society, individuals and in politics, he challenges the century-old conventions and religious orthodoxy which hamper all the prospects of social, economic, mental and spiritual development of Indian people

All the novels of the first phase were written during the pre-Independence period, and their central themes are pivoted around social evils such as untouchability, women's oppression, exploitation of children and labourers. There is only a feeble echo of independence movement in these novels.

In *Untouchable*, Anand's sympathy is fully reserved for the excommunicated section of society. In order to convince the reader that he is telling the story of India, Anand introduces so many references to Indian myths, puranas, history and characters in his novels. He finds likeness between Charat Singh who has a number of scars on his body and who always stands leaning by the goalpost and the character of the great Rajput warrior, 'Rana Sanga, the conqueror of Akbar, the great Mughal.'[5]

Coolie, in fact, is an elaborated metaphor of unequal distribution of social, political and economic rights and resources among the Indian people. Daulatpur grain market provides a picture of an Indian market stuffed with filth, rubbish, dirt and deadly reeking remnants and Munoo wanders with Tulsi to earn something to help his kind master, Prabha Dayal. Even in such a polluted atmosphere of the market, the coolie remembers the name of God. Anand mocks at the religious blindness of Indian people who all the time chant the name of God in vain. Munoo bearing the son and daughter of Hari on his shoulder, reminds the novelist of the power-god, Hanuman. This reference seems to be wrong because in *The Ramayana* it is described that Lord Rama was offered a Pushpak viman by the god of wealth, Kuber to come from Ceylon to Oudh. At another point in the great epic, Hanuman carries the two brothers, Ram and Laxman on his shoulders from the demon king Ahiravana's prison-house.

Anand shows his earnest concern with the economic and political slavery of the poor coolies and labourers. One of them, Mohan, thus incites his fellowmen to rise against tyranny and oppression. Charles Croft Crooke's hatred for coolies in *Two Leaves and a Bud* is in its lowest form where he says to De la Havre, 'You and your bloody coolies ought all to be shot dead against a wall.' De la Havre holds not only the English people but also the Indians' philosophy of poverty responsible for their pitiable condition. By making passing references to the characters of Indian history such as Jehangir, Nur Mahal and Shah Jehan, the novelist tries to assure the readers that he is narrating a tale related to India. The reference to the Indian God Indra, the king of heaven in Indian mythology, brings out the Indianness of description.

Anand's artistic vision encompasses all: Indian culture, customs, rituals, ethics and myths. In *The Big Heart* he chooses a few individuals to depict the conflict between the old conventions and the new modernity. He seems to have developed the power of getting into the inmost essence of a character and finding out the situations and emotions which moulded them. There are many symbols, images and pictures from Indian myths or even local myths in *The Big Heart*. The philosophy of Lord Buddha (62), references to the Mahabharat war (67), Gautam Buddha (66), Jalian Wala Bagh massacre (67), Maharaja Ranjit Singh (86), Rani Jindan (86), the remorseless wheel of Jagannath (88), Bombay strike of 1939 (88), Arya

Samajis and Gandhiji—all indicate the Indian background of *The Big Heart*.

The double standards of morality of the old Punjabi peasants is criticized by Lal Singh in *The Village*. He thus assails the practice of keeping Katch, Kara, Kirpan, Kesh and Kanga followed by the conservative Sikhs even today. *Across the Black Waters* begins with Lal Singh's escape from his village and ends with his becoming a prisoner of war in Germany. In this war novel, the hero has to give up his obsessional assumptions about his country's glory. By observing the fashionable European girls he comes to realize Indian women's negligence about themselves. *The Sword and the Sickle* is also sprinkled with images, symbols, references and rituals drawn from Indian bucolic life.

Anand's linguistic experimentations in the first phase of his career are undeniably carried out for the purpose of art as well as for the expression of fictional reality.

NOTES AND REFERENCES

1. Brunton, T.D. 'India in Fiction: The Heritage of Indianness', *Critical Essays on Indian Writing in English,* (ed.) M.K. Naik, S.K. Desai, G.S. Amur (Dharwar, 1972), 200.
2. '*U*' in the brackets stands for *Untouchable* (Arnold Heinemann, 1984) and the digits indicate the page numbers. Similarly *TLB.* stands for *Two Leaves and a Bud* (Arnold Heinemann, 1983), *C* for *Coolie, TBH* for *The Big Heart, TV* for *The Village, ATBW* for *Across the Black Waters, TSTS* for *The Sword and the Sickle* and show the page numbers of the novels.
3. Thakur, Guru Prasad. *Experimentation with Language in Indian Writing in English,* (ed.) S.K. Desai (Kolhapur, 1974).
4. Mukherjee, Meenakshi. 'Beyond the Village,' *Critical Essays on Indian Writing in English,* (Eds.) M.K. Naik, S.K. Desai, G.S. Amur (Dharwar, 1972).
5. Anand, M.R. *Untouchable* (A.H., 1984), 117.

2

Train to Pakistan: A Historical Novel

MALLIKARJUN PATIL

Khushwant Singh's *Train to Pakistan* is a classic by any literary standard. Though it was written long ago, still it appears fresh and frank in its delineation of a great cataclysm. It is full of comic realities and human touch—though embodying a human tragedy.

A critical analysis of the novel demands that one should go through it closely. *Train to Pakistan* is in four parts such as 'Dacoity,' 'Kalyug,' 'Mano Majra' and 'Karma'—characteristically signifying a kaleidoscopic picture of a turbulent phase of Indian history and it runs into 158 pages. 'Dacoity,' an anglicized form of a Hindu word, means cultural robbery. In Vasant Sahane's view: "This section constitutes a true-to-life description of cultural robbery committed in Mano Majra village, but its ramifications and remote echoes go far beyond the inhuman and cruel actions of the robbery of Malli and his gang" (76). The first part describes the harsh Indian summer of 1947. The summer is longer and drier and dustier. The climate is dry. There is no rain. Accordingly, Khushwant Singh presents man's hot state, his agonized heart and suffering and fate. He says "[...] no one could remember when the monsoon had been so late [...] people began to say that God was punishing them for their sins" (3). Some of them knew the country was partitioned into two—Hindustan and Pakistan—and the event had turned bloody. In fact, "Muslims said the Hindus had planned and started the killing." According to the Hindus, the Muslims were to blame. The fact is both sides killed. It is really a massacre [...]! About the title of the novel it is observed, "This natural phenomenon of the severe summer of 1947, combined with the popular notion of sin, is a significant element in the novel's narrative and dramatic design" (Sahane 77).

Mano Majra which was the earlier title of the novel, is a village on the Indo-Pak border. In fact, it is a major character in the novel. The only speciality of the village is that it has a railway junction and nothing else. The village is small one—just with seventy families. Yet people of all religions—Hindus, Muslims and Sikhs—thrive there harmoniously. The only three brick buildings—one belonging to the Gurudwara, one to the mosque and one to Mr Ram Lal, the Hindu moneylender—stand there as monuments of religious synchronization. What not? In midst of these there has grown an old peepul tree as if a symbol of peace and harmony.

Mano Majrans are farmers and coolies. Only a few of them pursue religion out of chance rather than out of necessity. Bhai Meet Singh, though a farmer, has been in charge of the Gurudwara not because he is interested in Sikhism but because he is lazy to work at fields, while Imam Sahib is in charge of the mosque as he is blind and unable to work elsewhere. Not to speak of, no Hindu is there for any religious activities. Yet all the people live there together.

Life in Mano Majra runs in accordance with the train schedule. Train is highly symbolic of Mano Majran life. Coming of a train in the morning towards Lahore means the dawn, while the reverse ends people's daily activities. For instance, a goods train that passes at 9 p.m. indicates rest. The public life goes on and on by train timings. Khushwant Singh describes it vividly with a touch of realism and comedy:

> All this has made Mano Majra very conscicus of trains. Before daybreak, the mail train rushes through on its way to Lahore, and as it approaches the bridge, the driver

> invariably blows two long blasts of the whistle. In the instant, all Mano Majra comes awake. Crows begin to caw in the keekar trees. Bats fly back in long silent relays and begin to quarrel for their perches in the peepul. The mullah at the mosque knows that it is time for the Morning Prayer. He has a quick wash, stands facing west toward Mecca and with his fingers in his ears cries in long sonorous notes, '*Allah-o-Akbar.*' The priest at the Sikh temple lies in bed till the mullah has called. Then he too gets up, draws a bucket of water from the well in the temple courtyard, pours over himself, and intones his prayer in monotonous singsong to the sound of splashing water.
>
> By the time the 10:30 morning passenger train from Delhi comes in, life in Mano Majra has settled down to its dull daily routine. Men are in the fields. Women are busy with their daily chores. Children are out grazing cattle by the river. Persian wheels squeak and groan as bullocks go round and round, prodded on by curses and the jabs of goads in their hindquarters. Sparrows fly about the roofs trailing straw in their beaks. Pye-dogs seek the shade of the mud walls. Bats settle their arguments, fold their wings, and suspend themselves in sleep.
>
> As the noonday express goes by, Mano Majra stops to rest. Men and children come home for dinner and the siesta hour. When they have eaten, the men gather in the shade of the peepul tree and sit on the wooden platforms and talk and doze. Boys ride their buffaloes into the pond, jump off their backs, and splash about in the muddy wat r. Girls play under the trees, women rub clarified butter into each other's hair, pick lice from their children's heads, and discuss births, marriages and deaths (6).

The major events in the first part of the novel are the dacoity of Lala Ram Lal's house, opening up of Juggut Singh's love affair with a Muslim girl and the arrival of a communist worker. But these incidents though take place singly, have their own influence upon each other as if they are interconnected. One day upon a dreadful night, a five-member gang with arms gets to Mano Majra. No doubt, they come to rob Lala Ram Lal's treasure. The leader, in the initial, does not get a good response from Lala Ram Lal's family. But soon he discovers Ram Lal and kills him for treasure. However, nothing is as interesting as their throwing away some bangles into Juggut Singh's house, which works well.

Dacoity highlights the 'this worldliness' of Mano Majra. It has a deep materialistic reality as in Daniel Defoe's *Mall Flanders*. The world of dakus is marked by a stark, blatant, unvarnished materialism. Malli's gang as well as Juggut's amply displays this. Of course, the latter due to his passion of love embodies an ambivalence of moral values and the holiness of his heart reigns supreme when he thinks of Nooran.

In a curious event, we come to know Juggut Singh's life. Juggut Singh is a rowdy, a rowdy's son and even a rowdy's grandson—a rowdy family. As Gandhi says, the traditional swimmer is buried in water, the police bury both his father and grandfather. But Juggut Singh is lately fallen in love with Nooran. A belle Nooran is the blind mullah Imam Baksh's only daughter. One only wonders at love's invaluable strength in holding Juggut from all the crimes. In other words, Juggut is not indulging in robberies as his belle enamours him. Yet the relationship is unethical and the same tortures him later.

Iqbal is a communist from Delhi. He had his education in England. Being interested in Marxist ideals, he comes to Mano Majra for guiding people to safer destinies. Yet he is not a man of practical experience. Totally grounded in Western life styles he toys to improve the Indian lot. What a shame? He does not mix up with Bhai Meet Singh emotionally and his ways of life appear utterly strange. He does not drink tea offered by anyone. Nor does he give the details of his nativity, parentage and caste when the police arrest him. Not to speak of, his name is equally a curse to him, especially during the event of partition based on religious fanaticism. It is a small wonder that Iqbal is taken for a Hindu like 'Iqbal Chand,' for a Muslim like 'Iqbal Mohammad,' and for Sikh like 'Iqbal Singh.' So with doubts and deliberation, he is arrested by Hukum Chand's order within a few days of his arrival. But people as the police doubted of his arrest as he came there after Lala Ram Lal's murder. To be brief, Iqbal is a mysterious figure.

Part II called 'Kalyug' bears a title, which according to Hindu view of time means the fourth and last phase of human cycle of existence. In the novel it means the then time was the last phase of India and Pakistan's relations. It takes us to the momentous event of partition. The immediate precedent for it, of course, is the moneylender's murder. The days appear to be very bleak for the multi-religious communities. Things go wrong and this is the characteristic feature of the Hindu concept of Kalyug. Khushwant Singh writes:

> Early in September the time schedule in Mano Majra started going wrong. Trains became less punctual than ever before and many more started to run through at night. Some days it seemed as though the alarm clock had been set for the wrong hour. On others, it was as if no one had remembered to wind it. Imam Baksh waited for Meet Singh to make the first start. Meet Singh waited for the mullah's call to prayer before getting up. People stayed in bed late without realizing that times had changed and the mail train might not run through at all. Children did not know when to be hungry, and clamoured for food all the time. In the evenings, everyone was indoors before sunset and in bed before the express came by—if it comes by. Goods trains had stopped running altogether, so there was no lullaby to lull them to sleep. Instead, ghost trains went past at odd hours between midnight and dawn, disturbing the dreams of Mano Majra (68).

The village communities talk of the matter. The murder of Ram Lal, Juggut's affairs, the partition of India, the continued suppression of illiterate masses, so on and so forth. If men discuss these things at mosque and gurudwara, women talk of them in the company of their folk. Banta Singh is the headman otherwise known as lambardar. His duty is to distribute posts, look after the village law and order and make arrangements for the outsiders. Yet, he is virtuous.

The same evening there comes a Lahore-Delhi train with a load of corpses—all Hindus. This makes the Hindu-Sikh community, in retaliation to Muslims' massacre of Hindus, dispatch a trainload of Muslim corpses as 'A Gift to Pakistan.' Soon the Mano Majrans are made to part with a lot of firewood and kerosene, which help the police burn truckloads of dead bodies. All the same, Hukum Chand, the Deputy Commissioner shifts Muslims to safer places.

It is little before the arrival of dead bodies, both Iqbal and Juggut are arrested on the charge of murder. In the jail they exchange the moments of their hectic lives. Here what strikes us is Hukum Chand's lecherous life. Hukum Chand is a corrupt Hindu official, a lower middle class. He rose to power with his pleasing tactics with the higher-ups. Of course, he has his own dispassionate life with his illiterate and unattractive wife and family. These personal minus points in this VIP make him find an outlet elsewhere—say in having an enjoyment of an 'extramarital life.' A few things, readers understand of Hukum Chand, are that he is lecherous and inefficient besides unresponsive to sensitive matters.

Later the news of Hindu-Muslim massacre reach Mano Majra shaking people beyond imagination. The sub-inspector wonders about it. He says,

> "No, no. I just went round the servants' quarters. You are early. I hope all is well."
>
> "These days one should be grateful for being alive. There is no peace anywhere. One trouble after another [...]."
>
> The magistrate suddenly thought of the corpses.
>
> 'Did it rain'" (85).

'Mano Majra,' the third part of the novel continues the

theme. Khushwant Singh depicts the cup of sorrow filled up at the border village:

> When it was discovered that the train had brought a full load of corpses, a heavy brooding silence descended on the village. People barricaded their doors and many stayed up all night talking in whispers. Everyone felt his neighbour's hand against him, and thought of finding friends and allies. They did not notice the clouds blot out the stars nor smell the cool damp breeze. When they woke up in the morning and saw it was raining, their first thoughts were about the train and burning corpses. The whole village was on the roofs looking toward the station (103).

Consequently, by a mysterious turn, the kingpin of the murder case Mr Malli and his gang, after a due enquiry, is released at Mano Majra. But we must remember these people are not Mano Majrans, they are of a neighbouring village. When he releases Malli *et al.*, the head constable fails to take the stock of situation about Iqbal with Juggut still in jail. He is still under the wrong opinion that Iqbal is a Muslim in spite of the best effort Bhai Meet Singh and few others make.

'Mano Majra' is a microcosm of the world and as the name of the third part it suggests the reign of Kali:

A few days later the village Sikhs gather and discuss the current turbulence of communal trouble. After a word-to-word exchange, under the lambardar's auspices and advice, and partly in consultation with Imam Baksh who interrupts there, the villagers take a decision that the Muslims of Mano Majra, just for their own safety, must evacuate the village. What touches us is the event of Nooran's parting from Juggut Singh. The latter is still unreleased though he is not accused of the murder. It is something unfortunate—an irony of the circumstance. Mostly thinking, the 'bad acts yield a bitter harvest' (167), the police hold up his release. Anyway Nooran's dismay over her future touches our marrowbones when she has to talk to Juggut's mother about her affair with Juggut's.

Although the Muslims of Mano Majra decide to go, their brethren, the Sikhs remain humane to them. But the outside Muslim officers when they come there in trucks to evacuate Muslims to Pakistan, misunderstood the communal relations.

One says to a good Sikh:

> "Yesterday you wanted to kill them (Muslims), today you call them brothers. You may change your mind again tomorrow" (118).

Well. Within a day or two, the Muslim lot of Mano Majra, like the neighbouring villages Julandar, Chundunugger, Kapoora, Gujjoo, evacuate from Mano Majra with a heavy heart and subdued voice.

The fourth part of the novel 'Karma' is highly significant. It means the totality of a person's actions in one of the successive cycles of his existence, thought of as determining his fate in the next phase of his life. It is the novel's final part. The climax lies in it. The time the holocaust begins, summer ends and monsoon comes. There occurs a heavy downpour of rain causing great floods. Unfortunately some weak villages on the Sutlej are

of border villages get murdered and their corpses floated the downstream—all horrible.

The ghostly trains, the beastly people and the devastating floods complete the picture of degeneration!

First the scene of the flood:

Secondly the scene of the corpses brought from Pakistan turns spectacularly horrible. Bulldozers are used to bury the dead.

This angers the Sikhs—specially the refugees—to retaliate and one of them at Mano Majra gurudwara arouses the innocent for retaliation. The novel has wider scenes to display this.

The Sikh mob, along with the Hindus, more than thirty thousand men, well-armed kill their Muslim brethren forgetting the latter's humanity. The massacre continues.

These horrors of killing resemble the horrors of the world wars as depicted in Evelyn Waugh's *Decline and Fall* or in Norman Mailer's *The Naked and the Dead.*

Meanwhile both Juggut and Iqbal are released from the jail. The former goes frantically in search of Nooran, while the latter sleeps drunken.

Two more contrasting figures come to our mind—one is of Mr Hukum Chand's, a highly corrupt official and the other is of the noble-hearted sub-inspector's.

Hukum Chand is a man of Kalyug. At the time of train passing three events—dacoity, Juggut-Nooran love affair and Hukum Chand-Haseena sex contact—take place. It is said, dacoity is contrasted with love, and spiritual love is differentiated from sheer physical passion in this triangle. Hukum Chand, a top Punjab civil servant is a type of Indian bureaucracy. Yet he is shown more seasoned, experienced and balanced in his way of life and style of functioning.

Iqbal is a babu, a city-dweller. He is influenced by the ideas of proletarian revolution. But he is cornered by his plea for improving the village lot and his own inability to flung in the communist activity. So he becomes a trishanku, a split personality—rootless. He resembles Sher Singh of Khushwant Singh's *I Shall Not Hear the Nightingale.*

Khushwant Singh, in this part of the novel, has succeeded in his tirade against Hinduism, Indian bureaucracy and politics. Iqbal stands for the failure of communist ideals, while before a senile humankind Gandhi is heard no more. Just the rotten returns to dust.

Kalyug or the age of chaos is triumphantly seen in *Train to Pakistan.* It is an inversion of human values, destruction, division and negation. Khushwant Singh suggests 'the time is out of joint,' 'trains became less punctual than ever,' 'the clock is set with wrong hour,' 'Children did not know when to be hungry,' 'the ghostly trains' all disturbed the dreams of Mano Majra. Even when the trainload of dead bodies came, Imam Baksh and

Meet Singh's cry could not rise to the heavens to proclaim the glory of God.

Division and disharmony are the ruling principles of Mano Majra or in fact of the Kalyug. Sikhs and Muslims almost equal in number form the community. Both work together. Several families of sweepers have an ambivalent religious adherence. To add to this, all the people worship a local deity Deo.

Train to Pakistan displays Khushwant Singh's inborn sense of reality and, in turn, the resultant comic spirit. These two artistic features are predominant from cover to the cover.

Both plot and characterization, language and style, contribute to the realistic mode of fiction. In the novel the best realism is seen in the description of village life, different communities living together, the event of murder, Iqbal-Meet's conversations, bureaucratic ordeals, the Partition and its harsh consequences. Laughter is created when the bleak and ludicrous go together. For example, Iqbal's sophisticated life, his rootlessness and Meet Singh's down-to-earth reality make us laugh.

Train to Pakistan is a realistic novel. Yet its realism or comic spirit goes beyond a limit and in that stage of novelistic development, Khushwant Singh's novel, like that of Tolstoy's and Dostoevsky's, acquires a prophetic note.

The novel has a symbolic treatment too. Train symbolizes life or cycle of motions connected to birth, death and preservation. Imam means a religious person, Meet, an affectionate friend and Iqbal a compromise. Nooran's broken mirror stands for her broken future and evacuation symbolizes the blind force of history's repetition, while the irony of fate can be seen in Malli, a gangster becoming the custodian of a community's property.

NOTE

Sahane, Vasant. *Khushwant Singh*, New York: Twayne Publishers, Inc., 77. All the references to the novel are taken from Khushwant Singh's *Train to Pakistan*, The Collected Novels, Viking: Penguin India, 1996.

3

The Company of Women: A Tragedy of Lust

BASAVARAJ NAIKAR

Khushwant Singh's latest novel, *The Company of Women* (1999) has been widely dubbed by the Indian critics and puritanical readers as a pornographic novel. As he says in the Author's Note, "As a man gets older, his sex instincts travel from his middle to his head. What he wanted to do in his younger days but did not because of nervousness, lack of response or opportunity, he does in his mind. I started writing this novel when I was eighty-three. I finished it at eighty-five. An equally apt title for it could be 'The Fantasies of an Octogenarian.' No characters in this expose are real: they are figments of my senile fantasies" (vi). It has been condemned by many orthodox readers for its obscenity and demoralizing effect on the young minds of India. M.K. Naik and Shyamala Narayan come down very heavily on Khushwant Singh: "Singh's semen syndrome worsens in *The Company of Women*. In his Prefatory Note he tells us that an apt title for the novel could be, 'The Fantasies of an Octogenarian.' Another equally apt title could be: 'Phallic Frolic.' The protagonist, Mohan Kumar, is a businessman, whose only asset seems to be a member of equine proportions and prowess. His (mostly horizontal) career may be summed up as: 'He came, he undressed and he conquered.' This Alexander of Adultery, Caesar of Sex and Napoleon of Nudity finally contracts AIDS and dies in bed—the scene of his many tempestuous triumphs."[1] Somebody in Chennai has gone to the extent of filing a case against the novelist and the publisher in the public interest. It is indeed strange that the Indian critics should react to this novel so puritanically, forgetting the fact that a masterpiece of erotics, *i.e. Kama Sutra* was produced by Vatsayana in the ancient days in India. Like all semi- or fully-pornographic novels, *The Company of Women* is widely sold, secretly read and publicly condemned. Dismissing this novel purely on puritanical grounds will be tantamount to critical blindness. It is high time for Indian critics to revise their critical parameters in the light of new experiments in Indian writing. When we Indians read and enjoy similar novels by Henry Miller, Norman Mailer and John Updike of America and D.H. Lawrence of England without any demur, there is no reason why we should make such a hallaballoo about this novel. In spite of the preponderance of pornographic element in the novel, one may easily see a pattern of human behaviour and experience in a particular context and the operation of the law of life in it.

Any reader who takes up the novel to read it begins with an inference that it might be autobiographical, but soon finds out that it is not autobiographical, but biographical. The reader learns that the protagonist, Mohan Kumar has asked his friend Khushwant Singh to write down the experience narrated by the former to the latter. Thus there is a combination of the experiential richness of the former and the artistic expertise of the latter.

Mohan Kumar, the protagonist of the novel is a brilliant student of India studying at the prestigious Princeton University of America. He has achieved the highest academic distinction in his post-graduate degree in Business Management and computers. He is, therefore, offered a job in the same university. A youngman of his calibre would have easily settled down in America. But Mohan Kumar returns to India and begins a business of exporting ready-made garments with the help of dollar wealth that he has earned in America by way of scholarship. Having lost his mother quite early in life, he has no relative except his poor father who has been living in a small house in Delhi when he was studying at Princeton for six years. Thus Mohan Kumar's foreign education and dollar wealth have elevated him from a lower middle class status to an aristocratic one. That is the reason why he is able to start a big and profitable business and live an affluent life. What a rich bachelor needs is a wife. Mohan Kumar's father, who is a pious old man and who has none other than his son in the world, thinks seriously about arranging his marriage by selecting a suitable bride for him. He wishes to do the parental duty of settling the matrimonial life of his son and subsequently feel free to busy himself with the otherworldly concerns. Although Mohan Kumar is not in a hurry to get married, he is sensible enough to understand his father's anxiety and therefore concedes to his wish. Accordingly he sees a couple of brides and selects Sonu, daughter of Achint Ram as a suitable one. His father approves of the match on the grounds of equality of status, prestige and culture between the two families. Eventually the marriage takes place with great pomp. Mohan Kumar is happy to have a wife and see his father being happy about his matrimonial security. He buys a large house with a compound in order to be equal in status to his wife's family. Mohan Kumar, thus, attains the status of *nouveau riche* and wants to lead a comfortable life.

His matrimonial life runs smooth for a few years. When a son is born to him, he feels very happy about it and names the baby as Ranjit after his own grandfather. Mohan Kumar's father develops a deep attachment to his grandson and spends most of his time in playing with him or in telling him stories. Mohan Kumar's domestic happiness and peace remain rather brief. His wife Sonu, far from being a docile wife, turns out to be a very assertive and independent woman. Slowly she starts questioning him about his premarital sexual experiences. He replies to her rather casually about a couple of past incidents. But she asks him for more exact and detailed account of his premarital experiences, thereby irritating him. She begins to taunt and nag him constantly. Similarly she shows utter disrespect and indifference to her father-in-law who is a very pious and non-interfering man. She contemptuously calls him an 'old man' and complains that he spoils her little son Ranjit. The father-in-law, who senses that he is unwanted, gently excuses himself and goes away to the ashram at Haridwar. Mohan Kumar knows that it is the high-handed Sonu who is responsible for the father's departure from home. But he has deep love and great respect for his father. He, therefore, visits his father every full moon day and spends some peaceful hours in his company. Mohan Kumar tries his best to keep his wife in good humour. He returns home in the evening and takes her to parties and clubs for socialization. But she never stops arguing, taunting and nagging him. Although she lacks nothing in her life, she does not learn to be happy with her husband. In the meanwhile, Mohan Kumar receives a postcard from the ashram at Haridwar that his father passed away two days ago. He, therefore, rushes to Haridwar and performs the last rites of disbursing the ashes of his father into the Ganga. Mohan Kumar is deeply saddened by the loss of his father. He suffers from a sense of emotional insecurity and loneliness. When Sonu learns from her husband about his father's death, she informs all her relatives and friends about it and closes the firm for a couple of days for the sake of social prestige and formality, although she really never cared for her father-in-law when he was alive. Thus Sonu is neither an ideal, understanding and adjusting wife nor an ideal daughter-in-law sympathetic to her father-in-law. The temperamental incompatibility between husband and wife makes life intolerable to each of them. They drag on their mechanical life rather peremptorily for a few years. Mohan Kumar ceases to love Sonu and even reduces the frequency of sex with her. They have a second baby. Sonu feels very angry with her husband's accusation that she was ultimately responsible for his father's permanent departure from home. Any trivial reason is enough for her to pick on her husband. Mohan Kumar naturally feels more and more irritated by her pettifogging and quarrelsomeness. Although mentally he has snapped his attachment for her, he continues to rub along with her domestically. But extremely strong willed as she is, she says she does not want to live with him. Mohan Kumar is fed up so much with her that he is even prepared to divorce her. One day the difference of opinion between the two climaxes into a situation when he slaps her fiercely on the cheek. Far from swallowing the insult, Sonu lodges a police complaint against her husband and runs to her parents' home along with her children. Her affluent background, extremely independent nature, possessiveness, nagging, quarrelsomeness and unadjustability are the factors that compel her to go away from her husband.

The death of the father and the departure of wife and children from home aggravate Mohan Kumar's sense of loneliness to a great extent. Life appears to be blank and meaningless. He longs for companionship and suffers from an acute sense of sexual starvation appetised further from the memories of his premarital sexual experiences with Jessica Brown and Wanchoo. Besides, he has a lot of money as his business is flourishing fast. A man of lower middleclass shot up into aristocracy, he is free from middle-class morality. Rather, he has an aristocratic, *i.e.* amoral (or even immoral) and hedonistic attitude to life. He wants to enjoy all the material pleasures of life like smoking, drinking, eating flesh and womanizing. In fact, he becomes an amateur philosopher of marriage and love, although he is not given to introspection. He thinks that most of the marriages are based upon money or property rather than on mutual response and understanding; that after a few years of married life, sex becomes mechanical and therefore they begin to look for extra-marital diversions secretly or openly.

In accordance with his hedonistic philosophy, Mohan Kumar wants to have the company of women by turns on an experimental basis. His name, Mohan Kumar, which brings to our mind that of cowherd Krishna, has a tinge of irony in it. Like Krishna, the mythical figure, he wants to have the company of women, but unlike Krishna, he dwells only on the level of lust and never on that of love. He gives an advertisement in *The*

Times of India and *The Indian Express* as follows: "Forty-year-old-product of an Ivy League College (USA) living separately from his wife and two children. Divorce petition filed. Seeks a live-in companion for a mutually agreed time-duration. Willing to pay air fare to Delhi and back and Rs. 10,000 per month for expenses. Free board and lodging in comfortable home with three servants and chauffeur-driven car. Religion no bar. Relationship to be without strings attached on either side. If interested, enclose photograph and biodata. Correspond box no [...]" (11). Thus, Mohan Kumar undertakes the sexual odyssey with a religious zeal. Before the grand sexual adventure begins, he wants to preface it with a minor one. Knowing that getting responses to his advertisement in the newspaper may take some time, he decides to explore the possibility of having a quick and easy sexual partner. While searching for such an easy lay, he happens to cast eyes on his sweeperess at home, Dhanno. He gives her money and gets her very easily into his bed. He fucks her twice a week to streamline his grand sexual programme that is to follow.

For a divorcee like Mohan Kumar who has lots of money, position and freedom, it is not wrong to long for sexual company. He could easily have kept a permanent mistress who could have easily understood him and been an equivalent of a wife. But Mohan Kumar's tragic flaw happens to be his insatiable hunger for lust. Not only that. Even his interest in a particular woman is not lasting, but very brief. He wants to taste a variety of women in bed. After enjoying sex with Dhanno surreptitiously, he begins to lose interest in her and dreams of having new bed mates that are experts in erotics. One may easily see in Mohan Kumar an imbalance between love and lust. His exclusive and disproportionate pursuit of lust at the cost of love makes him a tragic figure. Although he resembles the mythical Lord Krishna in his grand programme of womanization, he has neither the lyrical, nor the philosophical nor the musical capacity of the latter. His purchase of lust is very business-like without any aesthetic dimension to it. His sex-mania is supported by his unusually large phallus universally admired by all the women who receive it into them. He believes that variety is the spice of life. He finds the unity of lust in the diversity of women. In keeping with his practical Philosophy of Lust, he invites the women who responded to his advertisement in the newspapers, one by one for short-term experiments.

The first woman he entertains is Sarojini Bharadwaj who has a Ph.D. in English and who is a Lecturer in English in a college at Rewari. She goes to stay with him in his house after getting a green signal from him. For the last seven years she has not had any sex with anyone (after the break of her marriage). She is, therefore, scared of having it with Mohan Kumar who has an unusually big sized penis: "My God you are big!" She exclaimed in alarm. "This thing will tear me to pieces." She clasped it between her thighs to prevent it piercing her. "Promise you won't hurt me. Remember I'm very small and have had no sex for a very, very long time" (47-48). But her fear is gone when she experiences the joy of sex with him: "She spread out her thighs and he entered her very slowly. 'Oh God, you will split me into two,' she said clasping him by the neck. She was fully aroused. In a hoarse voice she whispered urgently, 'Ram it in.' He did as he was told. She screamed. Not in agony but in the ecstasy of a multiple orgasm. She had never experienced it before nor believed it was possible. Her body quivered, relaxed [...]" (48).

Mohan Kumar enjoys sex with Dr Sarojini for about a month and then his attraction for her diminishes. By that time, he is a bit disturbed by the death of his father-in-law and by the insult by his own brother-in-law. He sends away Sarojini after giving her a gift of a gold ring and the monthly allowance of Rs. 10,000.

Mohan Kumar again feels lonely at home and tries to refresh himself with the memory of his forlorn childhood and younger days. Having lost his mother at his birth, he was looked after by his father who was a clerk in Northern Railway of Delhi.

Having topped the list in degree examination in Maths and Sanskrit, he won a scholarship and went to Princeton University for higher study. There also he achieved highest distinction and was offered various job opportunities.

Mohan Kumar remembers how he lost his ignorance and innocence by being initiated into many interesting experiences at Princeton. He was initiated into sexual experience by a tennis player called Jessica Brown. Having lost his virginity to her, he bedded countless other American girls. Then he happened to meet a Pakistani politician's wife, Yasmine Wanchoo in Comparative Religion class. Although Yasmine Wanchoo questioned many aspects of Hindu religion, she invited Mohan Kumar on the last day of her stay in America for food and asked him to make love to her. The sexual thrill given by her was radically different from that introduced by Jessica Brown to him. "She took me by my hand and led me to the bedroom. She took off everything save her jewellery. Her skin was soft but flabby. Her big breasts sagged and she had shaved her pubic hair. None of the girls I had bedded shaved their privates. I was surprised to see that a woman so large, who had borne two children, had such a small vagina. It looked vulnerable while I gazed at her figure, she took off my shirt and pulled down my trousers. She gasped at what she saw. " 'Mashallah' what have you got there? Do all Hindus have organs of this size? It must be their reward for worshipping the phallus. She fondled it for a while with her pudgy hands, her lips glued to mine. She pulled me over her and stretched her thighs wide to receive me. I entered her. She moaned with pleasure and locked her legs behind my back. She ate up my face with bites and passionate kisses. We came together" (109). Yasmine Wanchoo teased Mohan Kumar by linking the sexual intercourse with the India-Pakistan political relationship. At the second round of sex, she took the active role and enjoyed the paradise of orgasm: "She pulled off my trousers and fondled my limp lingam till it was ready for action. She sat astride my middle, spread her ample frame over me and directed my phallus into her [...]. She kissed me hungrily and noisily on my nose, lips and neck, leaving her saliva on me, while she heaved and thumped me with her huge buttocks. 'I haven't had sex for six months. I am famished,' she said as her movements became more frenzied. 'Fill me up with all you have, you miserable kafir,' she screamed. And with a spectacular shudder and a loud ha, ha, ha, she collapsed on me like a lifeless corpse. She did all the fucking. I was simply fucked. 'Wouldn't it be nicer if we settled Pak-India problems this way rather than by abusing each other and fighting?' she asked after a while.

'Sure,' I replied. 'And with Pakistan always on top?'

'Of course! Pakistan must always be on top'" (110-11).

Such exciting experiences remain green in Mohan Kumar's memory and entertain him in his lonely hours.

After the divorce, Mohan Kumar fucks the sweeperess Dhanno as and when he wants, until one day she is arrested by the police for thievery and prostitution. Then goaded by intolerable loneliness, Mohan Kumar gives green signal to Molly Gomes from Goa who had responded positively to his advertisement in the newspapers. Accordingly she goes to his house to be his temporary concubine. Mohan Kumar tells his cooks and servants that she is a doctor. Molly Gomes is a skilled masseuse and knows how to arouse a man and then satisfy him. When she feels his penis, she exclaims, "Man, I've never seen anything of this size before. And believe me I've seen quite a few" (221). Then she sleeps on top of him twitching and milking him. Then they change positions. Mohan Kumar begins to dip into her: "I began to pump into her. She crossed her legs behind my back and heaved up each time I plunged down. 'Harder!' she cried. 'For God's sake, don't stop!' she screamed. I put all I had into her. She slapped the carpet with both her hands and cried loudly, 'Oh God, this is heaven, heaven, heaven [...]'" (222). After enjoying the heavenly bliss of sex, Molly Gomes rubs every part of his anatomy with a towel soaked in hot water thereby giving him a soothing experience. Then they exchange their memories of loss of their virginity. After listening to Mohan Kumar's past experiences, Molly Gomes tells him without any hesitation how she was deflowered in the fourteenth year of her age by her mother's younger brother who was twenty years senior to her. She also confesses how she had sex with white people whom she massaged, but never wanted to sleep with Goans lest she might be dubbed as a slut. Molly Gomes entertains Mohan Kumar in many ways by giving him company in drinking, eating, smoking and dancing with him and by listening to music and shopping with him. Mohan Kumar has the sweetest experience when has a sunbath on the roof-top of his house and is given a memorable massage by Molly Gomes. He first lies on his stomach. Molly Gomes becomes stark naked and sits astride his back and massages every centimetre of his rear side. Then he lies on his back when Molly Gomes massages every part of his front side very dexterously. He enjoys a close-up view of her nakedness from different angles. Then he massages her in his own unskilled way. By the time both of them are excited, he enters her from behind, "I positioned myself between her thighs and began to massage her buttocks. Come to think of it, a woman's buttocks excite a man more than any other part of her body—more than her lips or breasts or her pussy. And Molly's were beautifully rounded and firm. I found them irresistible and slowly entered her cunt from the rear. She gave a long sigh of pleasure and let me go further and further into her [...]. Then we resumed our search for the ultimate truth of bodily existence: at times she pressed into me from above with my hands squeezing and pressing her buttocks to urge her on, then I on top with her nails stuck into my posterior. When neither of us could hold out any longer, we went at each other like wild animals, tearing and clawing each other's flesh. The climax was the most prolonged that either of us had experienced in our lives" (245-46). After enjoying a variety of picturesque experiences with Mohan Kumar for three months Molly Gomes returns to Goa.

Mohan Kumar feels lonely again after the departure of Molly Gomes. He is taunted by his friends when he goes to the local clubs of Delhi. Once he goes to Haridwar to visit his late father's ashram. There he meets a few foreigners including

Susanthika Goonatillake from the High Commission of Sri Lanka. She is a Buddhist. Mohan Kumar takes her to Har Ki Pauri to observe the beautiful sight of the evening *puja* on the bank of the Ganga, the waving of candelabra of lights to the river, the clangour of bells, etc. Sasanthika thanks him for taking her to the beautiful holy spot where she could observe the beauty of living Hindu religion. Then she invites him to her room in BHEL Guest House. After exchanging amicabilities, Susanthika sits on his lap and kisses him. Naturally Mohan Kumar is aroused. "She felt my member rise and throb under her. She stood up and tapped it with her bony hand. 'He's getting impatient for action. Come.' She took my hand and led me to her bed. She lay down on her back and pulled her sari up above the waist. She wore no panties. She had planned it all. I was surprised to see how big her cunt was. She had obviously had plenty of sex. As I mounted her, she expressed no surprise about the size of my penis as most other women had: she simply guided it in with her fingers and said, 'It feels like Ashoka's pillar entering me. I like it. Put in all you have.'

"I did. She squirmed with pleasure [...]. She climaxed with her teeth dug into my neck and her hands clutching my hair. I pulled out just in time and squirted my semen on her thighs.

"'My thighs are sticky, my sari is crumpled, and you've snapped the buttons of my bra, but it was worth it'" (265). Susanthika tells Mohan Kumar how she was deflowered by her uncle when she was barely sixteen and how by way of revenge, she seduced the fourteen-year-old son of the uncle. Then she meets Mohan Kumar regularly on Saturday afternoons for regular fucking sessions until she is transferred to New York where she is engaged to a Sri Lankan. She asks Mohan Kumar to stop phoning to her.

After the varied sexual adventures, Mohan Kumar feels lonely and remembers his children Ranjit and Mohini. He wants to see them, but finds them rather indifferent to him as they are brainwashed against him by their mother.

One may easily see a moral pattern in this so-called pornographic novel. Mohan Kumar who has overindulged in sex has to pay a very heavy price for that. He feels that he cannot have erection now. He fears about the possible impotence. Once he goes to Bombay and stays in Taj Mahal Hotel where he drinks whisky and orders for a woman and fucks her twice on two consecutive nights. The woman being a common prostitute does not reveal her real name, but calls herself a *bai*. Mohan Kumar is happy to realize that he has not become an impotent. But the sins of his past life have a greater punishment than the impotence that is in store for him. After returning to Delhi he begins to suffer from fever and consults the foreign-returned Dr Malhotra. The doctor conducts many tests and confirms that Mohan Kumar has HIV positive. Mohan Kumar is scared beyond measure and haunted by the idea of death. His practical sense is instantly awakened. He, therefore, consults a lawyer and registers his will thereby leaving his property to his son and daughter. Later Dr Malhotra tells him that he has developed tuberculosis in addition to AIDS. Death in the form of shameful disease comes to him as retribution to his sins. As he has negated the principle of health, he is going to be negated by the moral order of hygiene. Mohan Kumar turns out to be a tragic figure by becoming aware of his recklessness in womanization and of the inexorability of his sinful action. He thinks of how his social prestige will be ruined and how he cannot lead a respectable life in the society. Although he bought a variety of sexes with money, he realizes how, rather belatedly, that money cannot save him from the monstrous disease, AIDS. Mohan Kumar knows that none but he himself is responsible for his downfall. He suffers from a deep sense of loneliness like a tragic figure. But again like a tragic hero, he never indulges in self-pity, but accepts the punishment manfully and heroically. He utters the Gayatri mantra and reads the *Bhagavad-Gita* left by his father in the ashram at Haridwar. Like a typical tragic figure, he is reconciled to his lot. One day he coughs and vomits blood. He plans to commit suicide as there is no other way for him. He, therefore, takes thirty sleeping tablets one by one and uttering the *Gayatri mantra* after swallowing each tablet and sleeps permanently. His life awakens both pity and fear in the mind of readers thereby alerting them not to follow the negative path of Mohan Kumar. By highlighting the negation of negative approach to life, the novel upholds the affirmative principles and the moral order of the universe.

Condemning *The Company of Women* as a demoralizing pornographic novel will be tantamount to the exhibition of one's critical blindness. A sensible reader should know how to learn a moral from it. The novel may be taken as a powerful satire on the aristocratic or *nouveau riche* as well as middle class Indian society. The aristocratic people who have abundant money but no morality. Such people are an easy prey to bad habits like smoking, eating, drinking and womanizing beyond the limits imposed by human life. A lesson that emerges from such a situation is that man cannot achieve lasting happiness with the help of money alone. Money can buy all the pleasures of life but never the real happiness. Man's overindulgence in sensuality may give him temporary pleasures, which ruin him at the same time. As Basaveswara, a twelfth-century mystic of Karnataka says, a sensual man is like a dog licking the blade of a sword tasting not only the drops of blood of others on the sword but also his own blood. In a similar way, Mohan Kumar has enjoyed the pleasures of womanization thereby ruining his own vitals of life.

The novel may be taken as a satire not only on men like Mohan Kumar but on women as well. It throws light on a particular type of women to be found in the Indian society. Almost all the women that Mohan Kumar beds are compelled by the contingencies of their life like poverty, desire for fun and pleasure or escape from the drudgery of life. They are not at all bothered about virginity, chastity or sexual purity. They are secretly emancipated from sexual morality and seek secret sexual satisfaction and fun and earn money from Mohan Kumar. They are systematically hypocritical in their behaviour. After a brief enjoyment with Mohan Kumar for two or three months, they wish to go back to their former life and lead a 'respectable' life. There cannot be a clap until both the palms meet. Similarly sexual sin is not possible without the cooperation of the two parties, *i.e.* man and woman. The novel, therefore, is a satire as much about a rich man as about hypocritical and opportunistic women who happen to be part and parcel of Indian society. One should have the courage to look into the face of harsh reality presented so uninhibitedly and boldly by Khushwant Singh and not shy way from it puritanically.

In spite of the fact that *The Company of Women* is apparently a pornographic celebration of the commercialization of lust, it also has a concealed satirical element in it. Just as one is struck by the shameless pursuit of sex by the *nouveau riche* industrialist, Mohan Kumar, one is also surprised to notice the hypocritical behaviour of a number of women, both foreign and Indian, who come into his sexual life. Whereas the shameless pursuit of sex is abetted by an abundance of money with the people of aristocratic class of India (possibly of the world), the same is necessitated by lack of money with the low and the middle class people. Whereas Mohan Kumar is representative of the aristocratic male, the various women who come in contact with him are representative of their classes who indulge in sexual adventures with him either for thrill or economic necessity. The behaviour of the various women who come into Mohan Kumar's life may be studied carefully to understand the society represented by them. Broadly speaking, the women that Mohan Kumar has had may be classified into two categories: Western and Eastern, although there are many individual differences among them.

Jessica Browne is the first girl who seduces and devirginates Mohan Kumar in Princeton. She is an African girl who is quite free in her sexual morals like other American or European girls. When she comes to meet and know Mohan Kumar, she moves around with him freely and teaches him how to play tennis. After achieving some intimacy with him, she invites him to her room, kisses him lustily and reveals the full beauty of her nakedness to him thereby arousing him sexually. Then she orders him to strip himself. She examines his unusually big-sized member with admiration. Realizing that he is still a virgin, she guides him into herself thus initiating him into the pleasure of sex. Mohan Kumar is thus devirginated by the uninhibited Jessica Browne. A believer in free sex, she has no qualms of conscience about sexual morality, virginity or chastity. She converts Mohan Kumar from a boy into a man and gives him confidence about his manliness. But she is not attached to him or any boy in particular as she is very independent in her behaviour. She believes in pure lust. That is why their friendship comes to a close very soon. She wants to sleep around with any boy of her choice. Soon Mohan Kumar discovers that she gets irritated with him over small things. Once when he invites her to watch his tennis play for the freshmen, she flatly refuses to oblige him. Mohan Kumar feels hurt. When he tells her so, she snaps at him, "You Orientals are very possessive about your women. I'm not your property. I am not your wife" (95).

If Jessica Browne is known for her free sex and independent nature, Yasmeen is a Pakistani Muslim young lady who practises her extra-marital sex rather secretly and hypocritically. She happens to be Mohan Kumar's classmate at Princeton University in the Comparative Literature course offered by Dr Ashby. A spirited Muslim from Pakistan, she argues with her teacher as well as with her classmates including Mohan Kumar about the apparent contradictions of Hinduism and the Hindu worship of animals like monkeys, elephants and snakes and things like trees and water and even human anatomy like phallus and vagina. She finds fault with obscene sculptures in temples and Lord Krishna's sexy games with gopikas, etc. But after growing intimate with Mohan Kumar, she apologizes for her frankness and requests him to clarify her misgivings about Hinduism. She tells him about her personal life, that her husband is a Minister in Azad Kashmir (the present Pakistan) Government and that she is also active in politics and a Member of the Assembly; that she has three children. She is naturally proud of Muslim heroism and asserts that "one Muslim warrior can take on ten of you Hindus" (102). In spite of the national and religious pride, Yasmeen likes Mohan Kumar, a Hindu and gives him a gift of a Gold Cross-pen. He reciprocates it with a gift of a silver ring. Although Yasmeen is twenty years' older than Mohan Kumar, she seeks his company. In spite of all the ideological differences between the two, Yasmeen seems to have liked him secretly. That is why she invites him for an evening meal on the last day of her stay in Princeton. When he goes to her room, she cooks food for him and offers him scotch and beer. In the meanwhile, she goes to her bedroom, spreads a mat, genuflects on it and recites her prayer for a few minutes. Mohan Kumar watches her praying while he is drinking his whisky. When she comes out of her bedroom after the prayer, Mohan Kumar asks her also to have some drinks, but she refuses flatly, "*Tauba*! It is *haram*. You will make me a sinner, will you? You can fetch me a coke from the fridge!" Yasmeen does not want to commit the sin of drinking liquor. One may not fail to notice the contradictions in her behaviour. She who refuses to drink liquor on account of its sinfulness, does not mind having sex with him. "Then she held my hands in hers and looked into my eyes till I had to lower my gaze, embarrassed. Suddenly, she put her arms round my neck and said, 'It is our last evening together. Make love to me. Something to remember you by for the rest of my days'" (108). Then she leads him to the bedroom and enjoys sex with him in a normal posture. But in the second session of sex, she behaves like an aggressive woman by getting on top of him and fucking him rigorously thereby getting the maximum sexual pleasure as well as proving the superiority of Pakistan over India symbolically. After enjoying wonderful sex with Yasmeen, Mohan Kumar asks her a few awkward questions, "You must tell me how you square your belief in Islamic values, with what you and I have been doing" (111). After a long pause she admits, "What

I did was sinful" (111). She answers, "The body has its compulsions" (111). Yasmeen's sexual behaviour shows the in-built contradiction in her nature and her compromise with the Islamic values, which she upholds so spiritedly.

Having enjoyed free sex with foreign girls with abandon, Mohan Kumar returns to India and gets married to Sonu under the paternal pressure and gets the first baby in course of time. He appoints a day nurse called Mary Joseph, a Syrian Christian from Kerala, to look after the baby. Being a nurse by profession, Mary Joseph is quite free in her sexual morals. One night, when she goes to Mohan Kumar's room to say 'good night,' he makes advances on her. Far from resisting it, she yields willingly to him and admires his unusually large member. Their mating becomes a regular habit for both of them. When his wife Sonu suspects her behaviour, she dismisses her from service. Then Mohan Kumar invites her to posh hotels to enjoy sex with her. She admires his member wholeheartedly, "Saar, you have the biggest thing I have ever seen. So big no other man has" (181). When Mohan Kumar asks her rather mischievously, "How many have you seen?" (181), she reveals her interesting sexual history, "What seen? My husband not half as big. And so quick to finish. In out, in out. Phat. Once his younger brother had me. Also small and very quick, quick. The padre of our village church was much better. But he was sorry for doing it. After he finished he asked me to pardon him and made me pray with him to Jesus to ask him forgiveness. Imagine, no, still naked and sweating and kneeling on the floor and praying to God! He made me feel worse than a prostitute who did it without asking for money. Tell me, saar, is it a sin to do it with somebody you like?'" (181). Mary Joseph's behaviour is ample evidence of the great gap between the powerful biological urge and the familial, cultural and religious façade.

After getting a green signal from Mohan Kumar, Dr Sarojini travels from Rewari to Delhi and instructs Mohan not to come to the Railway Station "as one of her colleagues would be travelling with her" (40). She wants to go to his house in a taxi.

Although a married woman and a Doctor of Philosophy in English Literature, she wants to pursue her adulterous career very secretly thereby satisfying the expectations of a patriarchal society and retaining her reputation as a chaste wife. One may see systematic hypocrisy in-built in her behaviour. When Dr Sarojini is going into the market of Delhi in Mohan Kumar's car, she observes another woman in a nearby car and mentally calls her a 'slut.' When the cars start moving after the traffic lights have changed, "Sarojini realized what she had done. She had condemned a woman who perhaps was doing nothing worse than what she herself had agreed to do. Only, she, Sarojini Bharadwaj, Professor of English, did not look the type. For the second time that morning she felt ashamed of herself" (43).

Although Sarojini is initially hesitant to sleep with Mohan Kumar, she feels assured by his gentle behaviour. When Mohan Kumar gives her rigorous sexual pleasure, she enjoys the paradisal pleasure that is unprecedented. "She screamed, not in agony but in the ecstasy of a multiple orgasm. She had never experienced it before nor believed it was possible. Her body quivered, relaxed [...]. I'm a whore, a common tart! I'm a bitch" (48). Mohan Kumar, therefore, tries to pacify her by assuring her, "You are none of those, you are a nice gentlewoman who has not known love" (48).

After overcoming her initial sense of guilt and shyness, Sarojini responds to him uninhibitedly and has sex with him in many picturesque postures. But their three months' period is cut short by the gossip that has started in his social circles and Mohan Kumar's fear of his wife's detective and harmful attitude. Although Sarojini knows she would be called a 'slut' if people came to know about her adulterous adventure, she has the satisfaction of having enjoyed real sex quite secretly. Then she goes back to her parents and son and the daily grind of her college at Rewari, to lead a 'respectable' life in the patriarchal society.

After seeking divorce from his petulant, nagging, quarrelsome and non-cooperative wife Sonu, Mohan Kumar decides to have his usual arrangement of sexual companionship. He studies the photographs of different women who had responded to his advertisement and decides to invite Molly Gomes from Goa. Molly Gomes is a trained nurse specializing in physiotherapy. Like a majority of women of her profession, she is not innocent at all. She has a checkered sexual history. She was once married to a foreigner and soon divorced him as he was good for nothing. Although born as a Catholic Christian, "I have no hang-ups about religion. I go to church only to please my parents and relations" (214). When she joins Mohan Kumar she tells him her professional history of massaging women and old men. She uses all her professional skills to excite Mohan Kumar and offers him wonderful orgasmic ecstasy, through different postures and methods. Additionally, she satisfies him with her wonderful cooking. One day Mohan Kumar asks her mischievously, "How old were you Molly when you lost your virginity?" and narrates his own previous sexual adventures with a number of women. Then Molly Gomes confesses that she was seduced by her mother's younger brother when she was only fourteen years. She narrates how one day he came home and fondled her for some time and "Then he fumbled with his trouser buttons, managed to get his fat dick out and shoved it in me, all in one go. He was an impatient man. It hurt and I screamed in agony. He pulled after a violent thrust and spilt all his gooey stuff on my thighs. He made me promise I wouldn't tell my parents, or they'd kill us both. Of course I didn't tell them. I didn't even tell the padre at confession. I told nobody. You are the first person" (230).

After having lost her virginity at the young age of fourteen, she did not remain sexually pure later also. She had sex with a few foreigners, but did not want to sleep with Goans because she did not like her so-called reputation to be tarnished. She says, "I can't afford to sleep around with Goans. It would soon get around and I'd be branded a slut. With foreigners there's no such danger. And although they paid me, I did not feel I was whoring because there was no talk of money beforehand, no bargaining. Everyone gave me a tip after the massage. If I gave them more than a massage, the tips were not a few hundred rupees but a few thousand—you can't let that kind of easy money go. But my motto is: Have fun with the whites, marry only a Goan" (237). Molly Gomes's life testifies to the fact that she wants to practise adultery secretly and still marry a native man and enjoy the reputation of being a 'chaste wife' in the patriarchal society. Her hypocrisy is as practical as systematic.

Susanthika who has been working as a Second Secretary in the High Commission of Sri Lanka is very social and liberal in her behaviour. She introduces herself to Mohan Kumar at a cocktail party and shows her eagerness to go to Haridwar to see the Har Ki Pauri and evening worship there. They plan their trip to Haridwar and watch the ethereal beauty of the religious worship on the Ganga river. As their friendship grows more and more intimate every minute, they indulge in mating and continue it for several months. Susanthika's history reveals the fact that she is not a virgin although she is unmarried. She is quite emancipated in her sexual morals. As she confesses, "Well, I come from a large family: tea planters. I was a clever cookie, so I passed the civil service exam and opted for the Foreign Service. As for being liberated, yes I have no hang-ups about sex at all. If I like a chap and he likes me we get into bed. Nothing wrong in that, is there?" (266). When Mohan Kumar asks her rather mischievously about her sexual history, she narrates her chequered and colourful history very frankly. "But I'll tell you I was sixteen. Nothing romantic about the deflowering. My own uncle, my father's younger brother [...]. It seemed harmless enough at first kissing and cuddling that sort of thing. Then he thought he'd got me worked up and started playing with my breasts and stroking my crotch. He got frantic and tore into me" (266). Having thus been deflowered at the age of sixteen by her own uncle, Susanthika takes revenge upon him by seducing his son, "I taught the fellow a lesson by seducing his fourteen-year-old son, my cousin. The boy got so besotted with me he started writing me love letters and poems" (266).

Susanthika enjoys regular sex with Mohan Kumar for two months until she is posted to New York. When they are separated by the exigencies of life, they keep ringing up and corresponding with each other, using words of love. But gradually there is a decrease in their calls and correspondence. "Six months later she informed me that she was engaged to marry a fellow Sri Lankan diplomat posted in Washington and we should stop writing or calling each other on the phone. She assured me that she would for ever keep a secluded corner in her heart for me and love me as she had from the day we first met" (275). Susanthika's behaviour shows how in spite of being an emancipated woman with varied sexual experiences with men of her choice, she wants to hide it from her husband when married to him. She thus wants to conform to the patriarchal set-up of society at least outwardly, although she has violated the patriarchal norms secretly. The feminine hypocrisy of Susanthika is too obvious to be commented upon any further.

Although Mohan Kumar is a notorious and decadent womanizer, he has some positive qualities, which endear him to us. His deep love and respect for his father is really an admirable trait of his personality. His father had lost his wife as soon as Mohan Kumar was born. He worked as a Superintendent in the Office of the Northern Railway and lived with his son in the clerk's quarters close to New Delhi railway station. After Mohan Kumar's return from Princeton, his father arranges his marriage because "It is a father's duty to see his son married in his life-time. I am only fulfilling my dharma. If your mother had been alive, she would have been helping me. Now I have to do it alone" (125-26). He takes Mohan Kumar to Haridwar and shows him the evening worship of the river Ganga. Mohan Kumar is overwhelmed by the sublime and ethereal experience so much that he is haunted by it for the rest of his life. Then he is taken by his father to Har Ki Pauri where both of them have their holy bath in the Ganga. In spite of the ideological difference between father and son, the latter obeys the former out of reverence. Mohan Kumar's father arranges his marriage with Sonu, daughter of a rich man, Achint Ram, because he wants Mohan Kumar to settle down in life and live happily ever after. Accordingly the marriage takes place with great pomp and jubilation. Mohan Kumar is relieved of his depression when his father-in-law Achint Ram buys a three-bedroom flat in Maharani Bagh for his daughter and son-in-law. Within a year's time Sonu gives birth to a son whom they name as Ranjit Kumar. Mohan Kumar's father develops deep affection and attachment to his grandson, Ranjit Kumar. Ranjit Kumar spends most of his time playing with his grandfather. Sonu does not like it and she openly accuses her father-in-law, "Pitaji, you are spoiling him. He gets too excited when you are around and refuses to go to bed" (186). She continues to complain against her father-in-law. Mohan Kumar is angered by his wife's curtness and bad manners. His father senses the daughter-in-law's resentment. "My father sensed that Sonu did not like his living in the house. One day he told me, 'Puttar, I want to go to my ashram for a few days [...]. I need to be with myself for a while'" (187). Sonu is quite happy to get rid of her father-in-law. But Mohan Kumar who has great respect for his father does not want to hurt him. He wants to do his best to make him happy and comfortable. He, therefore, takes him in his car to Haridwar and puts him in a room in the ashram. Sonu does not like her father-in-law to return home and spoil her son. Her callous attitude to her pious father-in-law is very typical of that of many Indian daughters-in-law who do not want any one except their husbands in the family. In order to compensate for his wife's callousness, Mohan Kumar visits Haridwar every full moon day and spends a few days in the company of his father. When Mohan Kumar gets a second issue, a daughter, Mohini, his father comes home, stays for a week and blesses the grandchild and returns to Haridwar. Sonu contemptuously refers to her father as an 'old man.' Mohan Kumar does not allow his cantankerous wife to come between him and his father. He visits his father regularly on every full moon day for five years. One day he receives a postcard telling him of his father's death and cremation. Then he rushes to Haridwar and is taken to his father's room he breaks down. "I was conducted to my father's room. In the centre of the charpoy on which he had slept a few days earlier was a brass pot containing his ashes. It had garlands of marigold flowers twined around it. I took it in my arms and again broke down. I heard myself wailing: 'Hai Pitaji! Where have you gone without me? You did not even give me the chance to be with you when the end came!' Ashram inmates gathered round to condole with me and Jiwan Ram let me cry to my heart's content till I ran out of tears" (199). He carries the urn of his father's ashes and goes to Har Ki Pauri and waves it worshipfully. "I reached the clock-tower facing Har Ki Pauri a couple of minutes before the aarti. As the priests on the opposite bank started waving their candelabras and chanting hymns and the temple bells began to ring, I stood ankle deep in the stream and waved the brass urn, touching its base to the water. Each time, I brought it down I felt at peace with myself and the world [...]. After a long time I walked back to the car, still clutching the urn in my arm. I refused to eat all-night and slept fitfully, thinking of my father. I felt he was as close to me in death as he was in life" (200). The next morning he goes to the Ganga ghat and pours the ashes into the river. Then he undergoes the ritual of having his head shaved. He settles the account with the ashram and returns home. Mohan Kumar's love and respect for his father is, obviously, admirable. He emerges as an ideal son by clearing the debt that he owes to his father.

NOTE

Excerpts from *Indian English Literature: A Critical Survey, Points of View*, Vol. VIII, No. I, Summer 2001, ed. K.K. Sharma. Ghaziabad, 112.

WORK CITED

Singh, Khushwant. *The Company of Women* (New Delhi: Penguin Books, 2000). All the references to the text are from this edition.

4

Bigamy and the Byronic Hero in Bronte and Jhabvala

MARIE FERNANDES

Women writers have always had to work against the grain. They have had to struggle hard to be heard, to achieve the distinction of being regarded as an equal of man, whether it was Charlotte Bronte and her sisters trying to carve a niche for themselves in Victorian England, or Ruth Prawer Jhabvala in more recent times, with her present-day brand of feminine consciousness.

But somewhere, in the deep recesses of the unconscious mind, there exists a kind of submissiveness, a feeling of inadequacy and helplessness which is difficult to shrug off, which unconsciously gives over to the superior male force. This is made evident in the women protagonists in both Bronte's *Jane Eyre* and Jhabvala's *Heat and Dust.* Critics see in Jane's love for Rochester as "a woman's longing for a strong master", and Olivia's fascination is with a Nawab, a wild Indian prince. While the hero is allowed to deceive the unsuspecting heroine and be above the rules of society, the heroine must strictly abide by them. For her, anatomy is destiny. Virtue will ultimately be rewarded and an act of bravado will only lead to misfortune and tragedy.

Although these two great feminist writers lived almost a century apart, one notices certain very interesting plot developments and ideas that are notably similar and one wonders whether Jhabvala has unconsciously modelled *Heat and Dust* on Bronte's *Jane Eyre,* or to use Wittgenstein's expression, is it just a 'family resemblance' we see in works by women writers?

Both Bronte and Jhabvala use the first person narrative to tell their story. Jane Eyre tells the readers the story of her life, right from the time she was a little girl of ten, till the time she marries Rochester. Critics have found an interesting structure in *Jane Eyre* where the imagery points out to certain thematic parallels. The Rivers family in the latter part of the book can be seen as the revised version of the Reeds. There is the repeated pattern of two sisters and one brother. The brothers sharing the same Christian name, alerts to significant similarities. There are surprisingly common elements in the presentation of John Reed and his apparently saintly Reed counterpart. The literal meaning of their name suggests an association—reeds growing beside rivers, which surely is not accidental. Although St. John's vocation, and the intensity of his dedication to it, make him an impressive figure in Jane's eyes, he attempts to bully Jane spiritually, as John Reed did physically.

The narrator in *Heat and Dust* in trying to reconstruct the story of Olivia, her grandfather's first wife, repeats in her life some of Olivia's adventures, but with a somewhat reverse image, according to the changed times and circumstances. It is as much a story of Olivia as it is a story about herself. Jhabvala skilfully manages this double parallel. Interestingly, Jhabvala too uses the name Rivers in *Heat and Dust.* Douglas Rivers, Olivia's husband, in *Jane Eyre,* is like St. John Rivers, a man devoted to his duty. In Marcia's words, "He was just a *stick* and she was not in the least surprised that Olivia should have got bored to death with him and gone off with someone more interesting" (179). There is also, of course, the thematic parallel in *Heat and Dust*. There is no similarity in the early and later part of the book, as in *Jane Eyre,* but two themes run parallel. The story of Olivia is very similar to that of the narrator.

Elaine Showalter in *A Literature of Their Own* (1977) divides the tradition of women's writing into three phases. She would probably place Bronte in the first phase, the 'feminine phase' (1840-80), where women internalised the dominant male aesthetic standard and where the main sphere of their work was their immediate domestic and social circle. Jhabvala would obviously belong to the third, 'female' phase (1920 onwards) which inherited characteristics of the former phases and developed the idea of specifically female writing and female experience. Unlike women writers of the 'feminine phase' who were impervious to the political happenings, for Jhabvala and the others it becomes their *raison d'être* of writing their texts.

Women's texts can be interpreted variously. Kate Millet in *Sexual Politics* used the term 'patriarchy' to describe the cause of women's oppression. Power is exerted directly or indirectly in civil and domestic life, to constrain women. Gayatri Chakravorty Spivak in her essay *Three Women's Texts and a Critique of Imperialism* is convinced that even in a cult text like *Jane Eyre* with its emergent perspective of feminist criticism, the axiom of imperialism must not be disregarded. She argues that this is true of all of nineteenth century British literature. Jhabvala also unwittingly reflects this axiom in *Heat and Dust.*

According to Elizabeth Fox-Genovese the beautifully orchestrated opening of *Jane Eyre* is the scene of marginalisation and privatisation of the protagonist. The family at the centre withdraws into the sanctioned architectural space of the drawing room, whereas Jane 'slipped in'—into the margin. She withdraws into the small breakfast room, mounts the window seat, draws the red curtains close and is shrined in double retirement. Jhabvala's *Heat and Dust* opens with the mention of Olivia forfeiting her centralised position and going away with the Nawab to live in a small town of X, not to be his wife but his mistress. Douglas who is upright and just, travels back to the centre, to England, where he marries Tessie.

It is easy to understand why Jane can be seen as being marginalised. The first few opening chapters emphasise Jane's vulnerability. While clearly not a servant, she is nevertheless in a subordinate position, obliged to tolerate the young John Reed's abuse because she is an impoverished dependent. Jane has been in this situation since she was taken into her uncle's house as a 'parentless infant.' Finally her slight size gives her a sense of 'physical inferiority.' A child, a female, an orphan, a pauper and evidently unattractive, Jane is at every point disadvantaged. Olivia, in *Heat and Dust* while not being in anyway inferior like Jane has still to be content with her subordinate role. She must be a dutiful wife to Douglas Rivers, play the role of a good host to the Minnies and Crawfords, play the piano and in short remain in the margins. It is a man's duty to seek a life outside the house and be at the centre of life and activity.

It is very evident that *Jane Eyre* belongs to the realm of Romance. Rochester represents a change from the handsome hero of tradition. He is a Byronic hero—a rebel, dark and compelling in appearance, though not handsome: a man who exercises considerable charm over women, in spite of, or because of, a guilty secret from which he is trying to escape. He has a shade of Byronic gloom and appetising mystery. The Nawab in Jhabvala's *Heat and Dust* has been depicted in a similar Byronic fashion. An Indian prince, dark and mysterious, he succeeds in charming the fair Olivia and even has the nerve to tell her "Yes you like rough people who fight well and are mostly on a horse" (45).

Rochester is master of his house and is used to having his way. From Jane too he demands obedience, for like the others, she too lives in Thornfield, under the same roof and as governess to Adele, receives a wage from him. Although Olivia is in no way dependant on the Nawab, she finds that she cannot disregard his wishes. As Harry says, "I told you: one does not say no to such a person [...]" (34).

The theme of madness seems to be a recurrent theme with women writers. Phyllis Chester in her book *Women and Madness* writes, "Women more than men, and in greater numbers than their existence in the general population would predict, are involved in 'careers' as psychiatric patients" (xxii). She argues that the ethics of mental health seems to be masculine. The social role assigned to women is that of serving an image, authoritative and central, of man: a woman is first and foremost a daughter/a mother/a wife. Felman uses Jacques Derrida's analysis of the way that oppositional thinking dominates Western cultures which define things by their opposites and impose hierarchy upon the opposition: man/woman, sane/insane, speech/silence, same/other, to show the traditional ways of defining woman, as being always subordinate. She is man's 'other' and is therefore what he is not—insane and silent.

Rochester had been tricked into marrying Bertha Mason, daughter of a West Indian planter and merchant. Although she brought with her a handsome fortune of thirty thousand pounds, she was mad like her mother before her. Rochester's father and brother Rowland knew all this, but they thought only of the money and joined in the plot against him. Since Bertha Mason had been pronounced mad, she had to be locked up and Rochester at the age of twenty-six felt cheated and helpless. He soon took up to riotous living in the continent to forget his sorrow. He tried to conceal his wife, to give himself a chance to make a fresh start and this was his dark secret.

The Nawab, in *Heat and Dust* unlike Rochester fell in love with Zahira Cabobpur or Sandy, who belonged to a family who were considered much bigger royals than his, and by their standard the Nawab was not even considered rich. He married her against their wish, but like Bertha, she went mad and was sent back to the family. The Nawab retained her dowry and he continued to have trouble with them. Like Rochester, his mad wife Sandy is his nemesis whom he does not really hide from Olivia.

Bertha Mason is understood to be a figure produced by the axiomatic of imperialism, the white Jamaican Creole, who struggled to give herself a voice but collapsed under the strain. She has been described in less than human terms. She is cast off and finally jumps to her death and lies smashed on the pavement on which her brains and blood are scattered.

Sandy unlike Bertha Mason is neither seen nor heard. The writer is careful not to endow her with beast-like qualities that would rob her of her humanity. Even after the affair with Olivia, Sandy still occupies the privileged position as wife. It is Olivia who has to play second fiddle and be a mistress to the Nawab and live alone in the small town of X, while he travels to the centre to London to plead his cause. His wife Zahira is not left alone in some remote corner of India, but is at the white man's centre—Switzerland, where she is being treated for her mental illness. The Nawab too spends time with her.

Rochester seems to possess no moral scruple. While he resents the trap laid by his father to marry the mad Bertha Mason, he does not hesitate to entrap Jane into a bigamous relationship. He takes advantage of her innocence and dependant position knowing that she has no family to take her side. But Providence comes to her aid and she is saved just in time.

A post-colonial reading of *Heat and Dust* would show how patriarchy and colonialism collude to worsen women's predicament. The Nawab, like Rochester is without moral scruple. Although Olivia is in no way like Jane dependant on him, he thinks nothing of seducing her. He exploits her weakness. He visits her when she is alone and capitalises on her admiration of him. Olivia is not as fortunate as Jane. The Nawab is like Caliban, the crude and unconquerable master of the state of Khatm without self-restraint and self-discipline. Following his past, his upbringing in the stifling atmosphere of a petty prince's harem, there is his frustrating relationship with the British Prospero who have repressed him back to childhood by their infuriating colonial paternalism. For, left to his devices he might have given full rein to his obvious criminal and vicious proclivities, for he belonged to a savage race, a descendant of a robber chieftain. His seduction of Olivia is seen not merely in terms of exploitation by a patriarchal system but as a political act. The English see it as his crude attempt to seek vengeance to try to assert his power and prove his dominance.

The story of *Jane Eyre* ends on a happy note with Jane going back to Rochester and marrying him after his wife Bertha Mason has died. *Heat and Dust* does not end on this similarly happy note, for Olivia has not been faithful to her husband. She can no longer be with him, when her guilt has been exposed and she goes to the Nawab. But the Nawab for his part, after he has made his conquest, is no longer enamoured of his fair lady and spends his time between mother, wife and mistress. The narrator of *Heat and Dust* is also similarly treated. She lets Chid and Inder Lal use her for their sexual gratification and at the end of the novel, she is alone. She wants to move to an ashram in the mountain, for she is determined to have the baby she has conceived with Chid.

The fire imagery is very strong in *Jane Eyre.* The Red Room signifies the eruption of Jane's overheated emotions. Lowood is the place where she learns from Helen Burns and at the fireside of Miss Temple to discipline those feelings. Thornfield epitomises warmth, both physical and emotional, and the attendant danger of the all-consuming fire—as symbolic of passion. Moor House is the location where Jane is most threatened by spiritual and emotional chill, while Ferndean is the scene of reconciliation—warmth without burning, the coolness of the evening air without the chill—once the fire of Thornfield has burnt itself out.

Heat and Dust too has its share of fire imagery. There is the blazing heat of the sun. "The country they drove through lay broiling in the sun. It glittered like glass and seemed to stretch out endlessly" (41-42). Then there is the unpleasant incident of suttee, where a merchant's wife had died and the widow had been forced by her relatives to burn herself with him on his funeral pyre. Besides, in the first summer when Olivia was in India, there was rioting in Khatm on the Husband's Wedding Day and the communal troubles that broke out in Satipur, the adjoining state to Khatm, "tended to spread like forest fire" (68). The fire of passion is more destructive in *Heat and Dust* than it is in *Jane Eyre* and there is a sense of waste and loss. It is the all-consuming fire that reduces to ash and dust Olivia's baby and her dreams and hopes.

REFERENCES

1. Bronte, Charlotte. *Jane Eyre* (1847; London: Octopus,1986).
2. Jhabvala, Ruth Prawer. *Heat and Dust* (1975; London: Futura, 1976).
3. Spivak, Gayatri Chakravorty. "Three Women's Texts and a Critique of Imperialism," *The Feminist Reader: Essays in Gender and the Politics of Literary Criticism*, Eds. Catherine Belsey and Jane Moore (London: Macmillan, 1989).
4. Chester, Phyllis. *Women and Madness* (New York: Avon, 1973).

5

Crossing the Border: A Study of *Baumgartner's Bombay* (1988) and *Journey to Ithaca* (1995)

USHA RANI

Invariably in almost all Indian writers in English, the theme of East-West encounter forms quite a significant aspect of their ventures. It has been explored at various levels and through different angles. In the fictional canvas of Anita Desai, too many protagonists travel across the land with different aims and expectations. Sometimes these journeys result in bringing new information, knowledge and memorable experiences. At other times they simply end up in confusion, frustration and unfathomable depression of the heart.

In the present paper, this theme of 'moving across the border' has been studied from a different angle with reference to the two objectives with which the journey is usually taken up. The two later novels of Desai, namely: *Baumgartner's Bombay* and *Journey to Ithaca*, quite clearly explain that journey, earlier referred to as 'moving across the border,' has been made the very leitmotif in these novels. Many characters in these two novels are always on the move from one place to another. However, in this paper, the main focus shall be placed on the principal characters only, *i.e.*, Hugo Baumgartner (*Baumgartner's Bombay*) and Matteo and Sophie (*Journey to Ithaca*). The paper poses two questions: whether the journey taken by the protagonists is a kind of an escape; or does it provide a platform or a means for a new search.

And finally, do these protagonists succeed fully in their purpose or not.

On the surface levels both these queries (escape/search) just appear to be the two sides of the same coin. And partly they are; but going into the details we realize that they point not only towards different factors, which are responsible for these escapes/searches, but also the end results too vary respectively.

The beginning and the end of *Baumgartner's Bombay* point towards almost the same situation: Kurt, another native of his own country, murders Hugo. The people gather around his flat; blood splattered body of Hugo is lying on the floor; the whole of flat is stinking badly with the smell of death and the dirtiness created around by the cats and kittens. Lottee, an old friend of Hugo takes in her custody the bloodstained old brittle papered postcards and rushes out of the flat, as she cannot control herself any more. This forms the end of the last chapter. And in the beginning, Lottee, still shocked with the incident of death of her friend, a cup of tea besides, arranges those letters chronologically, and goes deep down the life of her friend Hugo Baumgartner. She is also at the same time, ' […] trying to prevent those words from entering her—invading her—the assault of sweetness—cramming her mouth […] enough to embrace her, enough to stifle her, enough to obliterate her' (4, 5). These are the postcards, which Hugo had received at intervals in India from his land. Through these letters Hugo steps into life—shutting the door behind and coming out of it. The whole of Hugo's story is revealed through the flash-back technique of which Desai is the great master; partially it is from Lottee's point of view and partially from the narrator's angle and at times Hugo himself reveals his inner reality.

Hugo Baumgartner, a Jew by birth, lives in Berlin. While remembering his good childhood days he still can see very clearly his father ordering his employees to do various jobs […]

with special air of prosperity and satisfaction, '[...] like a bee that has stored much honey [...]' (27). And 'upstairs' was his mother's realm. The ash-tray in the form of a Prussian helmet [...] barometer shaped like a pistol that hung on the wall [...] the great mirror [...] table lamps with their domes of orange silk, fringed [...] her piano [...] all pointed towards a full life. He used to run with different errands between the shop and the apartment.

He had a great desire to go to the race courses (where his father often went) but he was never taken along. Even at that young age Hugo had come to realize that he did not belong to the picture-book world of the 'fir-tree,' the gifts and the celebration. He could not even accept [...] the Christmas gift [...] he could collapse into the dark ditch of his shame (36). Though he could neither understand it nor explain it—it baffled him and frightened him also. He *wanted to belong*. But then the circumstances changed. His father was first arrested and later he died. The house had to be vacated—the bad times had arrived—their life was no longer safe in Germany.

His father's friend told one day that now he could protect them (Hugo and his mama), so he must leave. Hugo did not want to leave his country though. He did not have any desire to escape or to make any kind of search. At least he wouldn't leave his country without his mother. He was asked to go to India with a recommendation letter to join the timber business in Calcutta. Unfortunately he could not persuade his mother to accompany him [...] though he painted a picture of their new beginning in the East—a crude picture, [...] all tigers and palm trees and sunsets [...] giving a laugh she asked—How will '*mein*' '*kleiner*' '*mann*' protect me from them? [...] '*Mutti*' he pleaded [...] 'No,' 'you get your work done [...] and then come quickly home again [...]' (56), that is how he left her. He was made to go, despite his desire to stay back. The family is displaced. There is no hope of any decent survival in his own land and Hugo is forced to escape this sordid, gloomy life and is pushed towards India.

'India,' for Hugo stands for a search of new life, a hope for livelihood—the quest for peace in an alien land, the image of home for his '*Mutti*.' He often wrote to her that when he is able to buy a new house for himself he would bring her there, and with lots of servants around she would always lead a comfortable life. A constant yearning for arrival and a constant failure to have arrived at pull Hugo apart in different directions. Hugo starts for India from Venice—the Western man in search of India. In Calcutta, with the introduction letter, Habibullah's help and instructions he could begin at last. But quite soon he realized that he had to build a new language to suit these new conditions. German language no longer sufficed, and English was elusive. Languages sprouted around him [...]. Like tropical foliage and he picked words from it without knowing if they were English or Hindi or Bengali—they were simply words he needed; as for instance *chai, khana, baraf, lao, jaldi, joota, chota peg, pant*, etc. He suspected it was not Indian but India's—the India he was marking out for himself.

His constant journeys from one place to another and endless reminders of unsavoury situation in Germany always kept him tensed. The small letters that came from his land—he kept on reading in between the lines foı finding assurances which those words lacked in. The war was declared—he was arrested and imprisoned in a camp. The letters too stopped coming. It was quite late when he came to know about the passing away of his *mütti* (mother). The poor Hugo, he could not even mourn the death of his mother. He was so innocent that he didn't know even the customs how to celebrate her death.

After Hugo is released from the camp he does not find his work secure in Calcutta. Now he is sent to Bombay with yet another introductory letter. In Bombay, the chances of his business seem to be quite bright. But Hugo always suffers the 'pangs of being alone' (133); 'Silence was his natural condition' (117). We learn quite early that even after spending so many years in India—he had not entered the mainstream. He felt relieved also for it, because it was getting more and more clamorous. He does not belong. He was not accepted in Germany, nor is he accepted in India. 'Germany there and India here' (216), both remain an elusive golden fish for him. He was always caught in the posture of either, 'running away' or 'standing helplessly.' Contrary to his expectations he finds India harsh and violent too. This man from Germany encounters feelings of joy, fear, envy, bewilderment, dullness, disappointment etc. in India. Indifferent land among different people, he also feels the pangs of alienation and loneliness even among the crowds. The realization of the sense of neither belonging nor having any identity of his own further depresses Hugo very much. He is 'too fair' for India and was 'too dark' for Germany. He can't even think of moving back under the circumstances, and is always repelled with the thought of going back, 'When Germany prosperous did not want him, how can the Germany destroyed shall ever need him?' 'Who is he' and 'whereto' he belongs—he keeps on questioning throughout and always remains a stranger, a firanghee; neither of this land nor of the land of his origin. So much so that once leaving his mother back home in a young age, Hugo is not able to see her ever again. His dream of finding a decent livelihood and a house for his 'mutti' always remains a dream in suspension. With the death of his mother, his last hope of ever returning to his country also disappears.

And 'when freedom came, Baumgartner was again on the fringe, looking on the Independence Day celebrations from a distance [...]' (190). Could he ever really escape? Could the search be ever over? Now return to Germany was out of question. The life in India of 50 years was still alien world to him [...] something he had (just) walked past quickly, not entered, not even glanced at.

What an irony of situation that the life he was made to escape always keeps a mental pressure on him. The memory of his Germany—his Mutti's letters—his papa's behaviour all keep on haunting his mind and also a secret desire of moving back to his birthplace never allow him to live in peace. Now, when he is actually present at the racecourses, enjoying riches with his partner Mr Chiman Lal in Bombay, he still can feel the pangs of yearning—how 30 years back he had requested his papa to take him to the racecourse and how indignantly he had refused. How he had hurt his mother in retaliation [...] now here he was at the races. 'Papa', he wanted to shout! 'Papa, what do you think? [...] Papa, do you see me here, at the races? [...]' 'Circular track that began in Berlin and ended here in Bombay which became by magic, the Berlin of 30 years ago' (195). How strongly is his past overshadowing his mind—can he really escape it?

And Baumgartner—a native of Hindustan [...]. He smiled, 'thinking of what *mü* would have said to that. And yet he had not met a single snake [...] he forgot [...] he would never hear from her [...]. There would be no communication [...]' (181). Hugo had not visited the tourist spots, not even Banaras. He had not been to temples or ashrams for he had not come with the purpose of finding the truth about India—the spiritual state for which many Westerners move to India, neither the escape nor the search was over.

On his way one day he lifted up a wounded cat. It died later on. Then he went to search the '[...] streets for a replacement for the first cat [...] in the end shame-facedly, he was reduced to capturing kittens [...] brought them home.' He provided them every comfort now he had found a purpose also to run back home to his flat in Hira Niwas. The more crowded and messy his home grew, the more comfortable Baumgartner felt in it (though his visitors did not). Hugo always remained haunted by the two worlds. It was always *Nacht Und Neble*, the Night and Fog.

'[...] Nothing made sense. Germany there, India here—India there—Germany here [...] impossible to capture [...] they all fell away from him, into an abyss.' He saw them following now, white shapes turning and turning [...] going gray [...] fell and floated [...] nothing to look at. It was all gone, and he shut his eyes, to receive the darkness that flooded in, poured in and filled the vacuum with the thick black ink of oblivion, of *Nacht Und Neble*.

Now let us discuss *Journey to Ithaca* in the context of the above statement. Many characters in this novel also take up journeys from one place to another with different aims and approaches. But in this paper I shall be mainly dealing with the two major protagonists, *i.e.*, Matteo and Sophie. The main common between these two novels (*Baumgartner's Bombay* and *Journey to Ithaca*) is that the major protagonists originally belong to the Western world and they moved towards India—the East—the land of the destination. Hugo starts from Germany, Matteo and Sophie move from Italy. Hugo is forced to leave his native land under the circumstances and is sent to India with a letter of recommendation to Habibullah in Calcutta. But on the other hand there is no such compulsion of circumstances for Matteo (*Journey to Ithaca*) to leave his land. And Sophie leaves her country to accompany her husband, Matteo. Whereas in the case of Hugo he started his journey at quite a young age, with many apprehensions in mind leaving behind his Mutti (who would not accompany him to such a far off and an unknown land) but with a firm faith that when the circumstances improve he would come back to his native land, Germany. Or if he were able to buy a house for himself he would send for his mama to India. Though it is a different matter that unfortunately neither he is able to come back to his birthplace nor does his mother survive to go and live with her son in India. But in the case of Matteo it was totally a different proposition. He is not forced to leave Italy—rather his parents don't like his going across the border to an alien land. And secondly, he felt he was not going to a strange land. He had known India quite well through the books and was moving towards it with a particular goal in mind. It was a deliberate attempt to escape from the land of his birth and also with a definite plan of search he entered the border of India along with his wife Sophie.

Let me first examine the reasons why did he want to run away from his native land. In the quite early pages of the novel, the grandmother explains to her grandchildren that, 'Matteo could not stand the school from first day to the last. [...] He couldn't take orders from the teachers. They couldn't make him do his lessons or sing or play football [...]' (11). And Matteo had to be taken out of school. Then he was tutored at home. One day he read the title of a book (*The Journey to the East* by Hermann Hesse) in the hand of his tutor. He wanted to read the book in English. Though his mama didn't like it, his papa allowed him. He borrowed the book and went through it page after page. Matteo was confused—what was it—a geography text? He read, 'It was my destiny to join in a great experience [...] a unique journey [...] and despair is the result of each earnest attempt to go through life with virtue, justice and understanding [...] children live on one side of despair, the awakened on the other [...]' (23). Matteo was greatly influenced by the reading of this book in his quite young age. He often murmured to himself, '[...] children live on one side of despair, the awakened on the other [...]' (24). He got a gift of yet another book from Hesse's 'Siddhartha.' Mama scolded him and didn't like it. Matteo was running once again. They couldn't stop him—he wouldn't stay in the house or garden, he would climb the walls or over the gate [...] run and run as if all he wanted was to place a distance between them and himself, a distance he drew out to greater and greater lengths with each run.

The people around too, 'saw Matteo fleeing like a Hare [...] he grew painfully thin [...] he no longer slept in his bed [...] he stayed away even at night [...] with the eyes of a man who is planning a long voyage' (27-28). There was another reason also for why he wanted to run away from his country. He was always surrounded by the material riches of the industrial age—the money, more money, the business, the car and hundreds of luxury items. He detested all these and like Wordsworth he too felt—the world is too much with us. He even found the sight of currency very sickening. 'He found the Villa with its velvet hangings and tapestries and brocades stifling. He thought the mountains hemmed him and shut off the view' (19). 'Money!—I don't wish to hear that word, Sophie!', he scolds Sophie. A big salary, car, all that junk, he considers these material things. Time and again Matteo felt that he does not belong to this world of his land—somewhere else lies his real life. He always 'tried to keep clear of others and to run if anyone came towards him [...]' (18).

And finally, 'in the summer of 1975, Sophie and Matteo, having first married to pacify their tearful and lamenting parents, left for India, dressed in identical blue jeans and T-shirts and Sports shoes [...]. Sophie still wore her hair very short and Matteo growing his long. They left on foot' (31). In Matteo's pocket was the copy of Hesse's *The Journey to the East*. This couple from Italy moves towards India in search of peace, tranquillity, the divinity, the meaning of existence and the ultimate Truth. All this is a well thought of and fully planned objective of Matteo. He knows what he wants to escape from and also what he wants to search in India. But as far as his life partner Sophie is concerned, the words 'escape' and 'search' both do not imply any special connotations. Sophie perfectly enjoys life in her own land and has no problems whatsoever with her existence over there. Nor is she any way keen to move to any foreign land in search of some particular truth. She comes to India simply because her husband won't stay back on any pretext. So to provide company to Matteo and with an anxiety to visit and experience the life in an unknown land, Sophie moves towards India. Here in India she does not like the new adventures much. The poverty around, the sickness, the unmanageable crowds of people, all are disgusting and she repeatedly requests Matteo to move back to his country. But for Matteo, '[...] There is a path of joy and the path of pleasure [...]. The wise one chooses the path of joy; the fool takes the path of pleasure [...]' (34). But to Sophie both were same—there was no difference between the two: the path of joy and the path of pleasure. In India Matteo was often hypnotized with the dancing performances. He had also given up wearing Western dresses. Now he dressed up in wide pajamas and a cotton vest. And whenever Sophie reminds him of his own country he feels disgusted, 'The past is over, Sophie, [...] over, over, over—not to be repeated. Don't repeat it, and he pressed his finger on her lip, hard' (43).

Matteo feels that by ourselves we'll never come to know India and Sophie tells 'Why not? [...] Go to Goa [...] to Kashmir [...] lie in the sun [...],' 'but that is not India!' Matteo shouts back. 'We must search for what it is [...]. We will go on a pilgrimage.' But Sophie could already visualize the ashram—she felt this whole country was populated with devotees; the Gods could not have enough; now they recruited them from abroad as well. And Matteo was bent upon to 'Find India, to understand India, and the mystery that is at the heart of India' (57). But Sophie felt very uncomfortable, her feet blistered with walking and everywhere she saw [...] people and more people—the mention of homes and families made them catch each other's eyes, smile. They knew what their families could never guess, shared what their families would never know [...].

In another town, 'Matteo visited a Yogi who had not slept for 25 years [...] Matteo (noticed) [...] a gold watch-strap on his wrist [...]' (65). He could not understand, 'Why did that Yogi, who did not need sleep, need a watch to tell him the time?' (65). Matteo was told, he could see only through faith and that he had to learn, to meditate. So Matteo rented a room for himself where he might be alone and meditate, concentrate [...] he wandered away to be alone, to be further away from everyone. In Goa too almost disappeared, receded. And when he fell ill he does not need a doctor—he needs a Guru. Matteo, the doctor asks, 'so I hear you are searching for divine light'—Matteo lay motionless, 'the divine light can kill...the Gods are destructive in this country' (71). And he advised him, the idea is not bad though—he should first acquire knowledge through the books—he can find the way for a flash of light. And in search of a Guru he was accepted in one ashram, where instructions were given—though foreigners were not served meals with Indian disciples [...] they were living in the filth and squalor—the hardship—people despised them—even exploited them. Sophie did not like all this. She always wanted to go back but Matteo wanted to stay and understand. He even started learning Sanskrit. When Sophie became pregnant they were moved to another ashram—the head there was a woman and the families were allowed to stay there—she was known as a mother.

Humility and penance were lessons he set himself to learn—moved from one place to another—always remained a wanderer. And Sophie always cursed, 'That damned book, the *Journey to the East*, but for that book you would not have thought of coming to India or of following this guru of yours to your death.' But Matteo feels, 'the book has opened my eyes—it does not lead to my death, but to my awakening I go.' The body does not matter, not even the earthly life. What matters is the search, my destiny seems to be—'never cease seeking' [...]. 'What do you hope to find Matteo?' 'I have found it, I have; what I never had before, what my life had been empty of—and now it is not' (88).

Matteo was very much impressed by the enlightening lecture of the 'mother' and her personality. He wanted to be one of her favourite disciples—he willingly did, whatever he was asked to do without any question and without any grumbling. He attended to the personal work of the mother; he even helped in the kitchen for cooking; so much so that he scrubbed dirty pans and pots day in and day out without any single frown and even without any hesitation. Sophie did not like all this, she could not tolerate it. She even could not understand what all this would ultimately lead to and what is the use of staying over here.

'The journey from Bihar to north exhausted Sophie—she (always) wanted to go back home—'send me home'—'I am dying—I am dying'—she often coaxed Matteo. But with Matteo it was different. Listening to the mother, he felt the 'experience of unity—spiritual with the physical—dark with the light—the human with the natural [...]. The Divine force is everywhere [...]. Everywhere we turn [...] we come upon the Divine power. Turn, Turn—and everywhere you turn [...]. Be open to the Divine' (99). 'Bliss! Bliss now, bliss here, forever bliss!' (103). The mother spoke. More and more words from the mother made Matteo spell-bound. She also told, 'Always remember the master [...]. I am here to drive away Darkness and remove screens so that [...]. See the master and his light [...]. Awake, o man, from thy deep sleep, Awake [...].' Matteo hovered in the vacuum, hardly breathing, hardly existing, only that particular moment mattered. Now Matteo realized, 'Why even the paradisaical surroundings of his home on the lakes had been for him empty and desperate—because no one had been there to show him that they were an expression of an eternal and essential truth' (107). The untiring devotion of Matteo—ungrumbling obedience from him pleased the mother and she expressed, '[...] yes, yes, Mat-t-eo is planning to join us. Mat-t-eo is going to stay' (123).

When Matteo brought Sophie also in the ashram he was shifted to the menial jobs of the kitchen, but he accepted it as a reward—throughout the day he was exhausted and at night he simply fell to the floor and slept. His wife didn't like it though. She wanted to escape from all this humiliation and often urged Matteo to return to his land, 'You won't work for your father's business, why do you work here for the Mother? What good is going to come out of it? I don't understand.' But Matteo shouted back, 'Mother does not make me work for anything—she teaches us, work without desire, work without fruit [...] the higher way of life.' Time and again he told Sophie, 'Money!—I don't wish to hear that word, Sophie!' Sophie could not understand. Matteo's disappearance into a world that remained shut to Sophie was so profound. Her uneasiness grew. She wanted to run away from here. Later on Sophie learnt that the mother actually belonged to Italy, she was a dancer and came to India with a dancing troupe. Now Sophie wanted to know everything about the mother. She again urges Matteo to go back, long conversation ensues without any result—Sophie of this world, Matteo of the other world—their arguments were turning into silences. These silences were further stretching and Matteo was disappearing into them, Sophie let him be very bitter. When Matteo was quite ill once more, she queried, 'When will we leave Matteo? [...] Must we wait till the mother's death?' (33).

Sophie wished to run away from all this and wanted to leave India immediately. She wanted to be among 'normal people' once again. For her it was the ashram that was the goal from which she had to escape. Matteo falls ill, Sophie again reminds him 'When you are well, Matteo, we will leave [...] if you stay, you will kill yourself.' But Matteo says, 'You will leave, Sophie, but not I [...]' 'Why, Matteo, why?'[...] 'Why can we not be together again, at home with the children?' [...] He shook his head very slightly [...] the gesture said '[...] they did not count, they were what he had left behind.'

'When will we leave Matteo?' And he answers, 'You are free to leave when you like, Sophie.' She feels not only insulted but disgusted too. Matteo tells her, '[...] I am waiting for a sign [...]. I have always waited for the signs. And then followed them [...] there is a design' (33). Sophie laughs sarcastically, how can a human being be so immune to his circumstances so absolutely? 'A design? [...] your destiny? [...] your great and glorious destiny [...] how glorious?' She pointed towards the sick room [...] metal tumbler [...] tray for pills and the patients slowly shuffling down the verandah [...] it was true [...] from the beginning [...] there were a design [...] pattern, to their wanderings [...]' (34-35). They seemed to be shown signs, given directions, drawn further, taken deeper [...]. Matteo was convinced and she never ceased to try [...] 'And go where? [...] we are waiting [...] and find the India that lies outside [...] although it was evening, it was oppressively hot, the air bottled in by the high buildings and the life that boiled inside them' (36-37).

Finally, when Sophie was no longer able to bear life in India, she went back to her parents' home in Frankfurt. But she could not share everything with her parents there. Her mother wanted too much of the children, she took them so completely. Sophie found it hard to reconcile with the situation. She rebelled and once again wanted to run away from there also. Another escape followed. Soon she packed up and along with the children moved to Matteo's home which was larger, warmer in Italy in the countryside. Here they could live and breathe. Sophie thought of not talking to them about India. She was silent about that entire time, that past and they were more grateful to have her back and be a part of their family. Now they believed Matteo too would surely follow. She relaxed and thought the children were safe in their grandparents' custody. The thought of Matteo living in the ashram in India with the mother tormented Sophie's soul. All this time she had been thinking that Matteo had been the cause of pain; all the years in India [...] to remove him would be to remove the pain. But now it seemed that one-half was ripped from her side. She felt hurt and wounded too. She might have put India behind her completely, but when a telegram informed that Matteo was taken to the hospital, she grasped the news. She reacted to it with such swiftness—it became clear to her that though physically away, her mind had been with Matteo all this time. She at once packed her bag, bought the ticket with such speed that it seemed nothing mattered to her now, she just wanted to be with her Matteo.

Sophie felt relieved at the thought that her children were safe with their grandparents but at the same time she felt hurt also to realize that they no longer needed her. One more realization also dawns upon her. She also realizes that in her determination to find out the truth about the mother she had actually abandoned her children as much as Matteo has abandoned her in his search [...] in following the mother she is entering an area of the chill, bleak, bitterness of renunciation.

Sophie is now very keen to meet Matteo, she is also keen to share the truth about the mother with him that she has found out. When Sophie reaches the hospital, they inform her that Matteo has left the hospital and gone. No one is able to tell her where could he go. Sophie is confused. Her urgency to see Matteo grows immense. She had never thought—that for Matteo too the wheel could turn. From the ashram she learns that the mother is dead and Matteo has left. He spent many days and nights lying on the gravel by her samadhi. He won't eat or drink and he wept so much. He had told that he would travel north to the mountains where the mother had received enlightenment and light—and might find peace. Sophie decides to follow him. But the success deludes her, she is not able to catch him (When asked, 'Will you follow him?' She says, 'I have to [...] What else?' (305). Even the children Giacomo and Isabel want to run away from their present circumstances. The grandmother does not want them to go to the parents and she does not want them here also. 'Where can we go?' They do not know any third place where they can go (28).

Thus from Matteo's point of view, his escape from his own world and his near and dear ones may have been complete, but we can't say that his search too was final, no, it was not. In the case of Sophie neither her escape nor her search was final. Away from Matteo, his memories haunted her and when she went all the way to India to meet him, he deluded her. The children too occupied her mind at times. Perhaps in a weak moment Matteo accepted or challenged Sophie, "You are trying to tell me I have failed [...] it is a sign of failure. I am not claiming it is glorious [...]" (34).

In the end we learn that one night Giacomo (son of Matteo and Sophie) comes home quite frightened and tells his grandpa—'I saw my father,' the boy repeats. 'Where?' "In the garden" [...]. "And I went to him. He was very thin. He smiled at me. He said, 'Giacomo,' 'Giacomo' [...] he talks like a foreigner [...]" (306-07). Whether it was a fact or not, the child is made quiet and no more queries follow.

Thus we see that all the three characters, which we have discussed in this paper, the factors responsible for their escape from certain conditions and circumstances were different. The aims of journeys taken up by them too were not the same and finally, the searches in all the three cases, which were conducted at different levels, remained incomplete at the end. No one could celebrate the final discovery or achievement. Proving once again the oft-repeated quote that happiness is found along the way only and not at the end of the road.

6

Journey to Ithaca: A Quest-Novel

SUMAN JANA

1

> There is no happiness for him who does not travel [...].
> Living in the society of man, the best man becomes a sinner [...].
> Therefore, wander!
> The feet of the wanderer's are like flowers, his soul is growing and
> reaping the fruit [...]. Therefore, wander!
> The fortune of him who is sitting, sits; it rises when he rises;
> [...] it moves when he moves. Therefore wander!
>
> 'Aitreya Brahmen' (*Rig Veda*)

This is the leitmotif of *Journey to Ithaca* (1995), a novel about the soul's journey to enlightenment and awakening. This novel, unlike Forester's *A Passage to India* which largely seems to grasp the 'mystery' and where the borderline between the 'muddle' and the 'mystery' is never clearly drawn, is Anita Desai's assertive statement that the truth, the enlightenment and the totality of an all-encompassing spirituality is in the heart of India. It is a direct negation of the rationalist/materialist Eurocentric vision which refuses to acknowledge or is not even aware of the existence of the mystery, the secret mystic truth of 'life.' Throughout the history of civilization, the journey motif is dominant in literature.

Professor Rama Kundu has aptly made an exhaustive statement on this journey motif that haunted the literary mind from time immemorial: "Demeter's journey across the sea, land and air to have her daughter restored, Orpheus' journey to the underworld to get back Euridyce, Odysseus's hazardous voyage over unknown seas for long-last home, Aeneid's fare to the underworld to benefit from his father's wisdom […]. Moses' long march through the sea [...] for the Promised land, the momentous journey of the Magi to Bethlehem, King Arthur's adventurous search for the Holy Grail [...]' to mention just a few." The crux of all these tortuous journeys is a goal, sometimes elusive, often tantalizing but always a shining beacon very meaningful to the realization of one's heart's truths. *Journey to Ithaca* is another such journey where Ithaca ceases to be a specific place, namely Ulysses's long-lost and yet long-cherished homeland. Ithaca in Desai's novel is the symbol of that unfailing beacon which eternally beckons man to wander, to be in quest of the heart's truth, a quest for reaching one's homeland. And man's true homeland is his inner self.

Desai's *Journey to Ithaca* is about one's journey within oneself, a journey which mostly ends in India, because India is the only land which recognizes the significance of the journey within, a land which is less a land and more a thought, a vision, a philosophy that stresses the truth of the search within.

2

Three journeys form the core of *Journey to Ithaca*: Matteo's journey from Italy to India and Sophie's journey to India and from India to Italy and back to India and her final quest for truth which begins from India; the itinerary-spanning Alexandria, Cairo, Paris, Venice, New York—suggests that the searching soul's real Ithaca is in India, within the self of the holy Mother. The third journey supplements the second, a journey undertaken half a century ago by a soul-searching pilgrim, Laila, who through her quest for Krishna ultimately finds her Lord in India. All these three journeys underscore the quoted motto of the novel 'Therefore, wander!' The value is not what you find at the journey's end, but the significance lies in one's undertaking the journey, the journey being more important than the destination, the search more meaningful than the object of search. It is the urge to search that makes a man of an ordinary biologically human entity; the search creates the soul. This is Desai's central concern who deliberately quotes C.P. Kavafy's poem *Ithaca* as the epigraph to her novel:

> Then pray that the journey is long.
> ....
> Always keep Ithaca fixed in your mind.
> To arrive there is our ultimate goal.
> But do not hurry the voyage at all.
> It is better to let it last for long years;
> ....
> Ithaca has given you a beautiful voyage
> ....
> And if you had found her poor, Ithaca has
> not defrauded you.
> With such wisdom you have gained, with so much
> experience
> You must surely have understood by then what Ithacas
> mean (3).

Matteo's journey to Ithaca forms the core of the first part of the novel. In one sense her journey is 'uni-dimensional' as Professor Kundu mentions. It is uni-dimensional because right from the start Matteo's aims are fixed; he knows that the heart of the matter, the mystic truth, the enigma of life's experience lies in India. For him his goal is clear; he has no ditherings about the road not taken. He knows that the world is cut into two, the path of pleasure and the path of joy. He tells Sophie what he has read in the *Katha Upanishad*:

> There is the path of joy and the path of pleasure [...]
> Pondering on them the wise one chooses the path of joy, the fool
> takes the path of pleasure (32).

That he would reject the Eurocentric zeitgeist of material attainment and rational appreciation and analysis of life is evident from his early childhood. As a child Matteo is uniquely displaced among his opulent ambience in a sprawling villa with beautiful gardens and lakes in Italy. He cannot scale the ladder of his cultural and family values. 'He could not stand the school from the first day to the last,' recollects his mother (11). The football, the symbol of Italian national vanity and the emblem of manly power and competitive prowess, failed him. 'The football was the worst [...]. He kicked the ball away from the goal, tackled a boy of his own term, not an opponent' and when chastised by the captain 'he sprawled in the mud in agony, then felt them trampling over him [...] and the greatest disgrace of all—he turned his back and ran for his life' (17-18). He felt 'repelled' staring at the face of his parents, hid himself among the startled eyes of parrots, stags' heads, rustling olive trees, blue irises and ground orchids. His favourite indoor pastime was sewing and looked 'like a grandmother sitting in that shawl with the sewing box' (15). Not only the school, and the family orders, all institutions traditionally valued by his European cultural lineage were like 'a theorem set within a larger theorem.' 'He was chilled by so much mathematical beauty, defeated by its logic' (17). Taken out of school, he was entrusted to the guardianship of a tutor, Fabian, who too seems to have thrown European values to the wind. Fabian would read out to him verses about some bright sphere, verses which equated life on earth as picking up fragments of dream. Fabian introduced him to a world outside the worldly and injected within him the spirit of a search:

> [...] Die
> If thou wouldst be with that which thou dost seek!
> Follow where all is fled?

Matteo's mind is ravished by a book which Fabian gives him to read, Herman Hesse's *Journey to the East*, an account of an imaginative journey to the heart of the mystery that is Life—'It was my destiny to join in a great experience' (22). Matteo ultimately embraces the destiny of Hesse's protagonist and makes his journey in search of luminosity in the heart of his Ithaca—the mystery that is in India, the India which alone is aware of that mystery. In reply to Sophie's exasperated question—'I want to know why we are here'—his answer is that it is only in India that it is possible to understand the mystery—'over there people don't even know there is a mystery [...]. There are people—great sages—to guide you. I need such a person' (54). Right from the beginning he is ready for a 'sign' and is sure of a 'design' (31). It was Matteo's faith that right from the beginning there was a design, a pattern, to his sojourns. At every turn he seemed to be shown signs, given directions, drawn further, taken deeper. Thus from Hotel Monaco begins his designed journey. It is as if by design he meets Pierre Eduard, a sort of collector of saints. The first Indian saint Matteo and Sophie meet lived in a squalid suburb in Bombay, through merchants' quarters and shady narrow alleys, through cigarette and soda-water stalls. A gray haired woman/saint sat in a thick, cloudy and oppressive atmosphere in a room filled with the smells of perspiration, of hair oil, of spicy fried food and suddenly 'the conflicting noisy and obstreperous odours that had earlier filled the room' were swept by a surge of a fragrance of flowers—'tuberoses, spider lilies, jasmine and roses' (36). Though Pierre Edvard cries 'Miraculous! Miraculous!' and Matteo is under the impression of being swept with another sign, Sophie asks the right question—why should one come to India for party tricks and magic shows which are in abundance in Europe? This is the fake mask of spirituality, the sign of the power of the divine that has often deluded and hornswoggled many a naïve believer in India. Then comes a series of similar miracles—a babaji sitting in the lotus posture on the water, a woman who wore a string of wooden beads and lectured to a reverential crowd, a meditating yogi completely nonchalant of prowling tigers, a woman meditating day and night in a cave sitting amid snakes and scorpions to rouse her psychic powers, left ultimately with one portion of her heart missing and so forth. All these are images of the Westerner's vision of cheap miracles which are the masks hiding the real India. One has to work out one's salvation through a rigorous process and in order to be initiated into this process, Matteo takes refuge in an ashram. For Sophie it was a place to be trapped. Sophie finds it a threatening menace—'all the crows in Bombay seemed to have gathered to huddle' complaining and cawing against their fate. The crow image is of crucial significance in *Journey*. During the monsoon season, the 'crows maddened her with their cries [...] giving extra loud caws of indignation and outrage' (42). Later, when Laila-Lila comes over to India and is trapped in the stultifying atmosphere of a throttling cage-like flat in Bombay, under the threat of extinction and the spell of the fake Krishna, she too finds the cacophony of the crows maddening her:

> Outside black crows are fighting and screaming [...]. They swoop upon (garbage) [...]. They frighten me so (275).

The crows are symbols of a cawing jarring menace of destructive forces that can nullify the inner silence, calm, joy and vision of an individual. It is most interesting, that these discordant threatening crows can only be silenced once the journey within is complete, once peace and harmony well up from within. This happens with the Mother who, while giving her spiritual discourse, sees the crows in eventime gradually settling on the branches of trees atop and around her, and yet not one crow cawing for a moment:

> What Matteo noticed—and Sophie would have been incredulous [...] was that while she spoke crows had settled into the branches of the ficus tree, ruffling their feathers, but made no sounds [...] (94).

Crows, therefore, in the novel, take up an extra symbolic dimension, signifying the discordant cawings within man. Once the truth, the enlightenment, the Reality is achieved or attained, the crows can be silenced.

It is to silence the crows within that Matteo joins the ashram. The first experience is barren. There's nothing worth mentioning other than the initiation into a mechanically routinised community life—taking food along with other disciples, sitting and eating on the same level, rising early and chanting hymns, the evening discourses *et al.* The images of the crowded evening sessions were thronged by families who brought along sick relatives, physically disabled or mentally handicapped ones. This again is an image of fake religion, since truth does not deal with the bodily or psychic malaise. It is an unflinching light in which diseases dissolve; Truth is not about magic cures, about touch and go. Truth is about curing magic itself; tricks are too low for truth.

The most significant part of Matteo's stay in this ashram is his undertaking of a pilgrimage to a shrine outside the city. The pilgrims are huddled together with their baggages and following a racking bus journey they alight on the open fields in the scorching sun. Then follows an exhaustive walk down slippery tracks, sometimes like acrobats lest they slipped and got splashed and splattered. All along the pilgrims were chanting 'Hari Hari come to me/Hari, Hari, I pine for thee.' The sun beat down on them with the stridency of metal. Pilgrims were carrying a palanquin with shoes of some sage in it, shouting 'Gyanadeva, Gyanadeva,' 'Tukaram Tukaram.' In the centre of this pilgrimage lay the horrid image of a mother carrying her terribly sick child, her eighth one, the rest seven being already dead. She has joined the pilgrimage in the hope of saving her last child without whom she cannot be taken back to her hearth and home. The shrine is reached, but the pilgrimage over, what remains is the dead child:

> [...] it was the woman with the child; she had placed him on a fold of her saree spread on the ground and he was terribly still. The woman was not looking at him or at

> anyone; she held her head in her hands and stared at the ground (53-54).

For Sophie, the cynical rationalist, bringing such a sick child was a risk, a blunder. But for the mother the pilgrimage was a form of homage to faith, the only panacea to one who has no other source of sustenance. This is what Sophie is told when one of the pilgrims explained: 'What can she do? If you have nothing else you must have faith in God' (52). Sophie with her typical Eurocentric vision of India, cannot fathom the meaning of such a faith. She, therefore, leaves the ashram and joins a band of European freaks in Goa, smoking marijuana. She nearly severs contacts with Matteo and is lost in the company of Marc, Peggy, Gustave, Francis, Henri and Andrea—a whole community of white ragged mendicants in loose pyjamas who make a mess around ashram and sadhus and yogis and peddle with contraband of drugs hiding them from the Goan police. Instead of the pilgrims who chanted 'Hari, Hari, I pine for thee,' their community chanting is about realization of Hari through marijuana, hemp and cocaine:

> Take a puff, take a puff
> Feel yourself disappear.
> Hare Krishna, Hare Rama
> Hare Krishna, Hare Rama (56).

That this was a sheer travesty of a search is best proved by the fact, that however much Sophie immersed herself in her puffs, she could not dissolve her self from the awareness of agony and shame:

> Sometimes she cried herself [...] and seemed to be lying in a spreading pool of her own excrement [...] quite shamefully (56).

The tryst with marijuana being over, again Matteo is joined by Sophie, who once again starts another journey to another ashram in Bihar. Meanwhile Matteo is in a frenzy. Gripped by a fit of ecstasy he suddenly begins to dance wildly before a funeral procession; on another occasion he mistakes a tavern for a temple and falls amongst the feet of the drinking customers and is kicked by Sophie shimmering indignation. Again he nearly drowns himself and is taken to a doctor who pumps out sea-water from his lungs. What ultimately is realized is that 'Matteo doesn't need a doctor, he needs a Guru' (67). Hence the journey to the ashram in Bihar in search of a Guru. This is another fiasco that he experiences. The ashram 'behind a high iron gate and walls topped with barbed wire' (70) resembles a dungeon. He is rudely taught his first lesson—to cleanse him pure and offer obeisance at the feet of the Guru. But when he offers a bag of oranges, bananas and cheekoos, he peeps through a drawer half open and sees it 'filled with Wills Gold Flake cigarettes, fountain pens, a gold-plaited lighter, and even currency in several different denominations. Matteo's offering was clearly despicable in comparison' (71). Too filled with ardent faith and blind devotion, this surprise cannot, however, traumatize him. He stays in the ashram, goes through its banal rituals and devotes himself to learning Sanskrit. Sophie is soon to rip off the mask of spirituality in this ashram when to her chagrin she realizes that these ashramites discriminate between castes and religions and are too venomous in their ignorance which leads them to believe that Sophie's touch can spoil the purity of water. Despair gradually creeps in. Both Sophie and Matteo cannot regain the spirit of adventure with which they had set out for India. To begin with the possibilities had seemed endless and fascinating, but now they were reeking with filth and squalor, meanness and hardship. The devotees and the ashramites segregated them lest they, holy Hindus, be polluted. Sophie realizes that they had come to India together, to share an adventure, to realize the essence of love. Instead they face a religion manqué, a fake face of the truth that is India. Meanwhile, when Sophie discovers she is pregnant, she faces enormous hostility, overhearing women—disciples condemning her sexuality: 'What do they think, that they can come here and live like animals in our ashram?' (78). The next step towards their realization of this fake image of enlightenment comes when they are horrified with the revelation that a dedicated disciple who had gone so far in his meditative practices that he had fallen into samadhi and on another occasion had a fit of seizure, is cruelly dispatched out of the ashram. There were rumours of a servant girl being impregnated by another devotee, who too was summarily dismissed. And finally, the extreme shock comes in the form of the news that the chief priest or head swami employed hooligans and muscle-men to evict people from some premises which could have been the ashram property. Power and pelf were the ruling spirits and any sojourner to Ithaca cannot find his/her promised land here.

So long Matteo-Sophie encounter the fake mask of the Truth; the real face is only revealed to Matteo once he journeys north and finds the Mother's ashram. His very first experience as he enters is significant. Instead of devotees engaged in mechanical rituals, he finds himself placed among groves of oleander and hibiscus bushes in flower, and citrus and guava orchards bearing fragrant fruit; multicoloured bougainvillaea in bloom. 'Birds called to each other [...] in ringing voices' (89)—an elemental harmony so different from the crows that huddled together in the Bihar ashram. This immediately places him in his childhood ambience, and he is thus symbolically placed in his second childhood home. His first encounter with the Mother is epiphanic. Truth comes to him in the form of bliss. He realizes that the mystery he has so long been searching for is neither in bookish knowledge nor in dry as dust wisdom, nor even in blind faith—it is essentially an experience of bliss—"anandam anandam anandam kevalam" as the Upanishads have stressed. The Mother's discourse is extremely crucial in understanding the heart of the matter. The purpose of life, she says, is to 'feel,' 'to experience bliss,' a 'bliss' that comes with a sense of being 'loved' (93):

> It is not like going to the church [...]. Not like going to the Temple [...] (unlike the ashram in Bihar) we do not bring any offerings with us [...]. We have no religion [...]. We do not listen to the black scolding voices of religion here.

> Religion makes one ashamed, makes one guilty, makes one fearful [...] open your hearts to love and light and the joy of loving [...] (93).

This is one of the most revealing statements about the 'mystery,' the Truth, that journeymen to Ithaca-India find anchorage in. Matteo is immediately absorbed into the life of the ashram. In stark contrast with the inmates of the Bihar ashram who have no names, identityless cogs in the wheel of ignorance and material greed. Matteo finds in the Mother's abode of bliss characters like Kripa (mercy), Diya (the giver), Prema (love), etc. It is a community of bliss, of selfless love and joy. Matteo is deeply immersed in his role first as washerman in the kitchen sink, then as the letter-writer for the Mother and finally in charge of the new publication unit set by Her for the printing and publishing Her Master Prem-Krishnaji's messages and discourses. After her childbirth, when Sophie comes to this shelter, she still has her cynical questionings scorpioning her calm. She considers the Mother as a large mother spider in whose web are caught small flies like Matteo to be engulfed and destroyed for ever. But Matteo has comprehended the essence of the hard work that all the ashramites put in—'she teaches us to work without desiring the fruit from that work. Isn't that a higher way of life?' But Sophie still is full of her spleen; her Eurocentric points of view prevent her from comprehending the essential nature of bliss. For her 'work is work and should bear fruit [...]. If it doesn't bear fruit it doesn't serve its purpose' (120). For Sophie, the concept is materialistic/individualistic—work is for material ends and should have personal goals to fulfil. Matteo seems to have plunged into the genuine Indianised goal of work for the world, a negation of selfish interests in life, an obliteration of personal goals, goals which ever prevent one on embarking a glorious journey to Ithaca. Sophie cannot drown her rational analytical Europeanised mindset into the ever-flowing deluge of love. She wants a palpable tangible comprehension of the Truth through rational scanning. Her mind is like that of the child who must have a scientific explanation, who 'pulls a butterfly to bits so it can see what makes it fly' (103). Matteo is in the process of learning to drown his ego, to allow experiences to happen, to be on the receiving end, to appreciate the graces of total surrender. He gradually learns to stop struggling, to allow the Master to pick him up and carry him. The Mother's message guides him:

> You know the Saint Ramkrishna said we should be like Kittens—allow the Master to pick him up and carry you. Don't struggle, don't resist. The Master, the Mother—they are the mother cats, they will carry you, the Kittens (100).

The dyke, therefore, breaks between Sophie and Matteo's vision and she finds 'Matteo had vanished in the heart of the world that remained shut to her' (121). In search of scientific explanation she meets the ashramites, sometimes overhears their conversation, questions even the eldest of the devotees, Montu-da, and ultimately creates a quizzical myth of suspicion round the Mother's past. She gathers information that the Mother was a Muslim, an Egyptian, a professional dancer and then adds up the strings together to build a myth of a man-woman relationship between the Mother and her Master, the departed Guru Prem Krishna. With her frame of mind, she cannot believe as Montu-da says that the Mother and the Master were not as one man and wife, but as the body is one with the soul. The rumblings of doubt erupt within her, explode into a conflagration of revolt and she decides to leave the ashram, Matteo and both their pasts to be once again free from the snares and pitfalls of an illusory enigma for which Matteo surrenders his life. Meanwhile Sophie has her second child within the 'Abode of Bliss,' meets Dr Bishop who delivers her child in the hospital, finds the doctor immersed in his missionary goal for which he too had undertaken a long journey from home. However, missionaries cannot attract her, missions are mirages for her and she leaves the ashram to go back to Europe.

Sophie too has her revelation in the Abode of Bliss. Once she scrambles out on to the hillside at the back of the ashram, loses her way, and suddenly emerges on a slow directly above the Abode of Bliss where the Mother lives. And then comes the epiphany. She suddenly finds the Mother, early in the morning, seated on a small tool, without her voluminous pink robes, looking essentially fragile, a small shrunken creature slightly growing bald. But to her astonishment and consternation, she finds the grand image of a host of peacocks and peahens dancing in front of her. While the peahens were being fed by her, the peacocks displayed a thousand individual fans of brilliant bronze-like greens, blues and golds, displaying their glories with a preening expression of vanity. She felt that the peacocks in the explosion of colourful magnificence were dancing a pageant of obeisance to Her—'this display that was their tribute to her [...] surreal to Sophie in this landscape of silence and solitude' (123). Sophie is deeply engrossed by this image of phenomenal beauty and pride bowing at the feet of the Mother. In spite of all her scientific-analytical framework of mind, the paradoxical enigma of this image stayed within her. She keeps this epiphany a secret, but this secret unconsciously ravishes her. This is evidently proved from her reactions to the world outside the ashram, as and when she leaves it for Europe. Once she leaves the ashram to seek freedom and individual independence refusing to be a silly fly to be caught in the spider's web, she feels the real outer world thrusting 'itself at her like blows from its fists' (144). The real world appears in all its sinister manifestations—there is menace, squalor, poverty and unconcealed lust. The real world, to her dismay, she finds considering her as a sex object. 'If she had hated the ashram, Mother, Matteo and their lives there, it was nothing, she now felt, compared to the hate she felt for the world outside' (144). The sense of escape to freedom and self-assertion have entirely dissipated to be replaced by a bitter sense of loss and betrayal. Once out of it, Sophie realizes how the serenity and calm of the ashram life had unconsciously ravished her mind. She reaches home in Frankfurt but finds no roots in it. She is an alien amid her own biological moorings. She resents the elegant apartment, her father's reticence and her mother's voluble expression of solicitation. The final blow comes when her mother proposes that her children be baptised. The same Sophie who once refused to name her child after the Mother's wishes as Prem-Krishna and christens him 'Giacomo,' in the family traditions, now revolts at the prospect of baptising her own children in the Christian tradition:

> 'No, I did not leave India and all its superstitions and rituals to come here and submit to the tribal rites of Europe,' she stormed [...]. 'You believe a baby should be dumped in a basin of water by a priest and have some mumbo-jumbo said over its head or it won't go to heaven, eh?' (146).

She leaves her home and goes over to Italy to Matteo's home with her children. Though the larger warmer atmosphere in the Italian countryside proved more relaxing, she did not talk about India, the time passed. In a way she felt she was convalescing amid the Camellias which indefatigably produced their coral pink blossoms. But in spite of all, she was obsessed with Matteo 'who came surging back in a way she had not imagined would happen [...]. The Mother, the ashram—images of them rose to haunt her. She saw the ring of dancing peacocks, the old woman in their centre' (147). Matteo had been the cause of pain of all the years in India, and she believed to remove him would be to remove the pain. But there was no stillness and no calm; she was consumed by restlessness. One-half of her self was ripped from her side by Matteo; the other half reeling under the unconscious influence of the Mother. It is very significant that during her stay in Italy she meets Paolo who too seems to show some interest in India, but no sooner she realizes that his is a fake interest in the mask of India, in sex and drugs and miracles, than she dismisses him with rude disdain. So when Paolo proposes to visit Matteo and surprise him, she scornfully retorts, 'You? you are not fit to even enter his presence. He—he is a god' (148-49). Finally, comes her most crucial rejection of Christianity as a means of salvation. On her way home from Paolo, she stops for a visit to the famous Cathedral of San Simpliciano:

> Sophie stood under it, craning her head to look up at the furthest reaches of the huge Romanesque dome [...]. Then she turned abruptly and walked out, her heels sounding loudly on the bare brick floor (149).

And when shortly after a telegram arrives from India informing Matteo's illness and hospitalization, she immediately packs her bag, leaving everything inconsequential behind her. 'It was clear her mind had been with Matteo all this time' (150).

3

Thus begins the second journey to Ithaca. Once in India, she is racked by her old doubts, cajoles Matteo with possibilities of a resuscitation of family and personal love, questions his illness and tries to impinge upon him that it is India which is behind the root of his infective hepatitis. But once she realizes that Matteo is firm in his dedication and surrender to the Mother's cause, she instinctively decides to embark on her own journey to Ithaca, to search out the truth of the Mother's past, to unravel her mystery and if possible to explode the myth of this danseuse turned enlightened embodiment of Truth and bliss:

> 'I must find whatever there is to find [...]. It is the only way I'll ever be able to understand you, what you have done to yourself' (153).

Thus she begins her travel back, back in time, although not her own time now, but the Mother's. The Mother's life, her past, the reality behind legend, is rediscovered in pieces and plots, through which ultimately the whole emerges. It is not merely Sophie's journey through Alexandria, Cairo, Paris, Venice, and New York to India, that Sophie reaches her Ithaca, her truth, her enlightenment, it is ultimately a journey within, a real pilgrimage into the heart of the beckon, a meaningful journey, a sojourn into the awakened awareness of the real face of India where all masks dissolve into insignificance.

In Mazarite, a small suburb in Alexandria, a little girl plays by herself. Her childhood is symbiotically related to Matteo's childhood. Both the little girl, Laila, and Matteo are misfits, uniquely dislocated from their ambience. As Matteo fails to live up to the standards and ideals of his Italian parents, Laila too fails the expectations of her teacher-scholar parents. Matteo roams aimlessly among geranium pots, pergola of wisterias, marble pineapples, marble grapes, among beds of artemisia and rosemary, while Laila too feels trapped within the quotidian mechanically of home and walks aimlessly, dances and frolics through unknown destinations in Alexandria. Matteo has to be desperately searched after by his mother while Alma, a woman of French origin, waits anxiously at home for the late uncertain return of Laila who may come back home at night with bare legs and tattered dresses, but with daisies and alyssum stuck in her hair. Like Matteo, this gypsy child considers the home an inadequate shelter, it's like a prison trapping her freedom. "That is how I feel here—a prisoner," says Laila, the eternal rebel, who wants to be free and her means of freedom is visualized through dance, "I want to dance [...] then I would be free." As Matteo considers his school a stifling riddle, the accepted normality of institutions 'a theorem within a theorem,' Laila too feels oppressed when she is sent to school at Cairo in the American College for girls—"Laila saw a way of learning that had no opening to debate, discussion, doubt or argument" (163). The inherent surge of the overflowing multifarious forces of life lead her to join secret meetings of students planning political revolt against British domination. There too a free soul cannot be stuck for long. "She was drawn first in one direction, then another, wherever she saw passion taken to its extreme, whether celebratory or ascetic" (167). In the month of Ramadan, Laila takes the freedom from restrictive routines of the school, roves around the streets of Cairo. She is the image of the eternal itinerant, and in her journey she encounters her first fateful experience of meeting an old hagdah at Café Fishawy. This old woman makes a peculiar prophecy that grips her psyche—"In the north, a city stands in water. There God and Goddess meet [...] then eastwards to find a temple [...] the temple of the Mother Goddess of the World" (169-70).

Laila, however, completes schooling. Her parents decide to train her to be a woman of the world and send her to Paris to her French aunt Francoise. The moment of departure is tinged with symbolic overtones. While the ship to Paris starts sailing and her parents are waving her a bon voyage, Laila unpins her Egyptian kerchief, pulls it off her head and leaves it to the care of the sea breeze. To their amazement, the parents visualise her symbolic gesture of freedom from cultural moorings:

> [...] the wind tugged it out of her hand—and it floated through the air that flooded in between the boat and the land and descended lightly, tremulously upon the waves which dashed up [...] to receive it. Before a gull could swoop down and snatch at it, it sank and was gone (171).

This is how Laila drowns her past, her Egyptian roots, her unbiblical nexus and now she seems to be free, a woman among the elements of the Universe.

At Paris, Laila is equally misfit and a terrible rebel in her aunt's house. In the house on the rue des Bernardins, all the rooms were curtained against the streets and the lights, lest the sunrays intrude and spoil the shades of the colourful carpets and fade the gaudy interior decoration. Naturally, Laila who is a spirit of light herself, revolts against this dungeon of shady gloom and repeatedly removes the curtains. She deliberately dishevels the mechanical 'order' of the rooms and shatters the artificial aestheticism of the Francoise household. In an illuminating passage, probably one of the most moving ones in the entire novel, Laila point out the inherent ferocity of meat-eaters, already having taken to frugal vegetarian diet herself. She asks her cousins—"Have you been in a butcher's shop to see it when it is raw? or into an abattoir to see how they slaughter the bulls and the calves and lambs and pigs [...]?' And one evening at the dinner table 'Laila electrified them by suddenly picking up her knife and fork and attacking the meat with such ferocity that gobs and strips of it flew around' and when her infuriated aunt asks 'Oh what is it,' she blurts out the horrible trauma within her—'Killing the ox, killing the ox!' in tear-streaked fury (178). Laila's odyssey in Paris begins. From college she doesn't return home but roams around the city. Once she discovers Madame Beaunier's dancing class, gets herself admitted to it, but very soon she starts defying Madame Beaunier, refusing to be a mechanically dancing puppet. At Madame's question, she very significantly explains that for her dance is a divine expression of emotion, something which can never be learnt in routined mechanicality. Once she drifts towards the Jardin des Plantes, where she feels distressed at the sight of caged cockatoos, baboons, rabbits and pythons. It is most significant that she is immediately attracted to a black panther that refuses to be domesticated, 'which still prowled the jungles of its memory, still inhabited an unpopulated wilderness of the past' (183). The panther for her is a symbol of revolt against oppression. Like the panther, she too refuses to be refused and 'paced and paced' the streets of Paris. Here, most significantly, she is spiritually related to Sophie who while seeking a defiant freedom from the restrictive oppression of the Bihar ashram, visits a zoo and can emotionally identify herself to 'the most beautiful beast of all, a black leopard.' Even within the cage it refuses to accept its imprisonment and its ferocious ambulations attract Sophie immediately. 'It paced in its small cage without ceasing [...] on restless silent paws [...] betraying what churned in its unquiet heart' (75). The black panther in Paris and the black leopard in Bihar symbolically space Sophie and Laila on the same plane; though Sophie has her European moorings, on an unconscious level she too, like Laila, is a spiritual pilgrim. What Laila does consciously, Sophie does unconsciously. Both seek freedom from stultifying institutionalism which is the essential precondition for a quester of truth and enlightenment.

Finally, in Paris, Laila seems to have found the image of her Ithaca—'a strange statue of some dark metal that struck a dancer's pose within a circle of flames.' In a bookshop, piled around untidy heaps of books, she accosts the image of Lord Krishna who fascinates her. She finds temporary refuge in this bookstore, Madame Lacan's, in the repository of titles referring to l'Orient or l'Inde—*The Rig Veda, Samhita, Ratnavali, Brhadaranyake Upanishad, La Bhavad Gita,* etc. Rustling through, she discovers the passage, which voices the leitmotif of her life as well as Desai's novel, quoted right in the beginning of this essay. Then comes a sign in the form of a poster about a dance recital of Krishna Lila to be held by a troupe of Indian dancers. She manages a ticket as gift from Madame Lacan and is thoroughly enraptured by the image of the dancer impersonating Krishna—'a body of indigo blue' who wore around his waist 'a cloth of saffron yellow while his head was crowned with peacock feathers [...]. He stood beneath a tree, playing upon a flute [...]' (193). What mesmerised her in the dance pageant was the nature of the dance itself, so different from the rhythmic monotony of Madame Beaunier's dancing classes. She was inspired by the dancing bodies 'in their sweeping, leaping, elegant, ecstatic, joyous, anguished, effortless poses and postures' (194). Laila intensely desired 'to leap up and perform to that music.' Throughout the novel, all the journeymen/women to Ithaca encounter fake images of truth. Laila too in her ignorance encounters a fake image of Krishna equating the dancer under the mask to the Lord itself. 'It seemed to her that he, the dancer was also the figure she had first seen in a volume of paintings in Madame Lacan's bookshop. He was also the God. She had studied in the books [...]. He was also the country and the art and the religion that had become her obsession [...]. (219). Thus she desperately pleads to the dancer/Krishna to adopt her, train her and make her an Indian dancer, hoping to dance the Krishna Lila and in her dance offer herself to the real Krishna. It is through this dance that she hopes to find her enlightenment, her Ithaca. The dancer Krishna is but a fake image of the Lord. He is a [...] thoroughly mean career-monger, in search of fame and pelf, lust and lucre, though he talks big about Indian notions of dance as a form of spiritual experience and counterfeits the role of a Guru: '[...] In India a man who teaches dance is a Guru, and the guru is not only a teacher, he is a spiritual teacher. I do not smoke or touch alcohol' (203). Meanwhile Laila shocks her aunt by refusing to go to Church: 'I do not go to church,' she revolts, asserting, 'I am a seeker after truth and have given up all orthodox religions [...]. I find them the repositories of ignorance and suppression' (199). Here too, symbolically, she has a psychic bondage with Sophie who rejects Christianity. It is thus most apt for Sophie to journey through the past in search of the truth about Laila/Lila, the Mother Goddess in the north of India. For Laila, the truth lies in India and it is in India, through the means of dance, would she arrive at her Ithaca, her enlightenment. She runs after the dancer-Krishna in the hope of going back to India and find her spirit's moorings. She feels a peculiar psychic propensity to their world, 'a certainty that she had once been one of them, possessed what they had, lost it but now saw she must grasp and recover it [...]' (195). Her hopes are however shattered when Krishna and his troupe move to Venice and shift to New York for shows, money and fame. The traumatized Laila, by now translated by journalists into Lila, flies away from the clutches of the fake Krishna, is ultimately rescued, and finally sails to India, the 'real' India. But by now she knows that this dancer-Krishna cannot be her real Ithaca. Ithacas exist elsewhere, but of course in India. The fake Krishna, the false mask, brings her to a dingy flat in Bombay amid filth and squalor with crows cawing out the poise of her mind. She feels spiritually strangled and falls terribly ill, is transferred to a hospital for treatment and cure of hepatitis. Matteo too was infected by the same disease. This is of course symbolic. Through physical ailment it seems comes liberty from bodily consciousness and confinement; Matteo becomes the holy man after recovery, and it is from the hospital that Laila finds the route to her enlightenment. The fake-image dissolves and she embarks on a journey to the north, amid the mountains (symbolizing spiritual heights) to Guru Prem Krishna's ashram and spiritual shelter. The fake Krishna/dancer is now effaced and the real Prem-Krishna, the God of love, the incarnation of the spiritual beacon that beckons the spiritual quester, is found.

It is significant that while Laila receives her spiritual umbrella at Prem-Krishna's feet on a night tossed by torrential rains and devastating storms (293), Sophie too comes to the Mother's ashram on an equally tempestuous night (118). Symbolically, thus again these two spiritual questers are equated—their real calm and light is arrived, at once the storms within fade out. The entry into a world of serene enlightenment can only occur once the tempests of life are conquered. The message is clear enough.

4

Sophie pieces together all the fragments of the Mother's past as she travels to Alexandria, Cairo, Paris, Venice, New York and finally the crux of the mother is revealed to her once she comes back to India and meets the now wizened old dancer—Guru Krishnaji, Laila's false God. It is in Krishnaji's possession that she discovers Laila's diary in which her journey to her Ithaca is recorded. Thus Sophie's actual journey to Ithaca begins from India (after her second visit) and ends in India with the revelations from the Mother's diary which she, after her own journey's end, sends to Krishnaji for his perusal. The diary and its revelations help Sophie reconstruct the legend about the Mother which she once wished to deconstruct. On her finding the truth about the Mother's past odyssey, she finally goes back to the Mother's ashram, only to learn that the Mother is no longer any more and that Matteo too has left for an unknown destination. The mother's journey to Ithaca had ended in Prem-Krishnaji, Sophie's journey to Ithaca ends with her discovery of the Mother's past, but it is Matteo's journey to Ithaca that actually is on. Matteo's final journey begins from the Mother's ashram. He becomes a pilgrim of eternity.

In the very last pages of the novel, Giacomo, while playing in his grandfather's garden, has an overwhelming experience. He is utterly astounded and tense. 'I saw my father [...] in the garden,' says the child in an attitude of fright and bewilderment, but asserts that this was no figment of his own imagination, that Matteo had really come, called him by his name. He looked 'very thin. He was wearing no clothes [...],' '[...] He was wearing first a white cloth tied like an apron. No shoes. Nothing else [...]. He smiled at me. He said Giacomo Giacomo' (298). But as Matteo said something to his son, the little boy fails to understand what he said, because he talked 'like a foreigner' (299). Matteo's journey is on. Evidently, he has realized that life itself is an endless pilgrimage. He has donned the garb of a sage, abandoned the trappings of European civilization and journeys to a path of love which is like the wind, that embraces all, but never sticks to anything or anybody. Sophie, too, at the end has realized the meaning of the voyage. In the Mother's ashram, lying alone, after the Mother's death and Matteo's departure, Sophie meditates upon the first pilgrimage she went on in India that had ended in the death of a child. 'Now she knows why the mother (of the dead child) went on that pilgrimage, why anyone goes on a pilgrimage, and why she must go too. She says in a flat voice 'I'll have to,' and adds, 'what else?' (297). Both Sophie and Matteo have the same revelation and enlightenment in spite of physical separation—that the only significance of living is to visualize the truth that life is a pilgrimage—'what else?'

5

In Desai's novel, Ithaca, the symbol of a meaningful goal, merges into India. *Journey to Ithaca* is indeed an apotheosis of the real Indianised vision of life. But the vision that Desai projects is not free from contradictions. The present writer wishes to point out only the most glaring ones in the novel. First, that the essence of Indian spirituality (and not religion) that the Mother upholds and Sophie and Matteo realize at the end, stresses on the journey within—'Know Thyself.' Whether this journey has aptly received focus in the novel remains a large question, because on the narrative level major stress has been laid on the journeys that take the form of pilgrimages. Are these journeys ambi-dimensional? That the journey to Ithaca is also simultaneously a journey to one's inner essence, it seems, has eluded the narrative. The goals are in realizations outside the self, it seems, except of course for the Mother. Second, the Mother who herself has rejected the Cross as an 'ugly image' and sought for splendour of beauty, the beauty within, points out to Matteo, 'Read nothing. Nothing [...]. I beg you to close your books. Clear your mind. The way of jnana—the way of knowledge—is nothing compared to the way of bhakti—the way of love. Here we teach only Love.' She cites Ramkrishna and Sufi Inayat Khan in support of her statement ('The Sufi said, "It is not in the book'" 107). But here Desai leads the reader to a gross contradiction—she differentiates between the way of jnana and the way of bhakti. Indian enlightenment never differentiates between the two; in Indian spiritual ethos perfect jnana comes from perfect bhakti. If one doesn't have jnana, wherefrom will bhakti come? Moreover, in Indian spiritual traditions upheld by the Upanishads and the Vedas, jnana can never be found in books. In that case, there is no point suggesting that unless one abandons books bhakti cannot be attained, as if jnana can be an impediment to one's bhakti and jnana comes from reading of books. Possibly Desai flounders in failing to distinguish between the knowledge one acquires from books and jnana, or wisdom which is far beyond bookish knowledge. The next inevitable question that flummoxes the reader is, even if what the Mother says is her own realization, why does she then publish with all her ardour the books of her Master Prem-Krishnaji? The final and the most pathetic contradiction, the one that is most aesthetically unsatisfying is Giacomo's final statement about Matteo, that he 'talked like a foreigner' (299) and that the child could not comprehend him. This is utterly absurd—if Matteo is really enlightened, he should have spoken the language of love and the child could definitely have grasped his meaning in totality. In spite of all these, one feels that these contradictions rescue *Journey to Ithaca* from being a philosophical treatise. It is indeed a remarkably fresh creation, totally different from the other novels of Desai.

NOTE

All references to the text are from the Ravi Dayal edition of the text.

WORKS CITED

Desai, Anita. *Journey to Ithaca*. New Delhi: Ravi Dayal Publisher, 1996.

Kundu, Rama. "'Journey to the East' Once Again: Anita Desai's Journey to Ithaca," in *Post-Independence Indian English Fiction*. (Eds.) R. Mittapalli and A. Monti (New Delhi: Atlantic Publishers and Distributors, 2001).

7

A Critique of *Fasting, Feasting*

M.Q. KHAN

While, on the one hand, the post-1990 Indian English fiction has made significant progress in the direction of occupying a commendable place in the post-colonial Literature, on the other hand, it has gained considerable range and depth in the thematic as well as technical explorations. Apart from the various technical innovations and new thematic use, it is the variety of approaches and experimental modes that have added new dimension to the Indian English fiction. Some of the writers like Salman Rushdie, Arun Joshi and Anita Desai have been immensely successful in creating new images in their latest works. *Fasting, Feasting* (1999), Desai's latest novel marks a departure from all her earlier major works. Perhaps she intends to make it altogether a different work from all her earlier novels. Much of the elements like the deep psychological insight into her characters, the neuro-psychic analysis and the serious reactions of her woman characters against the unacceptable situations are completely missing.

The first striking feature of the novel is that the plot is laid bare in the most simple and lucid manner without any trace of complexity. It appears a simple long story in a straightforward narrative structure. Desai presents the story of a small family in which MamandPapa are the central figures around which their three children revolve unravelling the story of a family that exists in the society like thousands of such families with hope and fear, happiness and sorrow, gain and loss, which are integral parts of life on this earth. Desai writes: "MAMANDPAPA. MamaPapa PapaMama. It was hard to believe they had ever had separate existences, that they had been separate entities and not MamaPapa in one breath" (1999: 5). The novel is divided into two parts. The first part deals with the life of MamandPapa living a life in their quiet house with their three children. Uma, the eldest daughter, turns out to be dullest of all with a good deal of follies and foibles that make her a failure in every walk of life. She fails in the school to be withdrawn by the parents, fails to make any impression on the visitors regarding the high expectations of her MamandPapa and she also fails to get a happy moment in life. Her parents try their best to get a good groom of their standard only to be duped by the Goyals, the cloth-merchant family that takes a sum of Rupees one lakh in advance towards dowry. Soon after they break the engagement and refuse to make any refund. Finally, she is married to Harish, who swindles them in order to take thirty thousand to pay his own debt. He runs to join his factory leaving the bride untouched and uncared for on the very first day of their marriage. When the shocked parents realise their mistake, it is too late. Ultimately they take away Uma to their house when they come to know that Harish is a married man with four children. Uma, therefore, is resigned to live in the house like a dumb and mute animal unable to give vent to her feelings. Their second daughter, Aruna emerges as a beautiful and talented girl who gets a good husband and moves to Bombay to live an envious life. She presents not only a contrast to the character of Uma, but her story presents a different aspect of life that is much above the expectation of Uma.

The second part of the novel deals with Arun, the only son who after making good result at the final, is sent to America for his higher studies just to fulfil the wishes and expectations of his parents. Since the parents cannot meet all the needs of their son abroad, he has to live partly in the dorm and partly with Mrs Patton in a small room on the first floor on Bayberry Lane. He has to live here till the beginning of Semester and obviously has to go through all the ordeal that a young Indian has to face with Mr Patton Rod and especially their daughter Melanie who is suffering from blimia, anorexia, depression, withdrawal, compulsive behaviour or hysteria. Arun has had peculiar experiences by living with this American family with a sense of bewilderment and strangeness which he quietly accepts as part of life. As the Semester begins, Arun leaves the Pattons after presenting a box of tea and an Indian shawl, while Mrs Patton keeps sitting on the porch with the box of tea and the shawl around her shoulders. The novel ends here as quietly as it begins with the parents sitting on the verandah, overlooking the garden, the drive and the gate.

The novel, thus, has the plot laid in the simplest mode and the language has clarity and vividness as a result of which words twinkle like the clear and crystal ring of telephone. The entire narrative structure is built in concrete words which are mostly monosyllabic with simple diction and precise description. The narrative becomes all the more clear and excitingly moving when Mrs Desai comes to reveal the excitement of the father at the birth of their much desired and much expected son.

> Arriving home, however, he sprang out of the car, raced into the house and shouted the news to whoever was there to hear. Servants, elderly relatives, all gathered at the door, and then saw the most astounding sight of their lives—Papa, in his elation, leaping over three chairs in the hall one after the other, like a boy playing leap-frog, his arms flung up in the air and his hair flying. 'A boy!' he screamed, a bo-oy! Arun, Arun at last!' It turned out that when a second daughter had been born, the name Arun had already been chosen in anticipation of a son. It had had to be changed in disappointment, to Aruna (*ibidem* 17).

There is obviously something in the language that goes deep in mind of the readers like a lump of lead into the water. Much like her use of language, Desai's art of characterisation is made through the same vivid and lucid structure of her language.

What strikes most in her presentation of characters is the fact that each one of the characters appears alive and intimate; they appear full-blooded and living like the figures on the cine screen and this is achieved chiefly though her language.

Apart from the clarity of language, it is the device of contrast of time, situation and characters that adds to the structural organization of the novel. Uma is a sharp contrast to the character of Aruna in her approach to life, in her thinking and sensibility and in her temperament and understanding of life. But it is chiefly in her contrast of time that Desai appears to achieve great effect particularly when Papa describes his struggle in his early days:

> Papa said, 'We did not have electricity when we were children. If we wanted to study, we were sent out to sit under the streetlight with our books. During the examinations there would be a circle of students sitting and reciting their lessons aloud. It would be difficult to concentrate on law because others were reciting theorems or Sanskrit slokas or dates from British history. But we did it—we passed our exams' (*ibidem* 6).

Besides the devices of contrast, her use of similitude also discloses her utter simplicity of diction. It shows her sense of preciseness, exactitude and accuracy. Desai's account of Aruna's marriage proposals along with her dress, choice of shade and in her deportment, display her excellent use of the similes mainly drawn from nature.

> There were so many marriage proposals for Aruna that Uma's unmarried state was not only an embarrassment but an obstruction. Here was Aruna visibly ripening on the branch, asking to be plucked: no one had to teach her how to make samosas or help her to dress for an occasion. Instinctively, she knew. The pale, pale pink sari, the slender chain of seed pearls, the fresh flowers, the demure downcast turn of the eyes, the little foot in the red slipper thrusting out suddenly like a tongue, and the laughter low and sly. Mama watched and wondered,

> Papa humphed and hawed and scowled but Uma could see it was a façade and concealed a pleasure he would not allow himself to express (*ibidem* 85).

Along with this, one may also notice her use of the syntax, the balancing of phrases and the force of narrative texture that add much to the effect that Desai aims at driving in her work. The quarrel scene between the two families and the encounter between Harish and Uma's father, very well reveal the force of narrative impact in this novel:

> It consisted of Papa raving and ranting at one end, the mother-in-law screaming and screeching at the other, the brother shouting and threatening in between, and the sisters-in-law clustering together to watch all the parties in a kind of bitter satisfaction (*ibidem* 94).

It is pertinent to note here that Desai is known for her delineation of women characters who are the victims of society, the depressed lot, who either react to their situations or fall as victims. But this novel does not present such characters nor does Desai make Uma appear a depressed girl. Uma is made to appear a victim of her circumstances, a victim of her fate and as such she accepts her destiny quietly, ungrudgingly and tries to live like the dumb-driven cattle. But that does not mean that she is completely insensible and unthinkable. On the contrary, Uma is full of tender feelings; she has her wishes and desires, imagination and expectation, which she is unable to express. There is a sense of agony, a sense of irreparable loss and permanent shock in her which she deliberately hides in order to remain true to her nature. This is to be chiefly noticed in her dream that Desai has very effectively recorded:

> But in spite of her, in spite of them, it was a day to remember. It was a day as all days ought to be, not just a single one in the whole year, a single one in a whole lifetime. If Uma was asked to paint a picture of heaven, then heaven would have paper lanterns hanging from the trees along the drive and around the school courtyard, pots of white and yellow chrysanthemums like

> great boiled eggs in freshly painted flowerpots on the veranda stairs. It would have Tiny Lopez's band playing 'Rudolph the Red-nosed Reindeer,' and 'Away in a Manger'; in a marquee on the netball field. It would have stalls all along one length of it, where ladies stood frying potato fritters, and selling toffees in packets of crinkly pink crepe paper, bottled drinks and candy floss. It would have stalls all along the opposite length where girls in blue slips and white blouses and ribbons supervised games of chance-lucky dips, pin-the-tail-on-the-donkey, toss-the-hoop, guess-the-weight-of-the plum-cake (*ibidem* 128).

In this connection it is significant to note that Uma has been delineated in altogether a different way from all the other heroines of Desai. She is neither a psychic case nor a violent rebellion in the society; neither assertive nor demanding and yet she is a thinking, feeling human being. Unlike her sister Aruna, she cannot express nor can she register her thoughts and yet she appears to suffer under the circumstances against which she can make no resistance. Here she becomes the traditional archetypal woman who is born to live and suffer. This has been very well displayed when Desai probes into her heart and discloses Uma's secret wishes relating to her career:

> A CAREER. Leaving home. Living alone. These troubling, secret possibilities now entered Uma's mind—as Mama would have pointed out had she known—whenever Uma was idle. They were like seeds dropped on the stony, arid land that Uma inhabited. Sometimes, miraculously, they sprouted forth the idea: run away, escape. But Uma could not visualise escape in the form of a career. What was a career? She had no idea. Her vision of an escape, a refuge, took the form of a huge and ancient banyan tree with streaming grey air roots, leafy branches in which monkeys and parrots feasted on berries. Sometimes she heard the berries raining down on the zinc roof which backed in the clean white sun (*ibidem* 131).

Unlike her other novels it may be observed that here an attempt has been made by Desai to present Uma as a girl who has to live in the society accepting all the humiliations, injustices, sufferings and miseries without raising any voice or making resistance. Thus, the central meaning of the novel lies in the character of Uma, the woman who becomes the prototype of Sita and Draupadi in their sufferings which they had undergone willy-nilly. Like the traditional Indian woman, Uma suffers quietly only to prove her great sense of endurance and stoic acceptance. After her tragic withdrawal from her husband Harish, Aruna whispers to her in the dark and silences, "Uma, Uma Didi—did he touch you?" Uma buries her head in her pillow and howls—"No, No." There could not be a more tragic situation than the one that Uma faces! Who could explain the cause or the justification of such a situation? Here she could only remember her Mira-masi who had once told her that she is chosen by Lord Shiva for his bride:

> But then she would feel Mira-masi's hands descend on her shoulders and grasp her, and hear voice intoning, 'You are the Lord's child—I see His mark on you,' or The Lord has rejected the man you chose. He has chosen you for Himself and Uma would give a start, then begin thrashing her arms around and looking about her wildly, making Mama cry, Uma what's the matter? and she would subside, and as she subsided, feel herself drawn by an undercurrent into a secret depth, so dark that she could see nothing at all—just the darkness (*ibidem* 133).

Herein, is revealed the great artistic talent of Anita Desai as a novelist. Her novels are not meant to explain the theories of philosophy and psychology; on the other hand, they reveal her involvement in the deep feelings of her women who are seen as the worst sufferers, highly suppressed by social 'tantalization' or marital discord. Such preoccupation seems quite natural on her part, for she like her characters, is very sensitive that gives her an insight to make a very successful in-depth study of her women.

In sum, it may be concluded here that *Fasting, Feasting,* appears to deviate from all the earlier novels for it does not deal with the exclusively female dominated plots. In all her major works like *Cry, the Peacock, Voices in the City, Where Shall We Go This Summer?, Bye-Bye Black Bird. Fire on the Mountain,* and *In Custody,* she lays added emphasis on the feminine character and takes special interest in projecting the essential features that dominate these characters. In the mid-1980s she appears to shift to male-centred plots like *Baumgartner's Bombay.* Therefore, she moves to present the male—female dialectic as in *Clear Light of Day* perhaps to illustrate and support the theory of Coleridge and Virginia Wolf that the great Mind is "androgynous" which she had presented in her essay at the Commonwealth Institute, London. But none of these views or trends is present in this novel. It has no trace of Desai, the feminist, nor of Desai, the social critic. Above all, it does not present an oppressed woman reacting violently against the society nor the depressed woman rebelling against the society of one male-dominated consciousness. It is, in short, the story of a family that seeks to exist against the backdrop of the Indian society with all its common and universal elements. It draws our attention to the fact that Desai's novels, particularly the one in question, present their inherent Indianness and put the focus of attention on the probing of the essence of existence and ordeal of consciousness which is primarily a generic problem concerned with the human condition as such. In other words, it may be said that in this particular novel, Desai intends to transcend all her earlier limitations to present a simple human situation in the most simple way to establish her credibility as a contemporary Indian English fiction writer.

WORK CITED

Desai, Anita. *Fasting, Feasting.* London: Chatto and Windus, 1999.

8

Mothers and Daughters: A Comparative Critique of *Fasting, Feasting* and *Difficult Daughters*

ASHA CHOUBEY

All the world may not love a lover, but it certainly adores a mother. The word is full of love, affection, selfless devotion and all that is soft and sweet and noble in human nature. Between a mother and a child, only trust and love can exist. This should be especially true of a mother-daughter relationship. Belonging to the same gender, they are supposed to be united in a bond of understanding besides love and trust. Much has been written on this holy relation and much has been exposed. If we have traditional literature eulogizing this relationship, we also have literature that exposes the ground reality. The glory of motherhood comes from taking a sentimental approach to the phenomenon which comes but naturally. Feminists, however, have deprived motherhood of much of its halo. The kind of motherhood that has been celebrated through tradition is a myth created by the male of the species to chain their womenfolk. These feminists believe that this relationship is also based on selfish motives and is as much a give and take relationship as any. Daughters are not all that dependant, admiring lot and mothers are not all that doting, sacrificing one. Their relationship is shaped by the circumstances that dominate. In India, however, this tendency took a little time to catch on as Indians take delight in investing all natural phenomena with a little artificial halo. With women increasingly realizing their individuality and getting desperate to get recognition as persons and not as role models, there has been a visible change in the depiction of erstwhile romantic relationships. Mother-daughter relationship, which was wont to be highly romanticized, has come to be portrayed in more realistic light. The bitterness, the resentment, the dislike and even the envy that were often felt but never expressed, came to be accepted as dominant traits of this relationship. In recent years *Difficult Daughters* by Manju Kapur and *Fasting, Feasting* by Anita Desai are two novels which show mother-daughter relationship in a new light. The present paper proposes to make a comparative study of both these novels from this viewpoint.

Mother-daughter relationship is unique and determines the future development of a woman. It is a relationship which requires separation and fusion at the same time for the proper development of the daughter's personality. Sophie Freud (1991) notices negativity and cruelty in such relationships. It is this relationship that helps the daughter overcome the ambivalences and to gain confidence to go out into the world, to face the world as an individual. Even the love life of the daughter depends on her relationship with her mother and precisely on the relationship of her mother with her father. The first bonding of an infant is with the mother. This initial bonding is true for both the sexes, but boys break away at an early age to identify with their fathers. Nancy Chodorow maintains: 'A daughter continues to identify with the mother' (Nancy 292). It is because of this emotional bonding and initial identification that the daughters struggle all their lives to separate from their mothers. In their quest for autonomy, daughters face initial inhibition due to their identification with their mothers. The 'feminine mystique' which feminists warn against is a concept which mothers bequeath to their daughters. Mothers learn by their experiences to please their men by their essential femininity and they pass this lesson on to their daughters as well. This lesson is a survival device which mothers offer to their daughters. The relationship though full of strains and conflicts must still be properly balanced. Where the mixture goes awry, there are disturbances in self-representations, conflict in gender identification, career problems and even difficulties in intimate relationships with men. Carol Boyd seems to solicit the conclusion reached at by Lucy Fischer in her research work that though there is a sense of identification, 'daughters struggle all their lives to separate from their mothers' (Boyd 292). This is one issue whereupon mothers grudge their daughters' quest for identity. Mothers would want their daughters to be like them but daughters crave, naturally, for autonomy. Mothers would like their daughters to learn their lessons from the mothers' experiences but daughters would still like to learn it their own way.

I

Difficult Daughters is primarily the story of a daughter's journey towards self-realization vicariously through her mother's attainment of selfhood. The story is presented through the conscience of Ida who goes on to explore the life and times of not only her mother Virmati but her maternal grandmother Kasturi as well. Virmati, the oldest of eleven siblings is forced to nurse her younger brothers and sisters as her mother goes on giving birth to children after children. Kasturi is either ill due to pregnancy or she is bedridden because of delivery. Hence Virmati has to take care of the younger lot. Gradually it so happens that Kasturi starts taking Virmati for granted. She looks upon her daughter as the governess of her children. Virmati is expected to treat her studies as a secondary job, the primary one being her doing the household chores and caring for the children. While Virmati considers Shakuntala—her cousin who is pursuing her studies in Lahore—as her role model, Kasturi has other dreams for her daughter wherein studies do not find a place. She would like Virmati to marry a suitable boy of her elders' choice and settle down like a good girl. But luck has chalked out a different course for the girl. Virmati is attracted towards an English professor who falls passionately in love with her because his illiterate wife could never prove a soul mate. After his repeated overtures Virmati gives in, as she is also a soul thirsting for love. This illegitimate affair leads to many a trouble. Virmati has to bear the brunt alone. She is forced to abort the child of Harish as the professor is reluctant—rather afraid—to marry her. Finally at the insistence of a friend, the professor is forced into marrying her. But Virmati's hardships do not end here, they simply change colours. Most of her sufferings are caused by maternal apathy. Virmati does not have a sympathetic shoulder to weep on and this aggravates her agony. She suffers at the hands of the parochial society, her family and above all her paramour. She could never share her feelings with Kasturi. As a child she keeps craving for a little understanding from her mother but with the passing of time she learns to accept the situation as it is. This mother-daughter relationship marches from identification to alienation. Years later Ida—the daughter of Virmati—relives her relation with her mother, marching from alienation to identification. Thus the novel presents the paradigm of two mother-daughter relationships. What could be a simple self-exploration through the exploration of formative influences becomes quite amazing in view of Ida's reluctance to be like her mother. Her reflection at the very outset seems to prepare the background for her search of roots: the one thing I had wanted was not to be like my mother. (Kapur 1. All subsequent references to the book are from this edition). The whole story thereafter is an attempt to comprehend the kind of person her mother was. As the realization gradually dawns, one finds Ida getting drawn towards Virmati. So much so that the novel ends with Ida almost identifying with Virmati.

Fasting, Feasting is the story of human hungers and cravings on one hand and satiation and surfeit on the other. Anita Desai explores human psyche through her study of motives and actions. The novel is the story of Uma and captures her dreams and desires as well as her frustrations and despairs. Uma is a woman who becomes the victim of a patriarchal society where women are not allowed to hold their own. Uma is the oldest of three siblings. As a child she is quite normal despite the dictatorial attitude of her father. The father is a strict disciplinarian who exercises authority not only on his children but also on his wife. There is seen a special bond between the mother and the two girls, all of them being the victims of Papa. The mother indulges in many such activities as are not approved by Papa and the girls are her confidantes. But with the birth of Arun—the precious son— things change for the girls. The mother drifts away from the girls and the son becomes the central force in the family. All activities in the family revolve around him. Uma is forced to drop out of school on the pretext that she is not good in studies. She is burdened with the responsibility of Arun. Since then life becomes an arid journey in a desert for Uma. To make the matters worse, her marriage fails and there is no escape from the prison that is her home. She looks after all the household chores while the mother enjoys life with her husband. Uma is expected to choke her own yearnings and to live for Mamapapa who become all the more inseparable, as Uma is always there to take care of everything about the house. She has to be on her toes all the time. Her life becomes a tale of oppression and the strange fact about the matter is that it is the mother who is more to blame than the father. Uma is forced into a life of drudgery by the mother and she is denied even basic human rights. The bleak circumstances leave Uma hysterical. A perfectly normal girl is pushed into insanity by maternal indifference. The amazing fact, however, is that in this patriarchal world, Uma is oppressed not so much by the patriarch as by her mother. Mothers are such strong influences in the lives of their daughters that they have the power to make or mar their daughter's personality. In a patriarchal world, however mothers instead of protecting the interests of their daughters become instrumental in torturing them. Uma, a normal girl child grows into a dull, insipid shadow of a woman and going through various trials and tribulations finally attains a mental state which borders on insanity.

II

There is nothing more painful for a girl than the pressure to grow up even before she has enjoyed her childhood. The patriarchal set-up plots against women right since their birth. The conditioning begins at home and women are supposed to walk from mother's womb into mother's shoes. More so, if the girl child happens to be the eldest in the family. Uma in *Fasting, Feasting* is still a child when her baby brother Arun is born. Arun is no ordinary child; he is the precious only son of the family who needs special attention. Uma is, then, expected to provide this much needed attention to her brother. She is forced out of school and even before the little child could learn to do her hair properly, she is taught:

> The correct way of folding nappies, of preparing watered milk, of rocking the screaming infant to sleep when he was covered with prickly heat as with a burn (Desai 18).

An innocent life that is full of possibilities is maimed by the forces that connive to condition a girl child to prove conducive to the patriarchal set-up. The most pathetic fact arises out of the knowledge that it is the mother who proves instrumental in this type of connivance. The birth of Arun does not make any change in the life of the mother. And if there is a change it is for the better as is evidenced by the lady's chin held high with pride at becoming complete by giving birth to a son. But for Uma it proves the end of all her dreams, her aspirations and even her individuality. Before the girl could learn to assert herself, she is burdened with the responsibility of taking care of a baby brother.

Virmati in *Difficult Daughters* has to be a mother to all her ten siblings. The mother Kasturi is involved in the sole job of procreation leaving the young ones for Virmati to tend upon. The poor girl does her best to appease her mother and at the same time pursue her studies. The presence of Shakuntala inspires her with the thirst for knowledge but the maternal pressure on her psyche is too much to bear. Even her dreams of emancipation are not free of all apprehensions:

> She could hear her mother telling her not to waste her time; there were more important things to do. Like looking after the children, thought Virmati bitterly, and then, as she thought of Paro's clinging arms around her neck, she began to cry (18).

Thus it is that the long chain of conditioning of women starts from their mothers. Mothers, being women, were themselves conditioned by their mothers first and the society at large next. Mothers take it as their duty to condition their girl child into the norms of the patriarchal society. The sooner the process is begun, the better it is for the daughter. Virmati's mother fails to understand her despair about failing in her studies. Ida reflects:

> Kasturi found the fuss Virmati was making about failing unreasonable. It hardly made a difference to *the real business of her life*, which was getting married and looking after her own home (19). (Italics mine)

The Victorian approach of 'men for sword and women for hearth' has seeped so deep into our psyche that it seems hard to rub it off. The real business of life is a nightmare which threatens to murder the peace of the daughter's mind. The tale of Virmati is the tale of struggle of a woman against the parochial society. In this struggle women must be aided by women. The feminists talk about the concept of sisterhood. There have been many instances where this concept has been successfully materialized but mothers seldom rise up to this concept. This is one relationship wherein understanding and support are most expected but this is sadly one relationship where these ideas are lacking.

There may be seen absolute dearth of understanding and emotional bonding between mothers and daughters. This lack of understanding is also due to the fact that mothers take their own revenge on the society by avenging against their daughters. Since they had not been allowed freedom, their daughters must also be denied. Since they were not free to dream, their daughters must also learn to accept the breaking of their dreams. Since the mothers were not permitted to pursue education, their daughters must also suppress their yearnings. Uma's mother is herself an insipid shadow of her husband and she has meekly accepted the secondary position. She wants Uma to learn submissiveness and to choke the voice of her individuality. Quite contrary to her wishes, the woman had to give birth to a son because the patriarch so desired. The price of this Uma has to pay, as she has to drop out of school in order to look after the baby. These women force their daughters into servitude but they are never moved with a bit of sympathy for the poor soul. The daughters have to share the responsibility that belongs to their mothers. While towards their own ilk these women are cruel and uncomprehending, they reserve their affectionate self for their sons.

III

Maternal alienation can be sensed all through the thoughts and deeds of daughters. The apathy that starts from the mother gives birth to this sense of alienation. Daughters never feel oneness with their mothers. The relationship has always an aura of estrangement. Daughters suffer in silence but are not able to share their private sorrows with their mothers. Firstly, because the mother is not inclined to share and secondly but more importantly because most of these sorrows are inflicted by the mother herself. The absence or lack of mother's sympathetic shoulders at home forces these daughters to look for sympathy outside which in turn leads to deception. Daughters become vulnerable to outside influences. The sense of belonging that is the essence of a good relationship is found sadly missing from this relationship which is most vital in the life of a woman. Uma proves a failure at every front. She is not as educated and beautiful as her sister Aruna; she is also not as lucky as her. Twice she is packed off in marriage and twice she returns. Her life is jinxed, she bears the stigma on her face but there is no one to comfort her. Mama is busy indulging the whims of papa. She does not notice, does not bother to notice the wounds of Uma. She thinks that keeping Uma busy with the household chores is the only way to keep her mind away from her personal life. An unmarried daughter's existence is futile, meaningless; she can bring significance to her life only by proving useful at home. Uma is forced to take up the role of her mother immediately after the birth of Arun and since then there is no respite for her. The mother has her own life and she enjoys her freedom from Arun's responsibility at the cost of Uma. Uma is kept busy with the task of looking after her brother and by the time Arun grows up she is found stuck in multifarious household chores. While the mother used to indulge herself stealthily behind Papa's back, she does not realize Uma's need to be. Uma cannot go to her neighbour's if she enjoys an evening out with Ramu Bhai it is not with impunity that she does so. Virmati keeps thirsting for love and understanding but her mother Kasturi fails to understand her cravings. Ida tells the readers:

> At times Virmati yearned for affection, for some sign that she was special. However, when she put her head next to the youngest baby, feeding in the mother's arms, Kasturi would get irritated and push her away. 'Have you seen to their food-milk-clothes-studies?' (6)

Apart from this Virmati does not exist for Kasturi. Years later when Ida rebuilds Virmati's story from the information provided by her relatives she can still sense that: 'The language of feeling had never flowed between them' (11).

If Virmati drifts away to Harish it is primarily due to the contrast that she finds between her mother and Harish. Harish shows patience and sympathy. Also he makes quite clear at the outset itself that he needs her badly. Virmati feels loved, wanted—the feeling that her mother could never generate. Uma and Virmati both go about their household duties quite mechanically. Both these women manage their mother's home skilfully; both seem quite uninvolved and aloof. There is a sense of alienation—especially maternal alienation. They do not seem to belong to their mothers. As a young child, both crave for their mother's love but when it seems impossibility, their yearning for it dies down. Uma finds solace in her treasury of greeting cards and later in the fantastic world of shadows to which Mira Masi introduces her. Virmati finds refuge in the arms of Harish who promises Utopia. Thus, maternal alienation leads to strong changes in the lives of daughters. For Uma the living, breathing world becomes unbearable because it is inhabited by her mother who is impervious to maternal instinct. For Virmati, the love of Harish comes as the only escape from the otherwise dull convention ridden patriarchal world. In fact, it is not love but the lack of love that turns her life upside down.

IV

Identity crisis is an issue facing all alert and aware women in a patriarchal society where identity is considered a preposterous concept for women. A daughter's quest for identity begins with her identification with her mother. Daughters search for self-realization through their mothers. (Ida in *Difficult Daughters* begins a journey into the history of her mother with a purpose to discover herself.) Ironical it is then that the conflict in this relationship begins when daughters start their quest. For as long as daughters are asexual children and are not conscious of their individuality, the relationship runs quite smoothly. But as soon as the child becomes aware of her sexuality and starts asserting her individuality, the strain starts building up. Ida in her quest for identity begins the search of the person who was her mother. She begins with a resolution that she would not be like her mother but as the story unravels she finds herself identifying with her mother. What started as alienation ends up in complete identification. But not all daughters are as fortunate as Ida. Virmati herself could never belong to her mother Kasturi. Her pleasures, her pains, her pathetic life as a mistress and then a second wife all remained her private sorrows. She could never share them with her mother. Kasturi never understands her, never attempts to understand her. Virmati becomes used to the tartness in Kasturi's voice. There seems a barrier between them which Virmati fails to pull down. Ida tells the readers:

> From time to time Virmati glanced furtively at her mother, and the wall she encountered forbade her from making the attentive gestures that might have made the journey bearable for both (102).

Besides all other allegations, Kasturi grudges Virmati the fact that 'She's become so independent' (161).

Uma is a submissive, docile girl who seems to have come to terms with her subordinate position in her mother's home. All day, till late at might she works for the comforts of her parents. Her presence in the house has given much leisure to Mama who enjoys the freedom from household responsibilities. While Mamapapa attend parties, invitations and pay visits to their friends, Uma takes care of everything in the house. But Mama does not ever acknowledge the contribution of Uma. She is taken for granted and it is believed that she has no right to be aware of her needs. She cannot accept the invitation even from Mrs O'Henry lest she shall have to repay the invitation. She has no right even to telephone anyone because calls cost money. The girl has a servile existence in her own home. Her lot is worse than that of a married woman. If she happens to steal some moments of fun away from the dull, dreary existence at home, she is rebuked badly. An evening out with Ramu Bhai gives her immense joy but her mother is out of her mind with anger:

> 'Quiet, you hussy! Not another word from you, you idiot child!' Mama's face glints like a knife in the dark, growing narrower and fiercer as it comes closer. 'You, you disgrace to the family—nothing but disgrace, ever!' (52-53).

Parental apathy—more precisely maternal indifference—destroys a life full of possibilities. Uma is a normal girl despite her failure in studies and like any other normal girl she could realize her possibilities if only she were not laughed at by her mother. The indifference of her father could become bearable if only she had her mother's love and understanding. Virmati also jumps into a blind, bleak future with Harish because her mother could never understand her dreams. So many promising lives go down the drain due to maternal apathy. Virmati would not be a victim to a much married man like Harish and Uma would not be a prey to hysteria if they had understanding mothers. The very course of a daughter's life changes due to the mother's attitude. Daughters are difficult only when life becomes difficult for them. Though like all relationships, this one is also bilateral and is based on interdependence; the dependence of the daughter is greater than that of the mother. Authoritative and autocratic attitude of the mother may mar the very personality of daughter as in case of Uma and it may make a pseudo-rebel out of an otherwise disciplined and motivated daughter as in the case of Virmati.

WORKS CITED

Boyd, Carol J. "Mothers and Daughters: A Discussion of Theory and Research." *Journal of Marriage and Family.* No. 51, 1989.

Chodorow, Nancy. *The Reproduction of Mothering.* Berkeley: University of California Press, 1978.

Desai, Anita. *Fasting, Feasting.* London: Chatto and Windus, 1999.

Kapur, Manju. *Difficult Daughters.* New Delhi: Penguin, 1997.

9

From Computer to Mangalabibi: A Conglomeration of Heterogeneous Elements: A (Post) Post-Colonial Project

SOBHA CHATTOPADHYAY

It is often difficult to 'frame' Indian English writing of the 1990s, when the Indian post-colonial novel was passing through a post-modernist phase. Though we know that 'the Indian English novel began in post-coloniality and will continue as a post-colonial form long after the post-modern phase will have passed on' (Kirpal 23), the fact that it shows certain striking features of the post-modernist novel and yet reveals a deep post-colonial concern, lying embedded, makes it difficult to analyse, interpret or even problematize.

Amitav Ghosh's *The Calcutta Chromosome* (1996) presents a special problem for critics. It is unique among Ghosh's novels in the sense that it betrays some definite post-modernist characteristics, yet underneath there is an implicit post-colonial agenda, as well as a simultaneous critique of the post-colonial which makes it a very complex text. Thus it touches on the 'problematic site of interaction' between the post-modern and the post-colonial to which Linda Hutcheon refers (Hutcheon 170). Tossed between the open-ended and the closed form, it is an interesting piece of work precisely because it seeks 'to discover the opportunity for actively using post-modern challenges in post-colonialism's Self-questioning' (Tiffin and

Lawson 56). I shall first examine some of these post-modernist features, and try to find out if their post-modernism can really be differentiated from post-colonial characteristics.

Post-modernism is characterized by plurality and indeterminacy, multiplication and juxtaposition of perspectives. For post-modernists the novel is a space for foregrounding 'ontological' issues (McHale 10). Jean-Francois Lyotard presents a vision of post-modernity as a search for 'dissent' and recognition of heterogeneity, of a multiplicity of arguments never arriving at agreement, of 'language games' as contestation, jousting, language as duelling, as performance (Lyotard 55-56). A post-modern novel reveals multiple layers. The text is something like a huge multi-layered box, containing various small Chinese-box worlds (to use McHale's phrase) arranged horizontally and vertically, where every compartment, no matter how small it is, coexists with every other compartment, retaining its separate identity. The author pulls the past into the present, the future into the past. One thinks of Rushdie's richly multidimensional and cosmopolitan novel *Midnight's Children*, the way it brings together diverse historical, political, social and psychological strands. This novel sets the trend for the 1990s novel. The way it cuts across three different epochs and juxtaposes the Mughal empire with British colonial rule and Indira Gandhi's Emergency rule in 1976 foreshadows Amitav Ghosh's *The Calcutta Chromosome*. Here again Ghosh spans three centuries, subtly moving back and forth in time and place between Ronald Ross's Calcutta in the 1890s, the 1995 Calcutta of Murugan and the journalists Sonali Das and Urmila Roy and the twenty-first century New York of Antar, the Egyptian-American computer programmer.

A post-modern novel is often an amalgam of disparate components like fact and fiction, history and myth, realism and fantasy. It often tries to close the gap between elite and mass culture, incorporating popular genres like the detective story or thriller, science fiction, the Western pornography and even pop art: 'Genres [...] continuously reproduce conventions while they transform them, reverse them, parody them [...] always introducing new idioms by playing off, interacting with, contesting each other' (Docker 113). The 'boundaries' of genre writing, so useful for criticism's mapping exercises, are like borders or territories. Borders are ambivalent in that they demarcate, but also invite crossing, by their mere presence. And cross-generic writing should be seen against the background of the increasing internationalization of the literary market, the geographical and cultural crossing and recrossing of boundaries, developments that gain unprecedented intensity in the 1990s. The earlier concept of 'purity' of form gives way to 'mixed genre' and 'hybridity'—terms evoking a new 'transcultural' form, which sets different points of view against each other in a 'conflictual structure' retaining 'a certain elemental, organic energy and openhandedness' (Young 22). Bakhtin's concept of the 'polyphonic' novel helps to understand the nature of the post-modern text: its polyphony is pluralistic and multi-voiced; it represents 'reality in all its polyphonic complexity,' and its structure is a dialogue between different voices and discourses, that 'do not merge in the unity of an evolving spirit' (Bakhtin 126). One recognizes this polyphony in Ghosh's novel, as some of the diverse components are presented as polarities. Nevertheless, through a sensitive use of language, voices and genres, Ghosh succeeds in balancing a complex set of concerns, some of them post-modern, others definitely post-colonial.

On the surface *The Calcutta Chromosome* strikes us as a mystery or a thriller. Right from the word 'go,' as the image of a damaged I.D. card, pops up on the computer screen and the insistent computer Ava demands enquiry, a strange, compelling tale of suspense is unfolded. The card belongs to Antar's former Indian colleague Murugan who vanished in Calcutta in 1995. As Antar investigates the cause of Murugan's mysterious disappearance through supercomputers and archives, a mystery unravels centring round Murugan's pursuit of a cranky obsession with Ronald Ross. As Murugan and his helpers all try to dig up information we find ourselves involved in secret research and ethnic rituals. We get caught up as the story jumps back and forth in time spanning centuries weaving together numerous characters. With Murugan and one of the assisting investigators, Urmila, we try to understand and expose a subtext of counter-science, occultism and intrigue round Ross and his associates. It is as mesmerizing as a Rubik's Cube.

The Calcutta Chromosome is science fiction too. Not just because it delves deep into the history of medical science or genetic science, but because with Antar we enter a new twenty-first century world of 'cyberspace,' plugging the brain into the worldwide computer network of the future. 'Cyberspace' is the visual image produced when one dons a headset linked into the universal network that facilitates the handling and exchange of massive quantities of data (Shippey 34). Science fiction is intrinsically a 'high information' genre-based on 'novum'—information recognizable as not-true but also not-unlike-true, not flatly impossible. We realize it is as yet an imaginary stage, but also that the existence of such stages is by no means imaginary. The fictive exploration of emergent futures takes a new turn with post-modern science fiction like *The Calcutta Chromosome*, new in the role it assigns to the Internet, trying to link up different cultures and ages:

> Ava had been speaking to him in the appropriate rural dialect of the Nile Delta. Her voice-reproduction capabilities had been upgraded so that she could even switch intonations depending on what was being said—from young to old, male to female (Ghosh 11).[1]

Yet there is something disconcerting about the Internet—an all-seeing consciousness throwing surprises and reminding man of his inability to explore the abyss of the awesome universe. Like many post-modernist texts *The Calcutta Chromosome* seems to show 'the way individuals are unable to deal with the great global multinational and decentred communicational network in which we find ourselves caught as individual subjects' (Berger 103-04). At times there is a sense of machine going out of control as when disgusted Antar leaves Ava in Penn Station. Technology takes the shape of magic, fantasy transforms into post-modern science fiction.

The fantasy element is quite prominent in post-modern novels like D.M. Thomas's *The White Hotel,* or in Rushdie's work. According to Brian Attebery, 'Fantasy invokes wonder by making the impossible seem familiar and the familiar seem new and strange' (Attebery 3). Baudrillard's concept of 'hyperreality' seems relevant here. As Ghosh dips into Indian mystic cult and transmigration of souls, we delve deep into the world of fantasy. Mangala, who is a laboratory technologist involved in Ross's research, also appears as the priestess of a cult that centres around the elixir of life; such unexpected double roles invest these characters with magic realism: 'These people who came to see Mangala may have believed that she was a witch or a magician or a god' (*CC* 204).

> Her treatment often produced weird side-effects—what looked like strange personality disorders. Except that they weren't really disorders but transpositions [...] what she had on her hands was a cross-over of randomly assorted personality traits, from the malaria donor to the recipient—via the bird of course [...] she could control the ways in which these cross-overs worked (*CC* 206).

To add to this sense of weirdness, Ghosh even introduces an arresting ghost story—the eerie incidents at Renupur. Everything in Ghosh's novel seems to be shrouded in mystery. The spirit of post-modern game playing pervades the novel. One could read a Bakhtinian 'carnivalesque' quality here, for a strong comic spirit lies at the novel's heart. *The Calcutta Chromosome* is sprinkled all over with humour and irony.

But there is even a stronger reason to read the novel as post-modern: its similarity with metafiction. According to McCaffery, metafiction is a self-conscious approach to the art of fiction-making, commenting on the nature of meaning itself. It 'either directly examines its own construction as it proceeds' or 'comments or speculates about the forms and language of previous fiction' (McCaffery 16). By virtue of its elements of parody, and its problematizing of history, Amitav Ghosh's *The Calcutta Chromosome* could well be examined under the category of historical metafiction. The novel is in fact a project of contradicting the official version of history. It explores the history of Sir Ronald Ross, the Nobel laureate, the British Army doctor who discovered the role of anopheles mosquito in the transmission of malaria in colonial Calcutta of the 1890s. It is mainly done through Murugan, the Indian expert on Ross, who leaves his job in New York to travel to Calcutta in 1995 pursuing his unrelenting scientific research. And as in metafiction, Murugan's version is a new satiric reconstruction of history questioning the traditional version. He gradually reveals how Ross's discoveries were fed to him by his Indian laboratory technologists Mangala and Lutchman. Mangala, according to Murugan, 'was way ahead of Cunnigham (Ross's predecessor) in her intuitive understanding of the fundamentals of the malaria problem' (*CC* 202). Ross may have had 'real talent.' But 'with this woman we're talking about a whole lot more than just talent; we may be talking genius here' (*CC* 203). And Lutchman 'was leading Ronnie by the nose': 'Every time Ron went running off in the wrong direction, Lutchman was waiting to [...] show him the way to go' (*CC* 200). But Mangala 'had bigger things in mind than the malaria bug.' She actually used the 'malaria bug' 'as a treatment in another disease,' syphilis which was 'incurable' in 1890s killing 'millions of people every year' (*CC* 204). According to Murugan, Mangala actually knew and demonstrated how 'artificially induced malaria' cured syphilitic paralysis and dementia thus anticipating the discovery of another Nobel laureate Wagner-Jauregg in 1927. In fact, 'she was working towards something altogether different' (*CC* 203)—immortality.

This approach to history invites a reference to the changed notion of history at the end of the twentieth century. Particularly after the new scepticism and suspicion about the writing of history expressed in the last quarter of the twentieth century by Barbara Foley, Hayden White and Dominick LaCapra, history and literature are now seen to share a similar inscribing of subjectivity in the very process of selection and interpretation. As Hayden White says, 'facts are not given but constructed by the kinds of questions we ask of events' (White 43). 'Every representation of the past has ideological implications' (White 69). This relation between history and fiction is addressed and problematized in that special kind of post-modern fiction, which Linda Hutcheon describes as 'historiographic metafiction,' a genre to which Ghosh's novel is very close.

True to the spirit of historigraphic metafiction, Murugan uses the historical data gathered by his avid research of Ross not by smoothly assimilating them, but by merely incorporating his data, in such a way that the reader gets to see his very efforts to create coherence. He is particularly tentative when it comes to Mangalabibi, the sweeper:

> 'The Calcutta chromosome' said Murugan. 'That's my name for what she was working towards.'
>
> 'Now I'm really lost,' said Urmila 'I've lived here all my life and I've never heard of this thing you're talking about.'
>
> 'And who knows if you ever will?' said Murugan. 'Or whether I will. Or whether it exists or has ever existed. At this point in time it's still all guesswork on my part' (*CC* 203).

As readers we see him both collecting the historical facts and trying to make sense of them. He is conscious of the inaccessibility of facts and 'truth.' Sometimes the entire activity of research is called into question. Murugan even problematizes the notion of knowledge: 'Maybe this other team started with the idea that knowledge is self-contradictory [...]. Maybe they thought that knowledge couldn't begin without acknowledging the possibility of knowledge' (*CC* 88).

The way Ghosh describes the famous scientist Ross, as sloppy, calculating and ambitious, led by the nose by the sinister 'other' team, makes us wonder if Ghosh is out to debunk the orthodox version of the past. This 'demystifying impulse' is 'typical of much post-modernist revisionist historical fiction' (McHale 91). 'Trouble is Ron doesn't know a goddam thing about mosquitoes: he's never even heard the word anopheles' (*CC* 66).

But this demystifying impulse is not just post-modernist. Perhaps this is one of the points where a post-colonialist reading comes in. Ghosh's contradiction of the public record of 'official' history could be seen as a kind of post-colonial rewriting. While the traditional Western version focuses on the contribution of white men like Ross, Laveran and Jauregg, Murugan's account drags Indians like Mangala and Lutchman to the forefront. Interlinked with it is the post-colonial attitude to history writing. The question of *whose* history survives and *whose* truth gets told is significant. The history of colonial aggression has always been narrated from the colonizer's perspective. The voice of the colonized has been silenced or wiped out. As the narrator in Rushdie's *Shame* puts it 'History loves those who dominate her' (Rushdie 124). The choice of protagonists and some of the major characters in Ghosh's novel is decidedly post-colonial. But there are more reasons why the novel can be regarded as post-colonial. The specific framework that is proposed for the understanding of history and the focus on social and political marginality and spirituality have to be taken into consideration.

Post-colonialism implies mental and cultural decolonization challenging received ideological paradigms of power relationship. The gaze of the colonizer is replaced by that of the colonized. In *The Calcutta Chromosome,* the male white figure of the ruling class is being debunked by the native Murugan. The central character of Mangala, the laboratory technologist and cult leader, is not an upper class Bengali but a subaltern, unlettered woman, a sweeper, very much marginalized. Her accomplice Lutchman is equally marginalized. As a boy in his teens he had 'nowhere to go [...] built a bamboo shack on the tracks' and lived in Renupur. The station-master 'told the villagers that the Laakhan was worse than untouchable, that he carried contagion; that he was probably the child of a prostitute; that his misshapen left hand was a mark of hereditary disease' (*CC* 233). If Ross stands for Western scientific rational thought, Mangala stands for non-rational thought or instinct. Ross was known as a harbinger of Western enlightenment, knowledge and benevolence, eradicating a great tropical scourge like malaria in nineteenth century Bengal. Malaria eradication seemed one of the pillars of success on which British pride and glory rested. Ghosh attacks the idea.

Wrapped into the historic account of Ross is a fantastic parallel drama of 'secret' research and rituals by which malaria-altered chromosomes are made to carry the characteristics of one human being to another leading to transmigration of personalities and hence immortality. Should we call it a principle of genetic imprinting by which an entire personality is imprinted on succeeding generations of host bodies? Any way Mangalabibi, Lutchman and others are gradually revealed as leaders of a secret cult, sworn to silence and secrecy. All this is very close to the Indian idea of reincarnation:

> For what we have here is a biological expression of human traits that is neither inherited from the immediate gene pool, nor transmitted into it. It's exactly the kind of entity that would be hardest for a conventional scientist to accept [....]. The left goes ballistic if they say anything at all about the biological expression of human traits: it's all consciousness and soul at the end of the spectrum (*CC* 207).

This introduces a specific Indian dimension into the novel. In fact, many expatriate writers like Rushdie or Bharati Mukherjee show this tendency to chase the echoes of some kind of a lost Paradise in their homeland India. Rushdie's novels seem to romanticize Bombay, where he spent his childhood. In Ghosh, the vision is not dark, neither is there any inclination to idealize India. His is more of an anthropologist's interest in India's ethnic past, a curiosity in such secret cults. It is presented in the form of an exploration of certain biological facts from the point of view of a zealous researcher.

This theme of transmigration of souls is here linked up with the post-colonial concept of identity, which cannot be fixed spatially or temporally, but is essentially fluid. This fluidity is opposed to the problematic colonial notions of the fixity of identity, a notion that underlies racism. Hence Rushdie's attempt to pluralize it; he talks of the hybrid nature of post-colonial identity—'our mongrel selves.' Amitav Ghosh is equally worried about violence, racial hatred and communal strife resulting from fanaticism, blind ideology and misconceptions of identity as fixed. His deep concern for the socio-political scenario comes out in his article in *New Yorker* (July 17, 1995) called 'The Ghosts of Mrs Gandhi'. He writes that the mass-slaughter and violence he lived through after the assassination of Mrs Gandhi 'had the greatest effect on my life': 'Experiences of that period were profoundly important to my development as a writer.'[2] One thinks of *The Shadow Lines*—the riot scenes in Calcutta or the picture of Dhaka, just after Partition, or the nightmarish experience of the people in Cambodia during the Pol Pot years, depicted with deep sympathy in Ghosh's latest travelogue *Dancing in Cambodia*. In novel after novel Ghosh shows how different cultures and communities become antagonistic, to a point of no return. His is a passionate plea for humane existence.

In *The Calcutta Chromosome,* the same concern comes out in a roundabout way. The idea of transmigration of souls itself becomes a sort of paradigm of the fluidity of identity. It is reminiscent of a similar concept in Rushdie's *The Ground Beneath Her Feet.* Ghosh wants to pluralize identity. The doubles, divided selves and shadow figures in Rushdie reveal a comparable concern. In *The Calcutta Chromosome* there is a hint at doubling of identity as a whole personality is transplanted on a second generation host body through genetic imprinting. By this analogy, the woman in 'crisply-starched saree,' 'carrying a bamboo bird-cage' trying to heal a 'body' lying prostrate in front of the fire, in the midnight orgy scene, whom Sonali later recognizes as the Armenian lady Mrs Aratounian, seems to be a shadow of Mangalabibi. The body she calls Laakhan, Sonali realizes, was Romen's. Is Romen a shadow of Laakhan or Lutchman? It is all veiled in mystery. In the last section Antar visualizes Murugan 'standing in the lobby of a large auditorium' (recalling Rabindra Sadan) and two women 'running up the stairs.' As they come closer Antar suddenly recognizes Tara and Maria (a Guyanese lady), both wearing sarees. Do Tara and Maria converge into Urmila and Sonali? Throughout the whole novel, characters are suddenly recognized as someone else, or they are eerily reminiscent of other characters. There is a constant doubling, a constant ambivalence of identity. The concept of reincarnation might explain some of these ambivalences, but it remains mysterious and difficult to put across. The novel prefers to represent identity as irrevocably fluid, hybrid and multicultural. The specific way in which this suggestion is created through ambivalent references to reincarnation makes a cross-cultural or post-colonial reading possible.

Ghosh makes the post-colonial critique also work through the structure and narrative techniques of the novel. He questions the linear progressive mode of traditional Western story-telling or the bildungsroman form. He replaces it by the circular multi-layered post-colonial mode of story-telling. This in itself is not a typically post-colonial strategy, but this specific narrative form comes closer to the digressions and juxtapositions used by the oral story-teller rooted in the Indian tradition. At the same time, the uprooting and fragmentation of identity due to traumatic colonial experience and the challenging of existing notion of history, culture, norms of continuity and cohesion lead to the deliberate breaking down of the boundaries of genre. As Fawzia Afzal Khan writes about Salman Rushdie's post-modernist narrative:

> The mode or genre equal to dealing with the exigencies of [...] fragmentation must perforce be equally fragmented. In fact, the narrative must be a mishmash of conflicting genres and modes [...] in which the Comic and the Tragic, the Real, Surreal and the Mythic all 'defuse' each other, so no one genre can predominate and 'unify' the others.[3]

In the case of Rushdie, this mode of narration is almost a political act, a strategy for liberation. Yet simultaneously the complex amalgam narrative displays the Indian trend of inclusiveness and absorption (the culture itself compared to a melting pot or a salad bowl). All this is also true of *The Calcutta Chromosome*, and this would be a reason to define both Rushdie and Ghosh as post-colonial writers.

At this point I can conclude that Ghosh, like Rushdie, borrows post-modernist techniques to bring home a post-colonialist agenda. It is not the style in itself that makes his texts post-colonial, but his characters, general themes, and the focus of his cultural critique. It has been suggested that one should read Indian English writers such as Rushdie and Ghosh as a separate brand of post-modernism, and differentiate them from Euro-American post-modernists. The Indian English post-modernists concentrate more on techniques, and their world-view *is* less pessimistic (there is less of the meaninglessness and nothingness of existence). But this observation could also be a reason to argue for a post-colonial reading of Rushdie and Ghosh. As Kwame Appiah suggested in 1991, a deep ethical concern may be characteristic of many post-colonial texts, as opposed to post-modern texts.

Ghosh does not stop at a smooth post-colonial critique. There seems to be a further critique of the post-colonial critique itself. The metafiction as a genre itself provides for such a scope. As Linda Hutcheon observes, 'The protagonists of historiographic metafiction are anything but proper types: they are the ex-centrics, the marginalized, the peripheral figures of fictional history' (Hutcheon 113-14). At times one wonders how reliable is Murugan as an erstwhile researcher, being syphilitic himself;

all his eccentricities and idiosyncrasies make him sound rather strange. As one critic observes, 'It's hard to determine whether he's crazy or brilliant or both.'[4] Apparently, the novel is not merely a project of undermining Ross. Ross just becomes a pawn in someone else's grand plan, his fate determined by other factors. Far from being idealized, Mangala does seem a poor substitute for Ross. Both Mangala and Lutchman strike us as queer and melodramatic. Ghosh creates a mumbo-jumbo world in which secret conspiracies lurk at every step, men and women stagger into and get trapped in the web of history, sucked into the centre gradually to be swallowed up. One may call it fatalism or a deterministic version of history. And indeed, India is seen as a cult-ridden culture which believes in fate or destiny and the occult. If the West comes out badly through the novel, India comes out even worse. Thus, Ghosh almost seems to be laughing at rabid post-colonials. Implicitly and explicitly he counterpoises an awareness of the limitations of the post-colonial agenda. And the subtitle 'A Novel of Fevers, Delirium and Discovery' leaves everything tentative and veiled in mystery.

All these points may give a handle to a group of critics like Kwame Anthony Appiah who prefer to see 'post-coloniality' as 'a comprador intelligentsia,' a small Western style, Western-trained group of writers mediating 'the trade in cultural commodities,' selling to the West an India 'they have invented for their world' thus capturing 'the Euro-American publisher and reader' (Ashcroft *et al.* 119-20). As Ghosh digs deep within the Indian tradition in search of a non-rational mythic past, he may seem to be exoticising India specially for a Western reading public. But then as a post-colonial writer he has to fall back on India's cultural identity and he insists on the fluidity of all cultural identities—including India's.

The theme of transmigration of personalities hints at some sort of convergence. In fact, at the turn of the century, the age of post-colonialism may already be over. Leaving behind resistant anti-colonialism, ethnic consciousness and pride as a reaction to expansionist European nationalism, we are gradually heading towards what Said calls 'an enlightened post-colonialism.' The movement is towards globalization, multicultural and blended identity. Of course, in no way should this assertion of a shared post-colonial identity betray a tendency to de-historicise and delocate cultures from their temporal, spatial or linguistic contexts, and we should not be tempted to adopt an abstract globalized concept, merging differences in a lustreless internationalism. Culture is the mark of a post-colonial person's identity, all the more when that culture is hybrid. India is a multilingual, multi-religious, multiracial country. In our plea for multiculturalism we often tend to overlook the plurality within our own culture. To be an Indian is to possess many identities. Particularly in the big metropolitan cities of India, in multicultural Bombay or Calcutta, there is ample space for a novelist to foreground the lives and cultures of different religions and ethnic communities, revealing how identity is shaped daily. Amitav Ghosh offers a new, both situated and transnational, post-colonial imagination that revels in continuous reshaping of identities and merging of boundaries.

NOTES

1. Ghosh, Amitav. *The Calcutta Chromosome,* A Novel of Fevers, Delirium and Discovery (Delhi, 1996), 11. Henceforth the abbreviation used is *CC.*
2. Ghosh, Amitav. 'The Ghosts of Mrs Gandhi,' *New Yorker,* July 17, 1995, 35.
3. Fawzia Afzal-Khan, 'Post-Modernist Strategies of Liberation in the Works of Salman Rushdie,' *Journal of South Asian Literature.* 23. 1 (1988), 139.
4. Steinberg, Sybil S. *The Calcutta Chromosome,* Book Review *Publishers Weekly,* August 11, 1997, 384.

WORKS CITED

Adam, I. and Tiffin, H. Eds. *Past The Last Post: Theorizing Post-Colonialism and Post-Modernism* (Hemel Hempstead: Harvester Wheatsheaf, 1991).

Ashcroft, Bill, Griffiths Gareth and Tiffin Helen, Eds. *The Postcolonial Studies Reader* (London and New York, 1995).

Ashcroft, Bill, Griffiths Gareth and Tiffin Helen, Eds. *Key Concepts in Post-Colonial Studies* (London and New York, 1998).

Attebery, Brian. *The Fantasy Tradition in American Literature* (Bloomington: Indiana University Press, 1980).

Bakhtin, Mikhail. *Problems of Dostoevsky's Poetics*, translated by Caryl Emerson (Minneapolis, 1984).

Berger, Asa, Ed. *The Post Modern Presence: Readings on Postmodernism in American Culture and Society* (London, New Delhi, 1998).

Docker, John. *Postmodernism and Popular Culture: A Cultural Study* (Cambridge University Press, 1994).

Ghosh, Amitav. *The Shadow Lines* (Delhi, 1988).

——. *The Calcutta Chromosome*, A Novel of Fevers, Delirium and Discovery (Delhi, 1996).

——. *Dancing in Cambodia* (Delhi, 1998).

Hutcheon, Linda. *A Poetics of Postmodernism; History, Theory, Fiction* (New York, 1988).

Kirpal, Viney, Ed. *The Postmodern Indian English Novel* (New Delhi : Allied Publishers Ltd., 1996).

Lyotard, Jean-Francois. *The Postmodern Condition: A Report On Knowledge*, translated by Geoff Bennington and Brian Massumi (Minneapolis, 1984).

McCaffery, Larry. *The Metafictional Muse*, The Works of Robert Coover, Donald Barthelme and William H. Gass (University of Pittsburgh Press, 1982).

McHale, Brian. *Postmodernist Fiction* (London and New York, 1987).

Rushdie, Salman *Shame* (London, 1983).

Shippey, Tom ed. *Fictional Space: Essays on Contemporary Science Fiction* (N.J.: Oxford Humanities Press, 1991).

Tiffin, Chris and Lawson, Alan, Eds. *De-Scribing Empire* (London and New York, 1994).

White, Hayden. *Tropics of Discourse: Essays in Cultural Criticism* (Baltimore, 1978).

Young, R.J.C. *Colonial Desire: Hybridity in Theory, Culture and Race* (London, 1995).

10

NISSIM EZEKIEL: THE POET

MALLIKARJUN PATIL

Nissim Ezekiel occupies an important place in post-Independence Indian English literature. He has wielded a great influence as a leading poet, editor and an occasional playwright. Besides, he is a well-known critic. Sometimes he also emerges as a politician in the guise of a fighter for cultural freedom in India. Ezekiel held many important positions. He was for many years a Professor of English in Bombay University. He is a noted name in the field of journalism. In this capacity he was editor of many journals including *Poetry India* (1966-67), *Quest* (1955-57) and *Imprint* (1961-70), He was an Associate Editor to the Indian P.E.N., Bombay.

As a man of letters Nissim Ezekiel is a 'Protean' figure. His achievements as a poet and playwright are considerable. K. Balachandran writes, "The post-Independence Indian poetry saw its new poetry in the fifties. Among the new poets A.K. Ramanujan, R. Parthasarathy, Shiv K. Kumar, Kamala Das, Monica Verma, O.P. Bhatnagar, Gauri Deshpande, Adil Jussawalla, Ezekiel occupies a prominent place. His versatile genius can be found in his poetry, plays, criticism, journalism and translation."[1]

Nissim Ezekiel has done a good work in Indian writing in English. He has written many volumes of poems—*A Time to Change* (1952), *Sixty Poems* (1953), *The Third* (1959), *The Unfinished Man* (1960), *The Exact Name* (1965) and others. His plays *Nalini, Marriage Poem, The Sleep-Walkers, Songs of Deprivation* and *Who Needs No Introduction* are already staged and published. He has also edited books *Indian Writers in Conference* (1964), *Writing in India* (1965), *An Emerson Reader* (1965), *A Martin Luther King Reader* (1965) and *Arthur Miller's All My Sons* (1972). His literary essays published in magazines and papers are innumerable. The notable among them are 'Ideas and Modern Poetry' (1964), 'The Knowledge of Dead Secrets' (1965), 'Poetry as Knowledge' (1972), 'Sri Aurobindo on Poetry' (1972), 'Should Poetry be Read to Audience?' (1972), 'K.N. Daruwalla' (1972), 'Poetry and Philosophy,' 'Hindu Society' (1966). He has written essays on art criticism 'Modern Art in India' (1970), 'How Good is Sabavala?' (1973), and 'Paintings of the Year 1973' (1973). His essays on social criticism 'Thoreau and Gandhi' (1971), 'Censorship and the Writer' (1963), 'How Normal is Normality' (1972), 'Tradition and All That a Case Against the Hippies' (1973), 'A Question of Sanity' (1972) and 'Our Academic Community' (1968) are varied and autotelic of his wide interest.

Ezekiel is not only a good poet in the post-Independence India, but also a cause of good poetry. Many poets including P. Lal and Dom Moraes have admitted that Nissim Ezekiel was their poetic father. What W.H. Auden and Philip Larkin think of Thomas Hardy as a poet, P. Lal and Dom Moraes think of Nissim Ezekiel. He is the doyen of English poetry in India. Ezekiel has nurtured many poetic talents. Dom Moraes acknowledging him as his Guru, writes: "When Ezekiel spoke to me of his views on poetry, it was as though he had unlocked a box full of unheard whispers."[2] Ezekiel is perhaps the first Indian poet consistently to show Indian readers that craftsmanship is as important to poem as its subject matter. He guided the young in craft and attitude. His suggestions to A.K. Ramanujan and Keki Daruwalla were very effective. He approves of Aravind Krishna Mahrotra and Saleem Peeradina, because of their capacity for sharp perception of environment and forthright statement. So Ezekiel is an influential critic as well.

Ezekiel is an editor of several journals encouraging writing poetry, plays and criticism. He also asked many writers for translation, affecting the theory and practice of the young poets. The writers like Rilke and W.B. Yeats influenced Ezekiel. Like Yeats, he treated poetry as the 'record of the mind's growth.' His poetic bulk indicates his growth as a poet-critic and shows his personal importance.

However much the West influences Ezekiel, he is none other than Nissim Ezekiel. All influences on him are secondary. Chetan Karnani states, "At the centre was that sincere devoted mind that wanted to discover itself. In the process, he managed to forge a unique achievement of his own."[3]

The poet Ezekiel has already published several volumes of poems. It seems he started to write poetry when he was hardly in his twenties. *A Time to Change* (1952) was his first book of poems. For him poetry-writing was a lofty vocation, a way of life. He treated life as a journey where poesy would be the main source of discovering and organising one's own self. In a sense, poetry to Ezekiel became a way for self-realisation. He calls life a texture of poetry. He identifies himself with poetry. So all of his volumes of verse are well-knit and they are in the poet's view, a continuation of each other. The following poem shows his concept of poetry:

A poem is an episode, completed
In an hour or two, but poetry
Is something more. It is the why
The how, the what, the flow
From which a poem comes,
In which the savage and the singular,
The gentle, familiar,
Are all dissolved; the residue
Is what you read, as a poem, the rest
Flows and is poetry.[4]

In the first volume of poems, which contains five sections that grow out of one another, the Berkleyian idealism is explicit.

The brooding protagonist of these poems evinces that man's self-realisation is hardly possible if he repeats mistakes. In the second section, Ezekiel expresses his disappointment and shows his search for an identity in poetry. In the third, he devises two ways for worldly fulfilment—first through material bliss and second, through human relationships. The former is revealed in the following poem with clarity and vividness:

> To own a singing voice and a talking voice,
> A bit of land, a woman and a child or two,
> Accommodated to their needs and changing moods
> And patiently to build a life with these [...].[5]

Poetry to Ezekiel appears to be a religion as evidenced in the fourth section. Grand views of poetry are implicit in Ezekiel's poetic vision. The final section ends on a deeply retrospective and penitential note. However, the book *A Time to Change* is a very important work in poetry. Michael Garman says that in this book, "the poet's religion sympathetically assumes a double aspect—the introspective—concept active and the outward-active."[6] Nonetheless all the poems of this maiden collection were not successful; they display Ezekiel's experiments in prose rhythms and his fine sense of structure and metrical ability. The verse rhythms of T.S. Eliot seem to haunt his mind.

Ezekiel's *Sixty Poems* (1953), his second volume of poems was published in 1953. But these poems are loose in structure and they are less appealing. Some critics have opined that poems like 'Invocation' could have been safely destroyed or omitted from the publication. In fact, after the brilliance of *A Time to Change*, this collection comes as an 'anti-climax.' However, Ezekiel writes a Yeatsian 'apology' to the volume to defend himself saying that these poems 'maintain some sort of continuity in his life.'

These poems show the impact of European poets on him. The collection begins with 'A Poem of Dedication.' The next poem 'The Stone' is influenced by Yeats' 'Easter 1916.' Likewise, the lyric simplicity of Herbert and Blake seems to have inspired the poem 'Song.' Even Blake, Rilke, Rumbaed and Baudelaire's impact is felt in Ezekiel's poems 'Speech and Silence' and 'Prayer.' The poems 'Situation' and 'A Short Story' bring Ezekiel's use of colloquial idioms and conversational poetic style. As a verbal portraitist, Ezekiel can make a person alive through the use of ordinary words and phrases. 'A Visitor' provides a fine illustration of this written in a familiar style. A person, forlorn in failure, fails to know how to avoid his repeated disasters. The poems 'Portrait' and 'Boss' display the ordinariness of modern man.

In her perceptive study of Indian-English poetry, Linda Hess characterises Ezekiel as "a poet of the body; and an endless explorer of the labyrinths of mind, the devious delving and twisting of the ego, and the ceaseless attempt of man and poet to define himself to find through all 'the myth and maze' a way to honesty and love."[7] So Ezekiel often deals with man-woman's sexual relationships in these poems and *The Third* (1959). According to Chetan Karnani, words like marrow, bone, blood, flesh, breast and thighs appear again and again. In this sense he is like Walt Whitman. Hence, Ezekiel's idea that the body cannot be ignored in sexual gratification is seen below:

> Then, wanting to be whole again, he prayed:
> That this his body may belong to him
> And let him understand that in the working
> Of his mind the body takes a hand.[8]

The significance that Ezekiel gives to body aspects is comparable to W.B. Yeats' lines:

> He with body waged a fight
> But body won; it walks upright.[9]

Ezekiel's poems on sex have a splendid personalism and frankness. His 'Love Song' proves the point in case:

> Beneath your dress I find you young,
> Rewarding to my explorations, certain,
> Soft and flowing
> And tender to the touch of love.[10]

These poems drive home the point that the life of repression brings mental neuroses. Therefore, Ezekiel points out that inner impulses must be given a healthy release. He returns to this theme with greater vitality and intensity in the third volume of *The Third*.

The Third was published in 1959. The book begins with 'Portrait' and ends with 'December.' However, unlike the pieces of *Sixty Poems*, these songs too show Ezekiel's maturity of thought. His views on poetry are reflected here. He thinks poets say 'What oft was thought but they never express it well.'

When the politician boasted
How he had made two hundred speeches,
"No Tom," his wife declared,
"You made the same speech two hundred times."
So are we all
Making the same speech over and over again.
And now I hear the first birds
Spasmodic and repetitive—
I know I shall repeat myself.[11]

'Division,' 'What Frightens Me' and 'Declaration' evince Ezekiel's mastery in versification. In the last, like Yeats and Hardy, he tries to depict a human situation:

Whatever is beyond my reach
    I shall not reach for, certain vases
And women are too expensive, or else
    Fragile, exacting, best enjoyed
From a distance, with delicate affection.
    Passion possesses, and beyond possession
All is in question, mood and mystery spent,
    But reconciled to long perspective
The sensual form may serve to calm
    The senses and keep the darkness pure.[12]

Linda Hess comments that "Every mature poet finds his art demanding again and again that he synthesises certain powerful and apparently opposite forces within himself. In Ezekiel the synthesis which has continually had to be made is that between the ever-abstracting intellect and the concrete irreducible experience of the senses in which, if there is not the comfort of symmetry and system, there is substance of life itself."[13] In the poems, 'Insectlore,' 'Cur,' 'Sparrows' and 'Aside,' Ezekiel deals with dumb creatures. 'The Pulley,' 'Episode' and 'In the Queue!' show the poet's depiction of human vices. The poem 'At the Party' portrays this:

Ethereal beauties, may you always be
Dedicate to love and reckless shopping,
Your midriffs moist and your thighs unruly,
Breasts beneath the fabric slyly plopping. [14]

Nissim Ezekiel's fourth volume *The Unfinished Man* (1960) is a significant book to Indian English poetry. It brought Ezekiel's searching and perceptive power to the light. The volume was soon reprinted earning the poet a name. Adil Jussawalla writes: "[...] the most perfect book of poems written by an Indian in English [...] Ezekiel at his most honest and lyrical best [...]."[15]

These poems are rhythmic and musically suggestive. Ezekiel makes an effective use of rhyme as T.S. Eliot did in his Sweeney poems. Like Yeats, Ezekiel writes about 'marsh' in human existence. His poem 'A Morning Walk' resembles Eliot's 'Wasteland.' He describes the present-day urbanisation in Bombay as follows:

Barbaric City sick with slums,
Deprived of seasons, blessed with rains,
Its hawkers, beggars, iron-lunged,
Processions led by frantic drums,
A million purgatorial lanes,
And childlike masses, many-tongued,
Whose wages are in words and crumbs.[16]

Bombay city seems rootless. He finds everything in chaos. The artificial city life leaves certain inexplicable spell upon the poet's subconsciousness.

'Love Sonnet' is about lovers' perpetual mysteries. The poem is in the line of John Donne's love lyrics. 'Island' expands the theme of 'A Morning Walk.' In 'Case Study' Ezekiel expresses the dilemma of a weak-willed man. There is a lot of self-indulgent scrutiny:

Ought he to practise yoga, study Greek,
Or bluff his way throughout with brazen cheek?
Beginning with a foolish love affair
After common school and rotten college,
He had the patient will but not the flair
To climb with quick assault the envied star;
Messed around instead with useless knowledge,
And staked on politics a fatal pledge.[17]

Commenting on the poem, David McCutchion remarks: "It is clear that there is no question here of the intense self-lacerating despair of Baudelaire's 'Examen de Minuit' but rather of a courteous, self-deprecatory uneasiness. Unlike Baudelaire Mr Ezekiel has considerable sympathy for his weak but well-intentioned persons [...]."[18]

Other poems of the volume are also good pieces. David McCutchion compares Ezekiel to W.H. Auden, the literary improviser of twentieth century. Chetan Karnani thinks it is because of *The Unfinished Man* more than anything else, that time will reserve similar laurels for Ezekiel.

Ezekiel's fifth book *The Exact Name* was published in 1965. The title poem shows his desire for accuracy of thought and clarity of expression:

Intelligence, give me
The exact name of things!
Let my word be
The thing itself,
Newly created by my soul.[19]

As in the earlier, in this book too, the poet extends the scope and subject-matter of his versification. However, Ezekiel seeks poetry in the ordinariness of the most events, employing the day-to-day language.

'A Warning' and 'Paradise Flycatcher,' display Ezekiel's attempt at beautifying the commonplace accidents of life. 'The Visitor' shows his fine gift as a verbal portraitist. 'Virginal' and 'A Woman Observed' transmute ordinary happenings into poetic perception. But the poem 'Night of the Scorpion' is an excellent piece that delineates an Indian theme with clarity of thought and vividness of imagination. The poem is a beautiful depiction that exposes Indian superstitious beliefs:

> May he sit still, they said.
> May the sins of your previous birth
> Be burned away tonight, they said.
> May your suffering decrease
> The misfortune of your next, they said.
> May the sun of evil
> Balanced in this unreal world
> Against the sum of good
> Become diminished by your pain.
> May the poison purify your flesh
> Of desire, and your spirit of ambition,
> They said, and they sat around
> On the floor with my mother in the centre,
> The peace of understanding on each face.[20]

The same human concern.is shown in 'Poetry Reading.' In 'Philosophy,' Ezekiel writes about his bent for the brighter aspects of life. 'In Retrospect' he dwells upon the invisible.

The best poem of this volume 'Poet, Lover, Bird-watcher' displays Ezekiel's views on poet's problems. He thinks the best poets wait for words, like ornithologists sitting in silence to see birds.

Like other Commonwealth poets, Ezekiel writes about the cultural milieux of his nation. What A.D. Hope in his poem 'Australia' writes, Ezekiel does about India in his. His robust Babu's Angrezi language in persistent in poems like 'Goodbye

Party for Miss Pushpa.' He writes about Indian English with lucidity:

Miss Pushpa is coming
From very high family.
Her father was renowned advocate
In Bulsar or Surat.
I am not remembering now which place
Surat? Ah, yes,
Once only I stayed in Surat
With family members
Of my uncle's very old friend.[21]

In Ezekiel, the very Indian is evinced. Despite his visits to the other parts of world, he is an Indian in blood and spirit. V.S. Naipaul found Ezekiel an exception in Indian writers. He was surprised to see Ezekiel's bearing of Indian heat and squalor. But Ezekiel is proud of his environment:

The Indian landscape sears my eyes.
I have become a part of it
To be observed by foreigners.
They say that I am singular.
Their letters overstate the case.
I have made my commitments now.
This is one to stay where I am,
As others choose to give themselves
In some remote and backward place.
My backward place is where I am.[22]

Ezekiel has also made experiment in poetry. 'A Very Indian Poem in Indian English,' 'Irani Restaurant Instructions' and 'Goodbye Party for Miss Pushpa' remain unrivalled as his poetic achievement.

Ezekiel is a playwright. Like W.B. Yeats and T.S. Eliot, he chooses another genre of literature to express his ideas to the readers. He thinks there is a dearth of plays in English language. True he regrets for the qualitative dearth of dramatic writings.

Ezekiel wrote five plays. The first three are significant. *Nalini* is a comedy in three acts, *Marriage Poem*, one act tragic-comedy and *The Sleep-walkers*, an Indo-American farce. All were published by the Writers' Workshop. His other two short-sketches *Who Needs No Introduction* and *Song of Deprivation* are of minor importance.

Nalini is Ezekiel's ambitious full-length play. It is a social comment with its interesting witty dialogues. The play begins with the presentation of two young friends—Bharat and Raj. It is a social satire. Ezekiel tries to show the immaturity of a whole class through the portraiture of two young men as a burlesque—not with a band but with a whimper.

Ezekiel's second play *Marriage Poem* is a one-act tragi-comedy reading more like comedy than tragedy. It depicts the light and shade that comprises the social institution called marriage. Naresh, the hero thinks that marriages done in haste cause regret. So Naresh has no love for his wife Mala, turning his married relationship into skirmishes and inanities:

Mala : [...] Shall I pour out some tea for you?

Naresh : Yes (satirically). And a slice of bread.
In it for me (she freezes). Put a slice of Bread dipped in tea into my mouth [...].

Mala : I will, I will [...].

Naresh : (chewing) Thank you. That was delicious.

Mala : I love it too.

Naresh : (Raising his voice) I hate it [...].[23]

The play *Marriage Poem* deals with a boring marriage-relationship. It indicates the futility of tradition-oriented system of wedding. Ezekiel's fine realistic approach is discernible here. His *The Sleep-Walkers* is a hilarious rollicking farce. Like some English satirist Ezekiel gives an elaborate stage directions, creating an impression that his plays are meant for stage rather than for reading.

Ezekiel is also an art critic. In this capacity, he has edited many journals. He joined *The Illustrated Weekly of India* as its sub-editor. As a critic, Ezekiel has written a good deal. Karnani observes, "As a thoughtful Indian poet, he has tried to establish certain literary norms. He has fearlessly condemned mediocre poetry so that Gresham's laws may not operate in this realm."[24] Ezekiel is a strong character, who disliked shallowness and duplication in poetry-criticism and allied arts. When he received Dilip K. Chakravarty's *Mimomsa* for criticism, he dared to expose the poet's 'narcissistic attitude.' In almost every review, Ezekiel shows similar intellectual toughness combined with a higher sense of enquiring spirit and critical standard. He is not happy about Shri Aurobindo's magnum opus *Savitri.* He thinks Shri Aurobindo wrote it in a foreign language and that too in decadent Edwardian style.

Ezekiel does not like obscurity in poetry save descriptions where some hard-truths are enshrined. He emphasises communicative efficacy as the main quality in lovely and fine verse. His essays 'Poetry and Philosophy' and 'Poetry as Knowledge' show his disciplind thinking. For three years Ezekiel was the art-critic of *The Times of India.* He helped in the creation of public taste. It is observed: 'With his fine aesthetic sense, gift for analogy, ruthless logic, and a certain ineffable sense of Indianness, Ezekiel has remained a force to reckon with whether in literature or art or social criticism. His contribution in this field has been as important in the domain of poetry because in his role as a critic he has made great poetry and great painting available to many by the help of his unfailing good taste and sound critical security."[25]

Ezekiel is a dedicated person to the rhyme, the extremes and pitfalls. No other Indian-English poet has today shown the ability to organise his experience into words as competently as Ezekiel. The remarkable aspect of his poetry is his sincerity and individuality. His poems generalise his own felt experience. It is neither repetitive nor shocking, but 'simple, introspective and analytical.' He treats poetry as a first-hand record of the growth of his mind. He loves simplicity. His love of the genuine is explicit in the following:

These I have dwelt upon, listening to rain,
And turning in, resoled
That I must wait and train myself
To recognise the real thing,
And in the verse or friends I make
To have no trunk with what is fake.[26]

Ezekiel's greatness lies in his effort to avoid the mistakes, which his fellow poets committed. He is a serious poet. His originality lies in his typical poems, which are firmly rooted in Indian soil. Ezekiel's impersonalism is another landmark. Indeed David McCutchion's observation is a tribute to this great Indian poet: "Ezekiel belongs with Thom Gunn, R.S. Thomas, Elizabeth Jennings, Anthony Thwaite, and others like them. He has their cautious, discriminating style, precise and analytical, with its conscious rejection of the heroic and passionate as also of the sentimental and cosy. The technique is immaculate: rhymes, and carefully varied yet regular rhythms, lines that run over with a poised deliberateness. But behind the casual assurance one senses the clenched first, the wounded tenderness."[27]

NOTES AND REFERENCES

1. Balachandran, K. 'The Company Nissim Ezekiel Keeps,' pt. *In Twentieth Century Literature in English*, ed. M.K. Bhatnagar. New Delhi: Atlantic Publishers and Distributors, 1996, 130.
2. Moraes, Dom. *My Son's Father*, qt. by Chetan Karnani, *Nissim Ezekiel*. New Delhi: Arnold Heinemann Publishers, 1974, 8.
3. Karnani 12.
4. Ezekiel, Nissim. *A Time to Change*. London: Fortune Press, 1952, 13.
5. *A Time to Change* 6.
6. Garman, Michael. 'Nissim Ezekiel—Pilgrimage and Myth' rept. *In Critical Essays on Indian Writing in English*. Dharwad: Karnatak University, 1967, 109.
7. Hess, Linda. *Quest*, No. 49, Spring, 1966, 30-31.
8. Ezekiel, Nissim. *Sixty Poems*. Bombay, 1953, 23.

9. Yeats, W.B. *Collected Poems*. London: Macmillan, 332.
10. *Sixty Poems* 36.
11. Ezekiel, Nissim. *The Third*. Bombay: The Strand Book Shop, 1959, 4.
12. *The Third* 10.
13. Linda 32.
14. *The Third* 16.
15. Jussawalla, Addil. *The Journal of Commonwealth Literature*, July 1968, No. 5, 69.
16. 'A Morning Walk,' *The Unfinished Man*, Writers' Workshop, 1960.
17. *The Unfinished Man* 16.
18. McCutchion, David. *Indian Writing in English—Critical Essays*, Writers' Workshop, 1969, 101.
19. Ezekiel, Nissim. *The Exact Name*, qt. by Chetan Karnani, *Nissim Ezekiel*, 76.
20. Karnani 83.
21. *Nissim Ezekiel* 97.
22. *Nissim Ezekiel* 105.
23. Ezekiel, Nissim. *Marriage Poem*, Writers' Workshop, 1969, 61.
24. Karnani 127-28.
25. Karnani 139.
26. *Sixty Poems* 21.
27. McCutchion, David. Examen de Midi—Review of *The Unfinished Man in Indian Writing in English—Critical Essays*, 100.

11

Nissim Ezekiel *vis-à-vis* His Contemporary India

QAMAR TALAT

Nissim Ezekiel looks upon both the European and Indian tradition from the point of view of new humanism that started during 1890's. At the same time he observes contemporary institutions and cultures from the point of view of tradition. The resultant essence of his poetry is the brilliant criticism of old as well as new conventions of life of our times. As a critic of life and morals, he always hoped for a new sensibility and new awareness in the process of appreciating life's delicate dimensions.

Nissim Ezekiel is a post-Independence Indo-Anglian poet, who had been continuously publishing his short poems from time to time, since 1952 till today. After 1947, a new India was born with its new institutions, new hopes and new ways of approach. The ideas of democracy, secularism and unity in diversity are the most important and urgent social innovations which needed a new clarity of approach. Ezekiel aims at poetically establishing the personal ways of arriving at that new clarity. To that extent, poetry for Ezekiel is a medium of personal experience. All these new institutional properties needed a tender care; and Ezekiel's poetry maintains that tenderness of approach towards these institutions.

As a matter of fact, the very concept of Indo-Anglian poetry more or less emerges with him. India is a land of many languages and poetry was written in those languages and in Sanskrit, the universal mother of all languages. But, however, with all the greatness of these poetries, it can be said that there was no single poetical movement which touched all the Indian languages in a unified manner. There were certainly competitive and self-contained poetic movements in various parts of India, during various times, all with various dimensional importance. As a result, we had Bengali poetry, Marathi poetry, Punjabi poetry, Telugu poetry and Urdu poetry flourishing variously in various times, at various places. If at all there was any unity in the whole creative atmosphere in India, it was there in the glorious *Vedic* traditions, the spirit of which was continuously maintained in almost all the local languages. The credit for this goes to Sanskrit and Prakrit as universal languages affecting the whole of India. Latterly, during the Mughal regime Arabic and Persian also contributed for the homogenous poetic spirit in the different Indian languages. It was the introduction of English into the Indian universities that could suddenly open up new vistas of humanism, which can be categorically considered as Western humanism inherited from ancient Greek and Romans and synthesized by Christianity. This, in particular, touched all the parts of India with intensity and vigour. The salient features of Western humanism will be elaborated. The concept of Indian poetry could be possibly experimented after the English touched the parts of India. As a result, we have plenty of Indian poetry independently practised and propagated through English. Thus, we have that *Indo-Anglian-poetic-movement.* For its largeness of appeal and for its synthetic homogeneity, Indo-Anglian poetry deserves a place of pride. Ezekiel, as a mouthpiece of this movement, establishes for himself a commendable claim and place, as an original creative writer of poetry in English in India.

Nissim Ezekiel is a romantic idealist nurturing in himself dreams of a free and felicitous India. However, it is worth noting that romanticism as a poetic movement died its natural death after W.B. Yeats, and a few other British poets. Thereby, Ezekiel, when he particularly stressed on the old romantic ideals, looks slightly outlandish and even decadent, not condescending however, to the decadent poetic purposes of the Georgian poets. At the same time, he inherits the immediate Western naturalist-realist traditions through education and culture. As a result, he develops a tone of defiance and non-conformism extending to skeptical dimensions. Hopelessness, depravity and loss of faith are everywhere for him to see; but, however, through his poetic endeavour he always wanted to arrive at 'a bold nectarean answer for the poison of the present' (to borrow the expression of K.R.S. Iyengar). His great search for the 'nectarean answer' always directed him towards maintaining hopeful deductions from out of what he felt to be a hopeless performance in operation. It is here that his authentic self falls at its either/or dilemma; and thereby, the division of his soul is there for everybody to see. However, one thing that consolidates his poetic stand is to be found in the unification of his personal experiences which ultimately go to take his analogical poetic forms. The apparent dilemma gets resolved in the uniqueness of his personal experiences. Ezekiel's poetry is a medium of personal experience, and the uniqueness of this 'personal' temper or temperament is found in Ezekiel's poetry.

Nissim Ezekiel's personal poetry has a profound social purpose. As a poet, he takes upon himself the fine art of telling people what all he considers to be an ideal process of human experience in a given situation. He is a bitter critic of traditional institutions. But, at the same time, he realizes the utter inevitable need of these institutions for the well-being of man. As such, he always wanted to reform the attitudes of the people towards the life-giving institutions. For that purpose, democracy, modern India, secularism and humanism are the glorious institutional essences to which he addresses himself as a fond lover and concerned critic. It is this quality of Ezekiel that wins him substantial place as a poet-thinker. It is with this thinker's attitude that he looks at what may be called the new Indian experience.

Ezekiel's ultimate concern is with India and its various ethnic groups that live in it. The traditional India, according to him, is always back-looking and primitive. To turn the huge Indian masses towards an achievable unified future, he hastens to attack the evils in very bitter tones, if necessary, and clarifies the visions of the people towards a par excellence human India. India is a land of innumerable cultures, languages and ethnic codes of conduct and behaviour. The only factor that unifies India quite ironically, of course, is its poverty. This poverty includes economic poverty and poverty of understanding. Ezekiel aimed at poetically dealing with the people against the dangers of poverty, ignorance and irresponsible manners of existence. According to Ezekiel, life has to be lived in perfect freedom of understanding in a depth analytical manner. He satirically denounces all inauthentic, superficial purposes serving styles of life. His ultimate aim is in creating the sort of human consciousness, free from all kinds of inhibitions and taboos. His poetic attempt is a sort of pathological operation on the vision of people. To that extent, he assumes upon himself the stylistic nuances of doctor in operation. Writing poetry, in the present context anywhere in the world, is not a pleasant job. The world's great aestheticians started addressing themselves towards the bitter social realities. Ezekiel takes up the same task and continues to write poetry on the same line.

In addressing himself to the Indian masses, Ezekiel always maintains a sort of poetical view towards the global human situations. His Indianism is a mere poetic address to the entire humanity. His poetry is essentially an individual appeal. At the same time, it is a great clarifier of the very stands and projects of a never-ending, ever continuous process in operation. For this operation, adjudication standards are exclusively prompted by the person within or the person's authentic self. With this amount of personal evocative touch, Ezekiel wants to establish a new human order where there will not be any interpersonal humiliations. The new human order of Ezekiel is informed by a sense of freedom and intimated by the liberty of imagination;

his liberty of imagination in its turn gets informed by pure humanism. In the practical world of Ezekiel, life should be easy, and enjoyable in all its proportions and dimensions. In this context, he does not plead for the prevalence or otherwise of the politicalisms. His whole purpose is happy living, good thinking and mutual trust in society. If so, Ezekiel's dreamland is a long way ahead.

In fact, Ezekiel developed for himself a real poetic theory, in the context of a sort of free and frank engagement of his imagination in the act of poetic creation. His poetic theory is similar to the poetic theories of modern Western poets. In a way, it can be said that he borrowed much in the name of poetic theory from his Western counterparts. But, at the same time, he introduces his own significant idea of creating a poem, as an act of freedom of engagement of his imagination.

12

Nissim Ezekiel's Concept of Poesy

SUKA JOSHUA

"In good poetry, prosody articulates the movement of feeling, and the total meaning of a poem includes the meaning of its rhythmic structures as these trace and define emotional and psychological processes."[1] Christopher Wiseman defines poetry thus and this definition best suits Ezekiel's poetry where the metrical patterns reflect the feeling the poem wants to convey, and where the emotional and psychological tensions of the poet are recorded and defined.

Ezekiel's concept of poetry can be well guessed from what he says of Daruwalla's poetry. Ezekiel says:

> Daruwalla's poetry finds its own form in a fine blend of freedom and discipline, metrical rhythms and the word order of prose, compact, harsh alternative phrasing and relaxed movement. To most Indian English poets, simple expressions of emotion with a sprinkling of imaginary exhaust the craftsmanship. They rarely attempt the dramatic, the creation of characters and situations, the poetic dialogue and the sustained reflection and experience. Even descriptive skill is rarely demonstrated. Daruwalla is in a different class.[2]

In Ezekiel we see this blend of freedom and discipline. Ezekiel's verse justifies the fact that excessive adherence to 'discipline' or conventional styles will hinder natural, poetic output, and that too much experimentation with modernity will make poetry vague. Ezekiel avoids obvious poeticism and sentimental reiteration by taking the safe means between excessive freedom and discipline. What Ezekiel expects of poetry is not extreme care in expression but the virtue of simplicity and clarity. As Ezekiel says in 'Something to pursue,' the texture of poetry is "only a limpid style of life."

Ezekiel's concept of poetry is that poetry should be treated as a method of discovering oneself at various stages. The influence of Yeats who treated poetry as the record of the mind's growth is obvious here. Ezekiel feels that one's inner self, his worldly experience, the knowledge of practical work, the pleasure of sexual exploration should form the source of one's poetry and should sustain the poet throughout. Only when these things become the source for poem, poetry will become a method of discovering oneself. Each volume of Ezekiel's poetry discovers Ezekiel's self at various stages of his life. He says he published the *Sixty Poems* because it gave him the 'sense of continuity.'

If poetry is to be treated as a method of discovering oneself or as a record of the mind's growth, it should inextricably be related to existence. Poetry, though related to existence, does not reflect existence with all its chaos and confusion. Poetry makes harmony out of this existence, as the poet formulates his life in terms of his poetry.

Since Ezekiel considers life as the main source of inspiration, he says in 'Something to pursue':

> Out of doors where the winds of God
> Make our minds sweet with love,
> The answer is: There shall be no more questions.
> No more expenditure of doubt
> But only a limpid style of life
> Whose texture is poetry.

The poem 'Poet, Lover, Birdwatcher' tells us of Ezekiel's expectations of good poetry and how such poetry can be created:

> To force the pace and never to be still
> Is not the way of those who study birds

Or women. The best poet waits for words.
The hunt is not an exercise of will
But patient love relaxing on a hill
To note the movement of timid wings;
Until the one he knows that she is loved
No longer waits but risks surrendering.
In this the poet finds his moral proved.
Who never spoke before his spirit moved.

Since Ezekiel believes in inspiration, he asks poet to wait patiently until his spirit is moved. A hasty lover wouldn't make a successful lover. A birdwatcher who does not with patience go along deserted lames, cannot get rarer birds. Ezekiel's view of poetry is that it should prove morals and open myths of light. Only the poet who patiently waits for words can get 'his mortal proved' and can write such poetry "That deaf can hear, the blind recover sight."

In 'Creation' Ezekiel talks of the 'dancing minute,' 'the spacious hour' which can be taken synonymous to the patience and the hour of inspiration suggested in 'Poet, Lover, Birdwatcher.' Even simple, ordinary things can be given poetic touch if the poet waits for the 'dancing minute.' 'Creation' expresses this idea:

Pavements or pools, traffic lights or lilies
Rivers or roast chicken, Cafes or Corn,
All are focused in a purer light, poems,
Waiting for transcription on the page
In the dancing minute or the spacious hour.

'A Poem of Dedication,' also suggests the same idea. Not everything at every time can be made poetry. Only particular seasons will give their peculiar fruits. The poet, for the fruition of his poetry should wait for the particular season of inspiration to come:

Both poetry and living illustrate;
Each season brings its own peculiar fruits
A time to act, a time to contemplate.

That is why in 'To a certain Lady' Ezekiel says 'I can't make poetry out of this" (altercation with the lady) though on many occasions, he has made poetry out of the altercations and misunderstandings in family life.

A poet's impatience leads to failure of getting the 'dancing minute.' At such a barren season, when the poet tries to produce poetry, the result will be futile. It is to such poets, who venture to write before 'the spirit is moved,' Ezekiel gives a mild rebuff in the poem, 'The Company I keep':

Damn all you sensitive poets
Seducers of experience
Self-worshippers and publishers
Editors of small magazines
Broadcasters of small weather woes
Victims of your own spontaneous fraud
You are in hell
And do not know it.
When did you last write
A real poem?

Ezekiel's concept is that writing poetry is not just a matter of inspiration but studying the skill of writing carefully. This study demands a lot of patience from the poet. Only when unskilled poets try their hands in poetry, poetry turns out to be self-advertisement.

Many of Ezekiel's poems express his view that poetry can be built in resolving the tension between two opposite forces and trying to maintain an equipoise. About this aspect Linda Hess says:

> Every mature poet finds his art demanding again and again that he synthesises certain powerful and apparently opposite forces within himself. In Nissim Ezekiel, the synthesis which has continually had to be made is that between the ever-abstracting intellect and the concrete irreducible experience of the sense in which if there is not the comfort of symmetry and system, there is the substance of life itself.[3]

'On an African Mask' clearly states Ezekiel's view that,

The mask evokes a muffled noise,
Of dialectic oppositions,
Which life is must slowly poise
Their various signs as good equations,
And in the passion of mind or heart
Acquire the equilibrium of art.

It is said of Frost, that he "had the power to hold in unity the ultimate irreconcilables, the power to bring a bursting unity of opposites and the power to make poetry out of those opposites."[4] This statement can be applied to Ezekiel too. His notion is that poetry should make an attempt to resolve the struggle in 'the primeval jungle' so that it can make sense in chaos and bring harmony out of it. This idea is suggested in 'Creation.'

Child of flesh and fancy,
Be equable, as the sages recommend
And God-like make a universe
From Chaos
Of fire and air and earth and water.

From the tribute that Ezekiel pays to William Carlos William, it can be understood that good poetry can be made not just by bringing together opposite forces but by adding to them the fusion of music and meaning, in fine proportion. The following lines from 'For William Carlos Williams':

Something comes
Through and through
I hear the music of it
I hear the meaning too.
I feel the flesh
Of the poem
Firm
And the bone hard

suggest if the fusion of opposite forces forms the bone of the poem, the fusion of music and meaning form its flesh, adding beauty to it.

'Something to Pursue' synthesises the secular and the religious elements. The poem also emphasises Ezekiel's view that fruition or creation is possible only when the intensities of tension get resolved.

> High endeavour with intensities
> Of feeling and of thought,
> That I may see myself
> No longer unresolved
> But definite as morning,
> Moving to fruition
> When the season comes.

Using this device, Ezekiel relates his life to poetry and it is obvious in his poetry that they are built out of the tension between the two opposite forces in Ezekiel's realisation of his failure to associate himself with the city and his wish to commit himself to life. This tension gets resolved when he accepts 'Home is where we have to gather grace.'

Ezekiel always insisted that existence should be the source for poetry. Vasant A. Sahane says of Ezekiel's poetry that it "projects his beliefs meaningfully in relation to the posture of the believer and his practices. Belief is not presented in isolation, in a mere theoretical or theological context but expressed poetically and also related to life's impluses."[5] If existence is to form the basis for poetry and if poetry is to be related to life's impulses, the poet should get completely involved in life and with his immediate surrounding; Ezekiel finds fault with V.S. Naipaul and says:

> My quarrel is that Mr Naipaul is so often uninvolved and unconcerned. He writes exclusively from the point of view of his own dilemmas, his temperamental alienation from his mixed background, his choice and his escape. That temperament is not universal not even widely distributed, [...] to forget this is to be wholly subjective, wholly self-righteous [...] it nearly undermines the validity of his arguments.[6]

Here Ezekiel expresses his doubt that when the poet is uninvolved, his work may become very subjective and may not get universality. So, involvement and commitment in life are very essential to make poetry.

Neither a saint nor a tyrant can have desires and passions and feel himself committed to life with all its pleasures and pains. Desire and passion are part of existence and they are essential requirements for the creation of poetry. Ezekiel insists "The blood must leap before the spirit sings" and this is not possible for one who has not the desire and passion and human commitments.

This is why Ezekiel says in 'A poem of Dedication':

> I do not want the yogi's concentration.
> I do not want the perfect charity
> Of saints nor the tyrant's endless power
> I want a human balance humanly
> Acquired, fruitful in the common hour.

Such a human balance can be acquired not by an angry poet but by a poet who is at peace with his surroundings.

Ezekiel's poetry is conditioned by the city to which he feels committed. The city has harmed his preparation and could no more illumine his poetic process. Still, as a poet committed to his city, he does justice to it when he says in 'A Morning Walk':

> Why had it [city] given him no light,
> His native place he could not shun,
> The marsh where things are what they seem.

Chetan Karnani has correctly said of Ezekiel's poetry that it "derives all its sustenance from his immediate environment though it is written within the broader framework of the tradition of English poetry."[7]

So, if poetry should be related to life's impulses, the poet must understand his own self first. A good judgment of one's self can be made not in isolation but in the context of his environment. This demands a fuller understanding of the society or environment, which ultimately demands the poet's commitment to existence and place of existence, which in turn forms the source of poetry and helps in relating poetry to life's impulses.

Ezekiel always insisted that poetry is not just a matter of saying things but it is a matter of how they are said. Anisur Rehman says of poetry and its form thus:

> I cannot think of poetry without at the same time thinking of its form. Both in reading and writing it, the form belongs to the spirit and substance of experience. To find the form inadequate is to question the adequacy of poetry, to doubt its full authenticity and significance. Right from the beginning into its inchoate sources, form is as much the main of the poet as meaning in all its modes.[8]

The epigraph in 'The Exact Name,'

> Intelligence, give me
> The Exact Name of things
> Let my word be
> The thing itself
> Newly created by my soul

justified Ezekiel's belief that the 'word' (matter) and the 'thing' (manner) should be given equal importance. Ezekiel stresses the need for the word to be clearly related to experience and that language and technique should be less artificial.

A comparison between Ezekiel and A.K. Ramanujan would help the reader see the different attitudes these two poets have towards the manner and matter of the poem. In Ramanujan's case, his poetry expresses an Indian sensibility sharpened and conditioned by Western education. Ramanujan himself says:

> English and my discipline (linguistics,
> Anthropology) give me 'outer' form—linguistic,
> Material, logical and other such ways of shaping
> Experience; and my first thirty years in India,
> My frequent visits and field-trips, my personal

Professional preoccupations with Kannada, Tamil,
The classics and folklore give me my substance,
My 'inner' forms, images and symbols.[9]

In Ezekiel's case it is different. For him substance and manner are not two different things that mutually shape each other. Ezekiel feels committed to his environment, to India, which becomes the source of his substance, which in turn shapes the manner of the poem. While Ramanujan's poetry is the reflection of memories of India recollected in tranquillity abroad, Ezekiel mocks at the concept of emotions recollected in tranquillity and terms it as self-advertisement.

Ezekiel shows unpretentiousness both in writing poetry and in his aim of writing poetry too. He does not consider his vocation as a mission of humanity. That is why, 'Flawless doctrines' and 'Certainty of God' receive human touch in his poetry. The poem 'A Time to change' justifies this view. His ambition is:

To know the various lives and dreams of men,
And show his deep affection for the world
With words emerging from a contrite heart.

The next section of this poem explains further:

The pure invention or the perfect poem,
Precise communication of a thought,
Love reciprocated to a quiver,
Flawless doctrine, certainty of God
These are merely dreams but I am human
And must justify to what they mean.

This explains that simplicity can be achieved when a poet speaks in human terms even of elevated things.

In the same poem, Ezekiel calls the process of writing poetry, a miracle of God but takes a commonplace methaphor to explain this:

The stubborn workman breaks the stone, loosens
Soil, allows the seed to die in it. Waits

Patiently for grapes of figs and even
Finds, on a lucky day, a metaphor
Leaping from the sod.
If this is not a miracle
Then I am God.

This metaphor is found in Robert Frost's 'Putting in the Seed,' where Frost talks metaphorically of the poetic process and compares the poetic thought to the seed that is put in the land which comes alive. Both the poets express their wonder in the miraculous fruition.

Ezekiel's poem 'Enterprise' is generally praised for its allegory of the pilgrimage theme. It can also be considered as the allegory of the process of writing poetry. As the pilgrims who start the journey with exalted mind, the poets start their venture of writing poetry with exalted aims to explore the realm of poetry. If the poets are not well-equipped, they will be discouraged when they meet with obstacles. They will lose the ability to perceive things, the ability which they had had in the initial stages. They wouldn't be able to perceive anything from the world outside. Such a poet will regain his ability to write poetry only when he finds the proper source of inspiration that is his own self and when he realises, "Home is where we have to gather grace."

A study of Ezekiel's concept of poesy exposes us to Ezekiel's dislike of pretentious structure and language, obvious poetism, loose-structure, extreme subjectivity and vague imagery. In his essay 'Ideas and Modern Poetry' Ezekiel emphasises that the imagery in a poem should perfectly suit the feeling expressed. Ezekiel expresses his disgust for obvious poeticisms and loose-structure in the poem 'The Tufted Owl.' He asks:

The lyric impulses frozen,
What is the poet but a bore?

and of looseness of structure in poems, he says:

A calculated couplet ends the game,
The tired poet quickly signs his name.

When the lyric impulse in the poet is frozen, what can be expected of a poet than a 'calculated couplet?' As Chetan Karnani says, "He [Ezekiel] tended to exclude the geniously colourful and the dramatic as extravagance. This leads to excessive faith on simplicity as a virtue.[10] That is why "he has often described his dislike for the profundities of the Indian metaphysical tradition even as he has shown supreme disregard for the cosmic platitudes of Aurobindo Ghosh."[11] Such virtue of simplicity and mastery of song can be achieved only when the poet achieves mastery of skill. He expects poets to cultivate this technique consciously. The lines from 'The Stone':

> I have learnt to revel in the stone,
> Hard, cold, heavy, shapeless, solid stone,
> To turn away from all that seems to flow
> Elusively; time, water, blood around the bone

bear evidence that Ezekiel has gained mastery of skill so as to turn away from elusive things and to revel in the 'stone.' 'Stone' here can be taken to refer to conventional modes of writing poetry which have stood the test of time. He has avoided the craze for modernity in expression, which he might have considered 'elusive.' Though he felt himself to be at ease with tradition, he believed that expression should not be marred by dogma or predetermined beliefs.

A thorough knowledge of Ezekiel's view of poetry will make one feel the same way as Dom Moraes. He says: "When Ezekiel spoke to me of his view on poetry, it was as though he had unlocked a box full of unheard whispers."[12] Chetan Karnani's comment on Ezekiel, in a compact manner conveys all the qualities that Ezekiel used to build good poetry:

> [...] Ezekiel is unpretentious yet disciplined. There is no intricate symbolism or far-fetched mythology haunting his work. Yet the thing clicks. Unlike A.K. Ramanujan or Keki Daruwalla, he believes neither in bogus repetition nor in stock statics. Instead as a record of life's growth, his poetry is simple, introspective and analytical.[13]

NOTES AND REFERENCES

1. Wiseman, Christopher. "The Development of Technique in the poetry of Nissim Ezekiel," *JSAI*, Vol. XI, Spring, Summer, 1976, No. 3 and 4, 241-42.
2. Karnani, Chetan. "Introduction," *Nissim Ezekiel* (New Delhi: Arnold Heinemann, 1974), 9.
3. Karnani 47.
4. Kemp, John C. "The poet from New England (1912-1915)," *Robert Frost and New England: The poet as Regionalist* (New Jersey: Princeton University Press, 1976) 90.
5. Sahane, Vasant A. "The Religious-Philosophical Strain in Nissim Ezekiel's Poetry," *JSAI*, Vol. XI, Spring, Summer, 1976, No. 3 and 4, 261.
6. Sahane 194-95.
7. Karnani, Chetan. "The Exact Name," *Nissim Ezekiel*, 84.
8. Rehman, Anisur. *Form and value in the poetry of Nissim Ezekiel* (New Delhi: Abhinav Publications, 1981) 7.
9. Quoted in: Dr Raghukul Tilak. *New Indian English poets and poetry: A study of Nissim Ezekiel, Kamaladas, A.K. Ramanujan,* Jayanta Mahapatra (New Delhi: Rama Brothers, 1982) 48.
10. Karnani, Chetan. *Nissim Ezekiel* (New Delhi: Arnold Heinemann) 1987, 12.
11. *Nissim Ezekiel* 28.
12. *Nissim Ezekiel* 8.
13. Sahane 226.

13

The Portrait of the Artist: A.K. Ramanujan

N. SHARADA IYER

A problem of post-colonial literature, and especially of writers living abroad in foreign lands is how to incorporate and express the diverse cultural influences on a writer in other ways than being merely thematic. Some writers have taken over the open forms of past-modernism to juxtapose contrasting passages from different languages and influences. Ramanujan is an example of a polished, sophisticated and profound multiculturalism. His English poetry incorporates and assimilates linguistic, literary and cultural features of Kannada and Tamil into the linguistic, literary and cultural form of English literature. Like the house in "Small Scale Reflections on a Great House" he absorbs the Western model to express a supposedly Indian way of being. He blended the India and European models into new forms. Along with his technique was his use of his South Indian Brahmin roots. Born in Mysore in 1929, he is an expatriate in USA where he teaches Dravidian and Linguistic studies. Despite his long stay away from India, one is struck by how much Ramanujan remains emotionally part of India. He has the ability to tolerate, accommodate and assimilate other cultures without losing consciousness of being an Indian.

"There is something to be said for exile. You learn your roots,"[1] writes R. Parthasarathy. There could be no better illustration of the truth of this statement than the life and poetry of Ramanujan. It is perhaps his long sojourn abroad that explains

Ramanujan's persistent obsession with his Indian past—both familial and racial—and it is this obsession that contributes as a major theme to all his poetry. Ramanujan's poetry is essentially Indian in material and sensibility. Ramanujan explains this paradox in a note to *Ten Twentieth Century Indian Poets:* "English and my disciplines (linguistics, anthropology) give me my 'outer' forms—linguistic, metrical, logical and other such ways of shaping experience, and my first thirty years in India, my frequent visits and field trips, my personal and professional preoccupation with Kannada, Tamil, the classics and folklores give me my substance, my 'Inner' forms, images and symbols. They are continuous with each other, and I no longer can tell what comes from where."[2]

The "outer" forms and "Inner" forms suggest the linguistic situation and cultural determinates respectively, which act upon him simultaneously. His poetry is the outcome of the interaction of these two forces. He has to convey the psyche of one culture in an alien language. Praising Ramanujan as the best of Indo-Anglian poets, R. Parthasarathy wrote, "Both *The Strider* (1966) and *Relations* (1974) are the heir of an interior tradition, a tradition very much of the subcontinent, the deposits of which are in Kannada and Tamil, and which have been assimilated into English. Ramanujan's deepest roots are in the Kannada and Tamil past and he has repossessed that past, in fact made it available, in English language. I consider this a significant achievement, one almost without a parallel in the history of Indian English verse. Ramanujan has, it seems to me, successfully conveyed in English what, at its subtlest and most incantational, is locked up in another linguistic tradition."[3]

His poetry exemplifies how an Indian poet in English could derive strength by forging back to his roots. In poem after poem he goes back to his childhood memories and experiences of life in India. There is no attempt to disown the richness of the past. This insistent preoccupation with the past produces a poetry in which memory plays a significant creative role. It is not 'emotion recollected in tranquillity but recollection emotionalised in untranquil'[4] moments that appear to be the driving force behind much of Ramanujan's poetry. Time and again "a hood/ of memory like a coil on a heath"[5] unfolds in the mind.

In *The Striders* and *Relation* poetry seems to grow out of Indian experience and sensibility with all its memories of family, local places, images, beliefs and history. His poems evoke the warmth of traditional Indian family and the closeness of long remembered relationships.

The memories are mostly seen through the eyes of a sensitive and observant boy growing up in a traditional middle class southern Hindu Brahmin family. In poem after poem he goes back to his childhood memories of life in South India. Recollected in adult tranquil or un-tranquil state abroad, these memories and experiences—once indelibly etched on the impressionable mind of a sensitive boy—now pulsate into life. The memory of the times when great aunt dies, or when a basketful of cobras come into the house, and a host of such other felt experiences gives a certain immediacy to his poems.

The poet's self is the theatre in which are staged a host of incidents from the past and across which move a number of dramatis personae like his grandparents, mother, father, wife, aunt, cousins, sisters, etc. In 'Small Scale Reflections on a Great House,' one witnesses a number of strange and bizarre figures coming to the house never to return, or to return even if they have been away. In the last stanza humour mingles with pathos, when the nephew after his heroic deeds on the battlefield, which had won him laurels, returns as a corpse on a particular 'chatty evening.' 'Love poem for a wife' stages a powerful psychic drama through a 'You & I' complex. There is a criss-cross pattern of memories which adequately convey the intensity of the poet's yearning for emotional fulfilment in the family relationships. In this way, the family figures and objects associated with his childhood become the sign and symbol—the alphabet for conveying the poet's emotions. As Ramanujan himself commented, "The authentic voice of the poet, his true 'language' does not solely depend upon the tongue in which he chooses to express himself; the landscape, the personal, the appropriate mood, all become a language within language."[6]

Ramanujan makes use of his South Indian Brahmin background in complex ways, seeing in the tight nature of an Indian family life both the security and closeness and also the bonds from which at times one wants to be liberated, only to go back to the family again. Cousins, nephews, sons-in-law, grannies, step-mothers, aunts, those who in the West, says William Walsh, are shadowy or invisible figures are substantial and influential in India. Fathers and mothers are both sacred and profane and their influences permanent and intimate. They are homely, limited and sad:

> Father when he passed on
> left dust
> on a table full of papers
> left debt and daughters
> a bed-wetting grandson
> name by the toss
> of a coin after him
> and he left us
> a changed mother
> and more than
> one annual ritual. ("Obituary")

There is a vein of melancholy in the portraits of father and mother, more deeply sorrowful in that of the mother, a cogent reminder of the power of the dead to affect the living.

> I smell upon this twisted
> backbone tree the silk and white
> petal of my mother's youth.
> From her earrings three diamonds
> Splash a handful of needles.
> And I can see my mother
> run back to the crying cradle.

My cold parchment tongue
licks bark
in the mouth when I see her four
still sensible fingers slowly
flex
to pick a grain of rice from
the kitchen floor.

("Of Mother, among other things")

The family is a system in which nothing human is alien and even oblivion has its function. The family is a tissue of relationships and coventions. The former supplies the poet with a rich store of human feeling, the latter with a structure against which to trace and analyse it. Ramanujan's poems enriched and patterned like this are both sensitive and disciplined, quiet and dramatic.

Poems like *Small Scale Reflections on a Great House,* 'Love Poems for a wife,' 'Mother among other things,' 'Real Estate,' 'A Leaking Tap after a Sister's wedding,' 'Looking for a cousin on a Swing,' *Relations* reveal an assured identity of the poet within the family, which he very much needs after he settled at Chicago. His physical displacement "has given a focus to his Indian experience so that the poems emerge as a sort of microcosm of his family history. They are indeed microcosm of the Hindu family which has enormously contributed to the stability and psychological health of the society for centuries and ensured the continuity of rich traditional culture."[7]

Ramanujan is neither a nostalgic traditionalist nor an advocate of modernisation and Westernisation. He is a product of both and his poems reflect a personality conscious of the change, enjoying its vitality, freedom and contradictions but also aware of memories of an unconscious namelessness, which are still alive at the foundation of the self.

The importance of memory to him is explained by Ramanujan to Rama Jain in interview where he says that his writing obtains its nourishment from Indian culture:

> Those are the roots. That is what binds us back to our childhood and all our early years.
>
> [...] One cannot live in the past, neither can you entirely live in the present, because we are not like that. The past never passes. Either the individual past or historical past or cultural past. It is with us, it is what gives us the richness—of understanding and the richness of expression [...].
>
> An expatriate, he lives in two different worlds—the one within, the one without—creativity comes out of a sustained attention to one's own experience, one's own locality and one's own landscape you know. And the circumstances which one can feel and experience deeply without any scheme, without learning this, that and other [...].
>
> Whatever world it may be. It may be a personal world, it may be a social world, but a world which is fully embodied in poetry. We need enough of that, some part of our experience—to explore it as best as we can.[8]

The use of the private experience and especially the inner world of memories and the continuity and discontinuity with the past can be seen as the basis of many of his poems. The core of this essential self remained as an inner world, but this is modified by changed circumstances and decisions. The essential self develops, evolves, changes, it grows from seeds in the past, towards a future which, though unknowable, is already formed. The inner world consists of fears and desires as well as memories, anxiety—growing from the past towards an unwanted future imprisoned by an unhealthy sense of tradition. The tension between the inner world of the past and the need to be freed from its fears and traditions is a major concern of the poems in *Some Indian Uses of History on a Rainy Day.*

A preoccupation with personal familial memories leads to a search for racial roots. The vital connection between the two is clearly stated in "Self Portrait" in which the speaker declares: "I resemble everyone/ but myself," and sees in a mirror "the portrait of a stranger/ date unknown/ often signed in a corner/ by my father."[9] In another place, the poet's persona finds his entire personality "bred in an ancestor's bone"[10] and "ancestral crocodiles and tortoises"[11] often haunt his imagination. The view of oneself as the only product of one's racial ethics leads the poet to ponder over his racial heritage, and assess its strength and weaknesses. "I must seek and will find/ my particular Hell in my Hindu mind,"[12] he declares.

Ramanujan's Hindu heritage has influenced his poetry profoundly. It is steeped in his Hindu portage from which he at no time could escape; even his stay abroad has not taken it away. No doubt he has been influenced by Western life and Western culture, but the traditions of Hinduism—the religion to which he belongs and the cultural values of it—have always clung to him with the result that there has been a sort of uneasy tension between the modernity of Western culture and the orthodoxy of ancient Hindu culture, with the further result that this tension has made its way into his poetry. The double influence—Indian and Western—faced by Indian poets in English had not before been handled so subtly and without self-consciousness.

Ramanujan's awareness of his Hindu heritage does not lead to a blind acceptance. He was alive both to its strength and shortcomings. He admires the Hindu vision of unity of all life as expressed in "Christmas" and contrasts this with the dichotomy between Man and Nature and Man and the lower creation which the Western tradition appears to make. "Christmas" is an evocative poem underscoring this essential difference between Oriental and Occidental cultures. There is oneness of all life on earth—human, animal and vegetable; "For a moment, I no/ longer know/ leaf from parrot/ or

I no
Longer know
Leaf from parrot
or branch from root

nor, for that matter
that tree
from you or me.[13]

In *Small Scale Reflections on a Great House,* he recognises the great absorbing power of Hinduism by describing a typical Hindu joint family. Despite the slight ironic tone employed throughout the poem, the final impression is one of admiration developing dangerously in sentimental adoration. The 'Great House' stands for the ancient house of Hinduism, feels M.K. Naik, the house that Krishna built—a house which in its motto of *Vasudhaiva Kutumbakam*—has absorbed from time to time numerous cults, cultures and races to create one of the greatest examples of synthesis in all human history.

When Ramanujan ponders over his racial ethos, he assesses its strength and weaknesses. He was aware of the flows and shortcomings of the followers of Hinduism, especially blind beliefs and superstitions. He is aware of the inability of Hinduism to satisfy the average modern mind, because it fails to logically explain the element of evil in life. The Hindu reads the *Gita* but does not find the calm within him; he does not hurt a fly or spider because of his cowardice though he pretends he does not hurt because of his gentleness.

But this does not make him want to change his faith; he does not see any valid reason to exchange one kind of despair for another. He has to establish his roots only in terms of the tradition to which he belongs, and one way of coming to terms with modernity is to accept the traditional concept of Karma. The Indian ethos pervades his poems, and it is according to the Indian ethos that the poet's predicament is the reality of a universal predicament, namely a quest for an individual identity.

Ramanujan shows in his poetry a historical sensibility which is sharp and acute. He links his familial experience with his historical consciousness in poems like 'Conventions of Despair' and even more in 'Prayer to Lord Murugan' and with his keen vision Ramanujan is able to evoke the recurring patterns of historical tragedy and individual suffering thus turning the 'poetry of reverie' into 'poetry of immediacy.' He perceives in the anxiety of the individual the anxiety of his people—long subjected to misery, and slavish colonial rule. Ramanujan's poetry does not convey the nostalgia of an individual for the things and times past, but the collective nostalgia of a whole nation which looks back often with an attitude of love-and-hate. His "particular hell" is our common heritage. By linking the familial experience with historical consciousness, he has been able to trace a pattern of permanence in the flux of individual experience.

NOTES AND REFERENCES

1. Parthasarathy, R. "Exile," *Ten Twentieth Century Indian Poets*. Delhi, 1976, 75.
2. *Ten Twentieth Century Indian Poets*, 95-96.
3. Parthasarthy, R. "Indian English Verse: The making of a Tradition," 31st English Teachers' Conference, B.H.U., Varanasi, 1980, 4.
4. Naik, M.K. *Dimensions of Indian English Literature* (Delhi: Sterling, 1964) 15.
5. Ramanujan, A.K. "Breaded Fish" *The Striders*, London, 1966, 5. Subsequent quotes from *The Striders* would refer to this edition.
6. Quoted by Ramji Lall in *Indo-Anglian Poetry* (Delhi: Rama Brothers, 1998) 20 (Part II).
7. Parthasarathy, R. "How it Strikes a Contemporary," *The Literary Criterion*, Vol. XII, Nos. 2-3, 1976, 192.
8. Jha, Rama. "A Conversation with A.K. Ramanujan," *The Humanities Review*, Vol. 3, No.1, Jan-June 1981, 5-13.
9. "Self Portrait," *The Striders*, 21.
10. "Excerpts from A Father's Wisdom," *The Striders*, 40.
11. Ramanujan, A.K. *Ralations*, London, 1971, 46 ("Some Relations").
12. 'Conventions of Despair,' *The Striders*, 32.
13. "Christmas," *The Striders*, 30-31.

14

The Feminist Stance in Kamala Das's Poetry

SANTOSH CHAKRABARTI

Kamala Das, recognized as one of India's foremost poets, has to her credit prose and poetical writings in which she highlights the plight of Indian women caught in the morass of effete conventions—social and familial. But at the first instance they portray her own joys and sorrows, happiness and agony that she herself experienced in different situations of her life. She is a sensitive soul recording in her poetry and novels all the intimations of wrong and turbulence that she feels she underwent through her life. What distinguishes her writings is her ability to transform her personal experiences into something general, to give a universal colouring to her personal sufferings. Through the presentation of her own experiences in her famous autobiography, *My Story*, in most of her poems and even essays and through the various situations depicted in her short stories, she 'has highlighted the various images and roles of an Indian woman, as a wife, a mother, a daughter, a mistress and even as a prostitute. She has focused her attention on the problems faced by a woman in a male-governed social set-up, the categorized roles assigned to her, the prejudiced attitude of man towards woman, the status and identity of a female child, the treatment of woman mainly as a sexual object, and the new concepts and problems arising for her in the wake of changing socio-cultural and economic scenario' (*Literary Voice* 11). As a matter of fact she empathizes with the numerous Indian women who daily suffer unspeakable tribulations, who are the victims of the same socio-familial set-up against which she herself takes the cudgel. She identifies herself with 'every woman who seeks love,' finds oneness with every woman who spends life in misery and bondage, sexual, familial and social, and participates in all the experiences of the woman in her life of sufferings.

In a brilliantly evocative poem—*An Introduction*—she maps out the effete social mores which seek to keep the woman in a perpetual bondage of conventions. The woman is asked to place herself in the stereotyped gender roles of mother, wife and daughter and forget her identity outside the known parameters of existence:

> Dress in sarees, be girl,
> Be wife, they said. Be embroiderer, be cook,
> Be a quarreller with servants. Fit in, Oh,
> Belong, cried the categorizers.

The point is that she wants to rebel against this injunction for docility and hence she even puts on an androgynic appearance:

> I wore a shirt and my
> Brother's trousers, cut my hair short and ignored
> My womanliness.

The *raison d'étre* of her rebellion is that in the tradition- and convention-bound Indian society it is the male notion and perception which govern the roles and perceptions of women. This obviously goes against the process of individuation in a woman. What she wants is to establish her individual identity in a world that seeks to marginalize women and seek an equal status with men:

> It is I who drink lonely
> Drink at twelve, midnight, in hotels of strange towns,
> It is I who laugh, it is I who drink lonely
> And then, feel shame, it is I who lie dying
> With a rattle in my throat. I am sinner,
> I am saint. I am the beloved and the

Betrayed. I have no joys which are not yours, no
Aches which are not yours. I too call myself I.

(*An Introduction*)

It is in her love poems that she articulates her feminine sensibility: her hankering and passion for love, the denial, the frustration, desperation and even fancy for adultery. In *An Introduction* she gives a brief picture of the history of her love:

I met a man, loved him. Call
Him not by any name, he is every man
Who wants a woman, just as I am every
Woman who seeks love. In him [...] the hungry haste
Of rivers, in me [...] the ocean's tireless
Waiting.

In her autobiography, *My Story*, she portrays the longing for love of a sensitive girl of fifteen who dreams of love as "a beautiful anguish" (12), fondly imagining life to be "so young, so happy, so full of promise" (57), but is thrust to the reality of marriage with a lustful man who "without warning [...] fell on me, surprising me by the extreme brutality of the attack" (79). There is an obvious echo of this traumatic sex experience and a sort of loveless husband-wife relationship in a number of poems that Kamala Das wrote. *The Stone Age* records the casual treatment of her husband with her in the most explicit and unabashed manner:

Fond husband, ancient settler in the mind,
Old fat spider, weaving webs of bewilderment,
Be kind. You turn me into a bird of stone, a granite
Dove, you build round me a shabby room,
And stroke my pitted face absent-mindedly while
You read. With loud talk you bruise my pre-morning sleep,
You stick a finger into my dreaming eye.

This experience of Kamala Das is reminiscent of Sue Bridehead's (in Thomas Hardy's most controversial novel *Jude the Obscure*), for in the latter's case her marriage with Phillotson under the contracted obligation of Victorian marriage laws has taught her that such obligations can involve one in [...] a daily, continuous tragedy. "A husband can absorb himself in his own activities throughout a whole evening to the exclusion of all else including his new young, and 'unusually silent, tense and restless' wife (*JO* 225); he can spend until midnight 'balancing the school registers,' and then, muttering on about school committees and draughty ventilators, he can ascend to the nuptial chamber quite as if sexual intercourse with his wife were just part of the day's functions (*JO* 228-29). Or, alternatively, he might sit up late 'as was often his custom, trying to get together the materials for his long-neglected hobby of Roman antiquities' when, at length, forgetting time and place, he might ascend 'mechanically to the room that he and his wife had occupied' but which is now hers exclusively, and go so far as to start undressing before, prompted by her terrified scream, he might recall she had wished to sleep alone" (*JO* 235; Morgan 121).

Kamala Das actually subverts the myth of conventional Indian marriage by exposing the hollowness of a loveless relationship in which the wife is nothing but a sex symbol. In the poem mentioned above, she writes with the anguish of a hurt soul:

> Through peep-holes, the neighbours watch, they watch
>   me come
> And go like rain. Ask me, everybody, ask me
> What he sees in me, ask me why he is called a lion,
> A libertine, ask me why his hand sways like a hooded snake
> Before it clasps my pubis. Ask me why like
> A great tree, felled, he slumps against my breasts,
> And sleeps.

She is not to give herself up to the sex hunger of her husband blindly; on the other hand she hungers for love as every woman does and articulates this hunger in her poetry. 'She is in the main a poet of love, of love from the woman's point of view. To her the centre is not blind worship of the husband but the consummation of love' (Das 42).

In *The Maggots,* a highly sensitized Radha of the Indian Radha-Krishna mythological lore feels the same kind of ossified feeling in her relationship with her husband:

That night in her husband's arms, Radha felt
So dead that he asked, What is wrong,
Do you mind my kisses, love? And she said,
No, not at all, but thought, What is
It to the corpse if the maggots nip?

This mythicization of discontent in love is obviously a carefully contrived by-product of her personal experience. Her distaste for physical love, sometimes casual and sometimes brutal as showered by her husband (cf., the above extracts from the poem *The Stone Age* and her autobiography) is to be juxtaposed against her hankering for real love devoid of sex hunger:

I want to be simple
I want to be loved
And
If love is not to be had
I want to be dead [...]. (*The Suicide*)

It is this craving for an emotional identity with her husband/ beloved and fulfilment which is sadly lacking in her life leaving a trail of agony and disappointment. Her poems of love are suffused with anguish and mortification, and script a litany of woes:

Who can
Help us who have lived so long
And have failed in love? (*The Freaks*)

Her love has resulted in generating unwarranted fear—

What is the use
Of love, all this love, if all it gives is

Fear, you the fear of storms asleep in you
And me the fear of hurting you? (*The End of Spring*)

and an apprehension of betrayal—

Betray me?
Yes he can, but never physically;
Only with words........................
....while
My body's wisdom tells and tells again
That I shall find my rest, my sleep, my peace
And even death nowhere else but here in
My betrayer's arms [...]. (*A Relationship*)

A brief space of blissful co-existence in love is a mirage in the vast desert sand of lovelessness. That is why there is very precious little reference to love and happiness in one of her early volumes of poems—

Now that I love you,
Curled like an old mongrel
My life lies, content
In you [...]. (*Love/ Summer in Calcutta*)

The contented spell of love life as imaged by the cosy comfort enjoyed by an old mongrel is to be contrasted with the image of the blinded and most frightened flight of a bat in an alien space of loveless relationship:

My soul today is on its blinded, most
Frightened flight, like a bat that finds itself
In an alien zone of light. (*The Bats*)

Such an incompatible and trying existence (for a bat to fly in a zone of light, alien or not, is trying indeed) spells a feeling of marginalization and privation. Das's use of the toy metaphor in this context reveals her anguish and feeling of her worthlessness:

With a cheap toy's indifference
I enter others'
Lives, and

Make of every trap of lust
A temporary home.

Her feeling of uselessness is overtly prominent in the poem called *Composition*:

To be frank,
I have failed.
I feel my age and my
Uselessness.

All this compounded grief and anguish generate in her a sense of bitterness which finds expression in a poem embodying a strange and odd request to her husband/beloved:

When I die
Do not throw
The meat and bones away
But pile them up
And let them tell
By their smell
What life was worth
On this earth
What love was worth
In the end. (*A Request*)

Her anguished cry to woman as an oppressed and marginalized class is a strident call to come out of the cocoon of repressed existence:

Woman, is this happiness, this lying buried
Beneath a man? (*The Conflagration*)

Sex bondage is the most repressive and unless the woman is roused to rebellion against this bondage—loveless sex as demanded by unfeeling husbands—there is no hope for the Indian woman's emancipation. What she advocates poetically as an antidote to a loveless home is also repeated in an interview with Shobha Warrier (Source: Internet). In a poem titled *Substitute,* she bitterly and rather cynically records how her loveless marital status led to adultery:

After that love became a swivel-door,
When one went out, another came in.

In an interview with Shobha Warrier she repeated the same sentiment—'I always wanted love, and if you don't get it within your home, you stray a little.' Now the question is whether Das's bold advocacy of adultery smacks of a nymphomaniac rebellion. The fact is that born into the matrilineal system of inheritance and succession, she was nurtured with an inherent spirit of independence. In the following passage from *Summer in Calcutta,* one gets a glimpse of this spirit:

I shall some day leave, leave the cocoon
You built around me with morning tea,
Love-words flung from doorways and of course
Your tired lust. I shall some day take
Wings, fly around [...].

While she speaks of the monotony and tiresome bind of a hollow married life, she also "speaks here as a 'liberated' woman, who resents 'the cocoon' built around her and desires to flit about without any restrictions. The fairer sex receives a better deal from this sensitive poetess, who airs out its grievances and sufferings in a striking fashion" (Dwivedi 21). Similarly in the call for adultery, one notices a mischievous glint of irony in her eye for in the following extract from a poem called *A Man is a Season* she enunciates how by a clever machination her husband thrust her into paramours' arms only to show that he is 'eternity' to whom she wants to revert ultimately:

A man is a season,
You are eternity.
To teach me this, you let me toss my youth like coins
In various hands, you let me mate with shadows,
You let me sing in empty shrines, you let your wife
Seek ecstasy in others' arms..................
.... Perhaps I lost my way, perhaps
I went astray. How would a blind wife trace her lost
Husband, how would a deaf wife hear her husband call?

The situation described here resembles Rabindranath Tagore's depiction of an identical scenario in his famous novel *The Home and the World* in which Nikhil, the protagonist, prevails upon his wife Bimala to go out of the confines of the 'home' into the 'outside' world even allowing her to come into close contact with a revolutionary friend Sandip whereupon she realizes her mistake of forsaking the tree for the woods and fervently seeks to revert to the 'home.' "In 'I Shall Some Day' (from *Summer in Calcutta*), the speaker visualizes herself as returning to 'your nest of familiar scorn' built around her 'with morning tea' and 'tired lust' by the men [...]." (*EPLE* 334). Of further relevance is the following extract from *The Freaks* in which she makes a frank confession of 'a limitless appetite for sex':

> It's only
> To save my face, I flaunt; at
> Times, a grand, flamboyant lust.

Commenting on the posturing that the poet takes here, a critic says, 'The impression should not be that she has a limitless appetite for sex but read carefully along with the title, the poem may reveal her endless quest for love. The reader should not be taken in just by the posture she adopts. Behind the lines there lurks a figure with a glint of irony in her eyes' (Sharma 15).

What she seeks to convey in her love poems is a fervent clamour for space for the woman—the Indian woman—emotionally tyrannized and sexually marginalized in the socio-familial set-up in which she lives. The most intriguing fact about her as a writer is the divergence between the apparent harmony with her husband and the vehemence of protest against the denial of marital happiness. In the Warrier interview it is recorded that her husband because of the age difference between them often played a fatherly role for both Das and her sons. Because of the great age difference between Kamala and her husband, he often encouraged her to associate with people of her age. Das says that he was always 'very understanding' [...]. As her career progressed, her greatest supporter was always her husband. Even when controversy swirled around Das's sexually charged poetry and her unabashed autobiography, *My Story*, her husband was "very proud" of her. Though he was sick for three years before he passed away, his presence brought her tremendous joy and comfort. She stated in the interview that there "shall not be another person so proud of me and my achievements." This divergence between an apparently compatible conjugal life and a strong sentiment expressed in her writings about the absence of it all needs further research to prove whether in her poetry she inflates her emotive experiences of sufferings to project a high-voltage feminism.

In her prose writings specially she builds a victim-victor syndrome (*Literary Voice* 40) and though in the two poems referred to above—*A Man is a Season* and *I Shall Some Day*—she condescends to the victim's role, she often reverses the position as in *Jaisurya* in which "the complex articulation [...] is an interplay of the kind of lyrical intensity one finds in Judith Wright's treatment of the relationship of man, woman and child (in 'Woman to Man' and 'Woman to Child'), on the one hand, and on the other, the subversive questioning of Margaret Drabble's novel *The Millstone*, in which the woman's discovery of her identity through the experience of motherhood is seen as marginally dependent on the male presence" (*EPLE* 333).

What distinguishes her among the women poets of India is her bold frankness in articulating sexual urges and feelings. She is the most renowned Indian woman poet of the confessional mode and easily places herself in the company of Sylvia Plath and Anne Sexton. The following extract from *Forest Fire* shows her in the frankest and yet most confessional mood which makes her a class apart:

> Of late I have begun to feel a hunger
> To take in with greed, like a forest-fire that
> Consumes, and, with each killing gains a wilder,

Brighter charm, all that comes my way [...]
My eyes lick at you like flames, my nerves
Consume; and, when I finish with you, in the
Pram, near the tree and, on the park bench, I spit
Out small heaps of ash, nothing else.

She may not command the intellectual vigour of the two poets of the confessional mode mentioned above, but 'she does not lag behind in lyrical outburst of unpremeditated thoughts and feelings and in emotional intensity. In truth, she is more aware of the pathos in the life of a common woman playing a very passive role in our tradition-bound society than some of these women poets highlighting a different cultural and moral ethos' (Dwivedi 118).

She finds a devotional means of self-fulfilment and elevation to the role of the victor by invoking the Mira Bai and Radha-Krishna myths. Just as Mira merges in the ultimate consciousness—God, and Radha surrenders herself in a blissful union with Lord Krishna, the eternal lover, so Kamala too merges with the eternal lover and thus escapes the travails of an unhappy love life:

Everything in me
Is melting, even the hardness at the core.
O Krishna, I am melting, melting, melting
Nothing remains but
You [...]. (*Radha*)

Whether this is panacea for the long-suffering marginalized Indian woman is another matter.

WORKS CITED

Das, Bijay Kumar. *Critical Essays on Post-colonial Literature*, 2001.

Dwivedi, A.N. *Kamala Das and Her Poetry* (Delhi: Doaba House, 1983).

Jha, Pashupati. 'Victim-Victor Interaction and the Image of Woman in Kamala Das,' in *Literary Voice*, February 2000.

Kaur, Tejinder. 'Images of Indian Women in Kamala Das's *Padmavati, the Harlot and Other Stories*' in *Literary Voice*, February 2000.

Kohli, Devindra. Entry on Kamala Das in *Encyclopedia of Post-colonial Literatures in English*, vol. 1, 1994. Cited as *EPLE*.

Morgan, Rosemarie. *Women and Sexuality in the Novels of Thomas Hardy*. Routledge, 1988.

Sharma, I.K. 'The Irony of Sex: The Gloss or the Teakwood (A Study of Kamala Das)' in *Indian Writings in English*, vol. 9, M. Bhatnagar and M. Rajeshwar, eds., 2000.

Warrier, Shobha. "The Rediff Interview/Kamala Das.' Rediff on the Net. 1996. Online. Internet.

15

LONELY KINGS: A COMPARATIVE STUDY OF KARNAD'S *TUGLAQ* AND SHAW'S *THE APPLE CART*

ANURAG CHAUHAN

Literary impulses do not remain delimited by time, place and milieu. If we consider the two plays—*The Apple Cart* and *Tuglaq*—by George Bernard Shaw and Girish Karnad respectively, this observation proves to be true.

The Apple Cart had a story set in future (after 1962), the play having been written in 1929. Called "a political extravaganza" by Shaw, the play centres around Magnus, the British king, whose well-meant actions make the inefficient democratic Prime Minister and his cabinet wary of him so that they think of putting a check on him.

But the king foils their designs successfully. The play drew both sentimental adoration for an aged Shaw and the feeling that it "blasphemed against democracy"[1] as Leon Hugo says. But Shaw maintains in the preface that the play exposes "The unreality of both democracy and royalty."[2] Neither was Shaw deterred from writing such a misinterpretable play at a time when there was a Labour Party government in England which favoured largely Shaw's socialist and democratic ideas: clearly, something was wanting in democracy as far as Shaw was concerned. Shaw wanted to give a guideline to democracy—which has become a part and parcel of modern political life—through his play.

On the other hand, *Tuglaq* is different from *The Apple Cart* in many respects. Although, it too is the story of a monarch, Tuglaq, it is a historical play set before 1350. Its story revolves around Delhi and Daulatabad. But it is not merely a historical play but as P. Bayapa Reddy remarks "a very imaginative reconstruction of some of the most significant events in the life of a great king [...] in India."[3] The play is largely allegorical too, reflecting the mood of disillusionment which prevailed in the post-Nehru era of 1960s in India—a fact accepted by Karnard too.[4]

The two plays, while dealing with history and future, have immediate, present concerns. Moreover, an analysis of both the plays shows us clearly that both Shaw and Karnad had wider concerns than simply holding mirrors or representing facts. Karnad certainly selected and altered historical facts to suit his purpose as Dr Satish Kumar has pointed out in his study.[5] The concerns of the two dramatists are not only worldly—of politics, administration and society—but also of the otherworldly—search for a system or philosophy.

In *The Apple Cart* we see a modern democracy which is in the hands of inefficient and corrupt ministers. Those that are honest like the Power Misteress General, Lysistrata, are contrasted with big-mouthed ones like Boanarges and corrupt ones like Crassus. Capitalists, too, bring such honest few to their knees. The public is misled by demagogues and democracy is on the rocks. Ironically, it is Magnus, who, though he is, in his own words, "An idol set up by a group of plutocrats so that they can rule the country with the king as their scapegoat and puppet,"[6] is really the democratic minded, "undemocratic guardian of extra-temporal values."[7] Shaw presents him as a wise, cool-headed person who wants to see a correctly functioning democracy but he is impeded by the fact that he has no powers. He finds politicians not up to the mark and says, "[...] thanks to the general belief in democracy you [ministers] can always pretend that what you do is done by the will of the people who,

God knows, never dreamt of it, and would not have understood it if they did" (33). Thus, he tries to use the little powers and freedom he has to influence the public opinion and to goad the ministers into conscientious working. His intentions, though understood to be so, are far from tyrannical. Behind the façade of a light-hearted person we have in him a deep-thinking and critical monarch who knows what is best for the people. If not exactly a down-to earth person, he is intensely practical and can foresee the future of the British democracy: corruption and capalists doing what tyranny used to do in earlier times. Up to the end of the play we find Magnus suave and unperturbable and having his say somehow.

Karnad's Tuglaq is of a more blood and flesh type, although, he too is a king. He is a hardened man and the circumstances he is in are more formidable than that faced by Magnus. He is, unlike Magnus, serious all the time both in action and thought. If Magnus is urbane, Tuglaq is unforgiving. He can be practical to the extent of cruelty and can get his father killed, send Sheikh Imam-ud-Din to a pre planned death, or those who refuse to move to his new capital Daulatabad punished severely. The staffs on which he leans are his conscience and Allah. A perfectionist, he is too demanding and one wonders what havoc he would have created if he was selfish too. In the face of rebellions by the likes of Ain-ul-Mulk, an untrusting people, corruption, and plans going haywire, he is able to remain practical and brilliant minded. He is deeply religious but is impartial and unorthodox. He is a more complex character than Magnus, an anomaly, wanting the moon in the midst of blood and dirt. About his dualistic character Ramamurthy says, "He is at once an idealist and a crafty politician, a humanist and a tyrant, a man who has murdered sleep and yet not a Macbeth hunted by supernatural solicitations, a man who thinks and broods too much and yet not a Hamlet incapable of action or guilty of delay."[8] He aims to establish an ideal state in which there is justice, religious freedom and has little patience with hypocrites, rebels and fools.

More than anything else, it is the prevailing conditions and social forces which act as a spur, bringing out the best, and sometimes the worst, in Magnus and Tuglaq. Magnus's case is of a monarch who is discontented with his apolitical status. The public has taken the king as an unavoidable entity but does not care for him. They look up to the persons for whom they voted for administration. The public in *The Apple Cart* is passive. They would not be affected by the honest imploring of Lysistrata but they get carried away by the songs and mimicry of Amanda and the high-winded speeches of Boanarges who says, "I talk democracy to these men and women. I tell them that they have the vote and that theirs is the kingdom and the power and the glory. I say to them 'You are supreme: exercise your power.' They say 'That's right: tell us what to do'; and I tell them. I say 'Exercise your vote intelligently by voting for me'" (12). The hoi polloi themselves are not above reproach: they remain unaware of the good work done or take it for granted; government authority and taxes are resented by them. Their fickle opinion can make demi-gods and aunt Sallies at the drop of a hat. In the preface Shaw says, "What we [the public] want to know is how little government we can get along without being murdered in our beds" (XVI). The public in a modern democracy can be innocent, misguided and utilitarian at the same time.

In *Tuglaq*, people in general do not get an opportunity to be utilitarian. They have been stuck in the rut of tyrants for aeons. To them, their Sultan, Tuglaq, is an enigma. We find an ambivalent attitude of the people towards Tuglaq; but mainly of doubts and misgivings. The play opens with a dialogue between an old man and a young man; the old man laments the rule but the young man says, "What are you worried about, grandfather? the country is in perfectly safe hands—safer than any you've seen before" (1). But, in general, in spite of Tuglaq's benevolence, impartiality and justice—power to people to file a case even against the Sultan, attempts at Hindu-Muslim amity, reorganisation of administration, making namaz five times a day compulsory—he fails to win the confidence of his people.

Firstly, because the people cannot see beyond their immediate material concerns; therefore taxes are abhorrent to them, prayers are painful and token currency an unnecessary farce. Secondly, Tuglaq's good acts are marred by the fact that they being ahead of the time are perceived just as whims by the people. So, his decisions to introduce token currency and to shift the capital fall flat. Moreover, they are punctuated by his cruelty and cunning, as evident by his remoured fratricide and patricide and compelling people to pay taxes or to leave Delhi. His inability to explain and express himself to the people is typically of an idealist; he is not an Antony who can mould public opinion.

Both Tuglaq and Magnus fight with opposing forces of the day although time and place make them deal with different forces in their different intensity. *Tuglaq* is the drama of an evolving society, which still has a little of barbarism and primitivism in it, in its cruelty, corruption and deceit. Aziz who can kill even his companion Aazam among others and can even deceive the Sultan, is an example. Thus, the forces in *Tuglaq* are religion, poverty, hunger and corruption. And their relationships with each other are not static. People are religious yet find it troublesome to pray; they want justice yet when a Hindu is allowed to file a case against the Sultan, they are sceptic; oppose corruption but would not deter from making counterfeit currency. No wonder that the utopian, idealistic reformer, Tuglaq, "On seeing the unbridgeable gulf between aspiration and reality [...] moves towards existential alienation."[9]

In *The Apple Cart,* however, we see stabilized society whose primitive impulses have subdued yet the stability brings mammon as the strongest motivating force. As Shaw aptly remaks, "[...] the conflict is not really between royalty and democracy. It is between both and plutocracy, which [...] has bought and swallowed democracy. Money talks: money prints: money broadcasts: money reigns [...]" (Preface VIII). Capitalism can make or mar a minister, can buy or break anything, even nations. The ills of democracy—corruptible public opinion, inefficient and corrupt ministers, demagogues, unreasonable laws—are there, but they are overshadowed and often generated by capitalism in *The Apple Cart.*

In spite of all the odds, the two kings try their best, be it understood or not. Magnus's philanthrophy is delimited by Constitution but he goes out of the way to have his way; and hence his ultimatum to abdicate and stand for the general elections, a decision which upsets the apple cart of Prime Minister Proteus. In him, unlike Tuglaq, we do not see any deeper psychological perturbations or developments. He is resourceful and firm and remains so.

In Tuglaq there is always a psychological conflict; the Sultan does not change in essence, he fights against the resisting forces when he can, and when he cannot, he can even fall at the feet of his amirs and say desperately, "If you don't understand me ask me to explain myself and I'll do it. If you don't understand my explanations, bear with me in patience until I can show you the results. But please don't let me down I beg you" (40). But he cannot abandon and go in the service of God, his most cherished desire. He says to Barani," Don't you see that the only way I can abdicate is by killing myself?" (56)

Magnus's ingenuity comes handy and where it does not, he does not overreach. But Tuglaq has no patience. He would kill even his father, get Sheikh Imam-ud-Din killed by guile; he would plead, force and adopt any means and would not stop; but the results that come do not satisfy him. Magnus's concerns cannot be overwhelming because he is only a cog in the political machinery. But Tuglaq is power itself, a power that divides its wielder. M.K. Naik points out, "In Tuglaq the focus is primarily not on the metaphysical aspect of the theme of the power but on its psychological implications in respect of a self-righteous idealist (the most dangerous combination possible) armed with absolute power over his subjects."[10]

Again, leaving aside the topical concerns of public good, problems, personal and otherwise, one can also perceive in both Magnus and Tuglaq a philosopher: their views of the world and universal good include a higher visionary philosophy. In the case of Tuglaq it is linked with Allah and religion but can go beyond it and is not sectarian. For Magnus, it is a power which chisels and betters. Thus he says "[...] there is a divine spark in us all; and the stupidest monarch or minister, if not wholly God, is a bit of a god—an attempt at god—however little the bit and unsuccessful the attempt" (10). He, being practical, would choose a cabbage over a rose; yet, in accordance with the Shavian philosophy of 'life-force' believes that "Some day perhaps Nature will graft the roses on the cabbages" (55). His visionary ideas, tinged with reality, come to the fore when he says:

> I stand for the great abstraction: for conscience and virtue; for the eternal against the expedient; for the evolutionary appetite against the day's gluttony; for intellectual integrity, for humanity, for the rescue of industry from commercialism and of science from professionalism [...]" (38).

Magnus is able to bring a compromise between his ethereal concepts and practical limitations. He views the affairs of the state as a state of affairs which is not ready for the 'life-force,' which wants perfections, and that is it, but man must not cease to struggle to make 'life-force' function.

Tuglaq, too, is visionary but his best laid plans are brought to nought. He compromises idealism with realism in his dealings: he can be benevolent yet hard on people, he is religious yet can ban the prayers too, he knows the heights reached by Buddha and Zarathustra yet can kill like a common murderer. But he refuses to compromise about his visionary ideas. There is no method in his madness, just frustration and paranoia, the price of being ahead of his times. He is in a mire, largely of his making and his hell is paved with good intentions. He cannot comprehend where he is at the end of the play after his sleep symbolic of his alienation. He says to Barani, "If justice was as simple as you think or logic as beautiful as I had hoped, life would have been so much clearer. I have been chasing these words now for five years and I don't know if I am pursuing a mirage or fleeing a shadow" (84-85). His rose garden, symbolic of visionary hopes, becomes a rubbish dump of copper coins—signifying the gulf between aspiration and achievement. He implored to his subjects to "be the light and cover the earth with greenery" but finds that he is unable to "spread his branches in the stars while the roots have yet to find their hold in earth" (10). An alienated person, as Erich Fromm says, starts viewing even persons as objects[11] and Tuglaq comes in this category. He can realise what he wanted to do, what he has done, and what he has not. Disillusioned, he cries to God, "God, god in Heaven, please help me [...]. I started in your path, Lord, why am I wandering naked in this desert now?" (67)

A wide gulf of more than six hundred years and geographical difference does not alter the fact that socio-political concerns are common in both the plays. There is a difference in the treatment though. Shaw laughs and derides and *The Apple Cart* can be safely called a comedy. Suffice it for Shaw to see, "[...] how many of them [readers], laughing or grave, are in the melting mood."[12] Karnad's tone, in keeping with the subject, is down to earth and certainly does not give an impression of a cloud-cucoo land and *Tuglaq* is an existentialist play[13] showing not only a person dealing with issues but, with more emphasis, the man himself. In *Tuglaq* literary concerns are more important from the dramatist's point of view. Here, delineation of a character in a life like manner, with deep character study was the chief concern. Though, the fact that it is not the story of self-centred individual, nor the personal aspect of an individual's life, make it different from plays like *Hamlet.* On the other hand, Shaw has deliberately chosen a problem and has made use of the personal life of Magnus only for diversion. Certainly, in the hands of Karnad and Shaw, the plays rise above the story of individuals and encompass not only concerns about the contemporary social and political scenario, but also philosophical and visionary ideas. The hallmark of any great play—criticism of life—has been retained by the two dramatists.

NOTES AND REFERENCES

1. Hugo, Lean. *Bernard Shaw* (London: Metheun, 1971) 217.
2. Shaw, Bernard. Preface to *The Apple Cart* (London: Constable, 1930) VI.
3. Reddy, P. Bayapa. *Studies in Indian Writing in English* (New Delhi: Prestige, 1990) 44.
4. Paul, Rajinder. "Girish Karnad interviewed," in *Enact,* 54, 1959, n.p.
5. Kumar, Satish. *Themes and Technique in the plays of Girish Karnad* (Bareilly: Student Store, 1987) 34-37.
6. Shaw, Bernard. *The Apple Cart* (London: Constable, 1930) 11.
7. Meisel, Martin. *Shaw and the Nineteenth Century Theatre* (Princeton: Princeton University Press, 1963) 402.
8. Ramamurti, K.S. "Some aspects of Indian drama with special reference to Tuglaq," in *Littcrit,* Vol. 5, No. 1, June 1979, 17.
9. Gomez, Christine. "Karnad's Tuglaq as an alienated protagonist," in *New directions in Girish Karnad's plays* ed. Sudhakar Pandey & Freya Barua (New Delhi: Prestige, 1994) 141.
10. Naik, M.K. "The limits of human power: A comparative study of Caligula and Tuglaq," in *Studies in Indian English Literature* (New Delhi: Sterling, 1987) 142.
11. Fromm, Erich. *The Sane Society* (London: Routledge and Kegan Paul, 1956) 126-27.
12. Shaw, Bernard. *Complete Prefaces* (London: Paul Hamlyn, 1965) 733.
13. Kumar 48-52.

16

HAYAVADANA: A STUDY OF KARNAD'S USE OF SOURCE-TEXTS AND FOLK FORM

MOHIT K. RAY

Girish Karnad was born on 19 May 1938 in Matheran, a town near Bombay. He comes from the semi-Marathi and semi-Kannada Saraswat community. While growing up in the small village of Sirsi in Karnataka, he had abundant opportunity to have first-hand experience of the indigenous folk theatre. He used to go to the Company Nataka performances with his father who being a doctor had a free pass. But to the Yakshagana performances—a form of folk theatre—he used to go with the servants, because his father considered it beneath his dignity to witness these plays. His encounter with the Nataka companies left a lasting impression on his mind and the effect of that is evident in various theatrical technicalities such as lighting, setting, etc. of Karnad's plays. In this connection Karnad writes: "I loved going to see them and the magic has stayed with me" (*NTQ* 360). The technical aspects of these two varieties of drama have gone into the making of Karnad's plays. During the formative period Karnad went through diversey influences. He was exposed to a literary scenario where there was a direct clash between the Western and the native traditions, between the new modernistic techniques, a legacy of the colonial rule and cultural nationalism, a bid for a return to and discovery of tradition inspired by search for roots and quest for identity. There was a growing trend to look more closely at the native tradition and explore its contemporary relevance. Karnad writes:

> My generation was the first to come of age after India became independent of British rule. It, therefore, had to face a situation in which tensions implicit until then had come out in the open and demanded to be resolved without apologia of self-justification: tensions between the cultural past of the country and the colonial past, between the attractions of Western modes of thought and our own traditions, and finally between the various visions of the future that opened up once the common cause of political freedom was achieved (Dodyia 21).

It is only natural that a sensitive artist who absorbs both the tensions would eventually turn out to be a dramatist in whose plays tradition and avant-garde are wonderfully reconciled into a harmonious whole.

After graduating from Karnataka University, Dharwad, in 1958 Karnad went to Bombay for further studies. Meanwhile, on receiving the Rhodes scholarship he went to England for further studies. On his return to India in 1963 he joined Oxford University Press, Madras (now Chennai). However, first and foremost he is a playwright. Between 1961 and 1998 he wrote nine plays and most of them have been successfully produced on the stage. He has translated many of his plays into English and has also translated some of the plays of Badal Sarkar, whose influence he publicly acknowledged, into English and has also written with great critical acumen on drama and theatre. In 1974 Karnad went to Pune as the Director of Film and Television Institute of India. And soon, acting, directing, script-writing, etc. came as grist to his mill as he began to appear in Hindi films and TV serials. In 1987 he went to USA as a Fulbright scholar-in-residence in the Department of South Asian Languages and Civilization, University of Chicago. From 1988 to 1993 he served as Chairman of the Sangeet Natak Akademi (National Academy of Performing Arts). In 1994 he was awarded Doctor of Philosophy (*Honoris Causa*) degree by his alma mater, Karnataka

University. At present Karnad is the Director of the Nehru Centre in London. Such is "the versatile personality like the ideal Renaissance man" (Dhanavel 15) whose particular play, *Hayavadana* (literally meaning one with a horse's head) we are going to discuss.

Hayavadana, a play in two acts, is Karnad's third play. Originally written in Kannada, the play was an immediate success on the stage and received the prestigious Kamala Devi Chattopadhyay award of 1971. Like Samuel Beckett translating his own play from French into English (*En attendant Godot/ Waiting for Godot*) Girish Karnad, also inspired by the success of his play translated it into English retaining, however, the original title, *Hayavadana*. Originally published in *Enact*, it was published by Oxford University Press in 1975 in the New Drama in India series, and since then it has been performed in different translations and adaptations around the world with great success.

II

Hayavadana which literally means "one with a horse's head" (haya=horse; vadana=face; hayavadana=one with a horse's face/ head) is a novel kind of drama which remarkably combines tradition and modernity. The drama has one main plot and one subplot. The story of Hayavadana constitutes the subplot, while the main plot of transposed heads can be traced back to *Vetalpanchavimsati* which is part of a larger *Kathasaritsagara* of Soma Deva of the 11th century.

The stories in *Vetalpanchavimsati* and *Kathasaritsagara* are basically the same except some changes in place names and in the cast of the characters. The story is as follows: Prince Dhavala married Madansundari, the daughter of a king named Suddhapata, through the favour of goddess Gauri in a temple in the city of Shovabati. Then one day Svetapata, Suddhapata's son, proceeded to his own country along with his sister and her husband. On the way he came to another temple of goddess Gauri. Dhavala went into the temple to pay homage to the goddess. Through some irresistible urge he cut off his head with a sword which he chanced to see there, and presented it to the goddess. As Dhavala did not come out for quite sometime Svetapata went inside. When he saw that Dhavala had killed himself, he also cut off his own head and offered it to the goddess. Then Madanasundari, realizing that her husband and brother had gone away for a long time, went into the temple and saw their dead bodies lying before the goddess. She also decided to cut off her own head. Just when she was about to kill herself, the goddess appeared before her, prevented her from killing herself and promised to give her what she wanted. Madanasundari naturally requested her to revive her husband and brother. The goddess asked her to set their heads on their shoulders and through excitement she mixed up things. She joined her husband's head to her brother's shoulders and *vice versa.* When they came back to life Madanasundari realized her mistake. Vetal's question is: "Who is Madanasundari's husband?" The king answers: "Of course the person with Dhavala's head on his shoulders."

Girish Karnad, however, writes emphatically that "the central episode in the play—the story of Devadatta and Kapila—is based on a tale from *Kathasaritsagara* but I have heavily drawn on Thomas Mann's reworking of the tale in 'The Transposed Heads.'" A brief summary of the story "The Transposed Heads" is as follows:

Sridaman, a Brahmin by birth but Vaishnava by profession, and Nanda, a cowherd and blacksmith, are close friends. Sridaman falls in love with Sita whom he happens to see when the two friends are travelling together, and wants to marry her. Nanda laughs at the idea but agrees to act as a messenger for his friend. Sita accepts the proposal and marries Sridaman. Some months later when Sita, Sridaman and Nanda are all travelling together in a cart to the house of Sita's parents, they lose track, come across a temple of Kali, and take a halt. Sridaman visits the temple alone, and overcome by an irresistible urge offers himself to the goddess as a sacrifice. Nanda goes in search of his friend, finds what has happened and, afraid of the charge that he killed his friend because he was in love with Sita, and also because he does not want to live without his friend, kills himself. Sita realizes what has happened and prepares to hang herself. The goddess appears before her, chides her, and grants life to the dead bodies asking Sita to fix the severed heads on the respective shoulders. Sita in her excitement fixes the heads wrongly. Now the problem is: who is her husband? The hermit Kamdaman whose advice is sought decides in favour of Sridaman's head. Nanda's head (with Sridaman's body) therefore, decides to become a hermit. Sita is happy to have the best of both worlds. But gradually Sridaman's head begins to control Nanda's body and the body becomes refined. Sita begins to pine for Nanda so much that she sets out to meet him, carrying the young child Andhak with her. They spend the day and the night in heavenly bliss. Next morning Sridaman appears on the scene. He suggests that they should kill each other in a combat and that Sita should perform *sati.* Sita thinks that if she lives the life of a widow, Andhak's future will be doomed, but if she performed *Sati* Andhak would be a *sati's* son and his social image will improve. So she gives her consent and burns herself on the pyre of her two husbands.

Mann avoids the incestuous aspect but obviously acts on the solution offered by *Kathasaritsagara* that since the head represents the man, the person with the husband's head is the husband and brings his relentless logic to bear upon the solution. As Karnad points out:

> If the head is the determining limb then the body should change to fit the head. At the end of Mann's version the bodies have changed again and adjusted themselves to the heads so perfectly that the men are physically exactly as they were at the beginning. We are back to square one—the problem remains unsolved (Dodyia 32).

Mann writes the story of *Kathasaritsagara* to use it as a vehicle for the expression of his favourite idea of mind-body dualism and the ironic confrontation between opposites in human life. But Karnad's focus is on the psychological and sociological dimension of human desire for completeness, the unattainable complete happiness. So while on his own account Karnad broadly follows the outline of Mann's story, he introduces many changes both in the form and content to highlight the contemporary relevance of the story. The most important change, of course, is the change of form: from story to drama and the introduction of the subplot. Even in the story there are some minor changes, but it is quite significant the way Karnad has changed the names. Sridaman, Nanda and Sita of Mann have become Devadatta, Kapila and Padmini in the Karnad play. By changing the names Karnad has on the one hand been able to make them generic or representative and thus give them a sense of universality and timelessness. The name of Devadatta (given by gods) reveals the Apollonian aspects whereas Kapila (dark and therefore earthy) reveals Kapila's Dionysian tendencies. Padmini, like a lotus, seeks to be a delicate bridge between the earth and the sky. Rooted to the earth and the lower turned skyward, Padmini symbolizes the fundamental nature of the human body: it is torn between the downward earth and the upward sky, fury and mire of the blood and the spiritual aspirations. Furthermore, in order to project his vision Karnad has introduced a new character, Hayavadana, a man with a horse's head, to the story of the transposed heads. In his version Karnad, like Mann, avoids the incest theme that lies at the core of the *Vetalpanchavimsati* version. The story of Hayavadana introduces a subplot—an original invention of Karnad—and it is thematically integrated to the main plot, so far as the theme of the identity crisis is concerned. The very fact that the title of the play is derived from the subplot or the story of Hayavadana suggests its thematic importance, and it is Hayavadana who raises the identity question more dramatically and more authentically than anybody else in the play. The subplot enables Karnad to provide a double perspective to the problem, at the metaphysical level and at the socio-cultural level. Karnad, in other words, handles the moral problem in the main plot and the philosophical problem in the subplot.

While writing the play Karnad felt that it would take the shape of a folk drama chiefly because of the change of heads which could be easily managed on the stage with masks. Here a brief reference to the genesis of the play may be quite relevant. Karnad writes in this connection:

> By the late sixties any seminar you went to in India, the question was what to do with folk theatre and this problem was endlessly debated and people said this was relevant and this was not relevant, what to do with it etc. [...]. All this meant that folk theatre was very much in the air and one day I was telling the story of transposed heads to my friend B.V. Kamath. I said here was a beautiful story, and why don't we make film and he said why a film, it could make a marvelous theatre. The moment he said I knew it would make a very good play. So while one confesses that one went consciously to some of the folk theatre, Yakshagna and others, one cannot deny that Brecht as well as Badal Sarkar were haunting one, and that went some way in the shaping of *Hayavadana* (*IL* 1989:98-99).

Thus while *Hayavadana* ostensibly uses the folk form, Karnad assimilates into it the tradition of Indian classical drama, the Western dramatic conventions to convey his perception of contemporary reality and thus the play is suffused with modern sensibility: search for completeness and search for identity, existential anguish, the predicament of the liberated woman in the contemporary Indian society. As a result, the play reverberates with echoes of Indian classical drama, Freudian id,[1] Lacanian notions of desire and lack[2] and profuse use of symbols and symbolic episodes. The play opens with the offering of worship accompanied by singing to the Lord Ganesha. This is perfectly in keeping with the Indian classical tradition where in the beginning of a drama some god or goddess is invoked for blessing. In Yakshagna it is Lord Ganesha, the god of success that is invoked. At the beginning of the performance, a mask of Ganesha is brought on the stage and kept on the chair. *Pooja* is done. In this song Ganesha is addressed as "single tasked destroyer of incompleteness" (73). The choice of the elephant-headed god is significant because Lord Ganesha with human body and animal head properly suggests the central theme of incompleteness of being. Yet it is paradoxical that Lord Ganesha who seems to be an embodiment of imperfection is worshipped as the "destroyer of incompleteness." The Bhagavata rightly comments: "An elephant body, a broken tusk and a cracked belly—whichever way you look at it he seems to be an embodiment of imperfection, of incompleteness" (73). In this connection Karnad comments: "[...] the elephant head also questioned the basic assumption behind the original riddle: that the head represents the thinking part of the person, the intellect" (Dodyia 33). By invoking the Lord Ganesha and by attributing the pivotal role to the Ganesha myth in *Hayavadana* Karnad achieves an admirable equation which accommodates the classical and folk conventions within the frame of contemporary theatre strategies, and thus reconciles the tradition and the avant-garde into a harmonious whole.

The Bhagavata who introduces the story is the Yakshagna version of the Sutradhara or the stage manager of the classical Sanskrit drama. By using the Bhagavata Karnad conforms to the folk form of Yakshagna but the kind of role he assigns to the Bhagavata far outgrows the traditional role. However, in keeping with the folk tradition he narrates the story in the manner of a folk-tale: "Our duty is merely to pay homage to the elephant-headed god and get on with the play" (73), and he begins: "This is the city of Dharmapura, ruled by King Dharmasheela whose fame and empire have already reached the ends of the eight directions [...]" (73). The Bhagavata who is a godlike omnipresence in the play is involved intimately with every character. Like Tiresius he presides over the everyday reality that keeps turning into the problem of the play. He initiates the discussion and invites responses to the actions of the characters. He expresses sympathy for Kapila when he is forsaken by Devadatta and Padmini after the transposition. It is to the Bhagavata's charge that Padmini entrusts her baby before she performs *sati.* He takes charge of the play's opening when the Nata, frightened by a speaking Hayavadana, creates a commotion on the stage. He also decides the time when the half-curtain must be brought in or withdrawn, symbolic for a god who decides the amount of illusion to be purveyed. It must be pointed out, however, that although the Bhagavata of Yakshagna folk drama is modelled on the Sutradhara of classical drama there is a difference between the two. The Sutradhara in the classical Sanskrit drama does not play so much active role as the Bhagavata does. In fact, after appearing at the beginning of the play to invoke the blessing of gods and to conduct the formalities with the audience he is rarely seen on the stage. In contrast, the Bhagavata remains on the stage practically all the time and controls the action in a significant way. In Karnad's play, the Bhagavata becomes a Brechtian type of narrator, and this is not surprising because we have already pointed out that Brecht has been a major influence on Karnad. Brecht himself, however, drew heavily on the Eastern theatrical tradition.[3]

We have already noted that Karnad uses mask in the play. The first mask to be used is that of Ganesha. Later Devadatta, in the opening of the play appears on the stage wearing a pale coloured mask and Kapila a dark mask. Later in the play masks are transposed to indicate the transposition of heads. Kali appears in a terrible mask, and Hayavadana at first appears wearing the mask of a horse's head and later when he becomes a complete horse he wears the mask of a complete horse. About the use of mask Karnad writes:

> [...] the story initially interested me for the scope it gave for the use of mask and music. Western theatre has developed a contrast between the *face* and the *mask*—the real inner person and the exterior one presents, or wishes to present to the world outside. But in traditional

> Indian theatre the mask is only the face 'writ large': since a character presents not a complex psychological entity but an ethical identity, the mask merely presents in enlarged details its essential moral nature (Dodyia 32-33).

In this respect Karnad's use of mask has an interesting affinity with the mask in Japanese Noh plays.

Another important device drawn from the folk theatre tradition is the use of half-curtain. The stage direction in the very first Act runs like this:

> Two stage hands enter and hold up a half curtain, about six feet in height—the sort of curtain used in Yakshagna or Kathakali (77).

Half-curtain is used throughout the play as a very important stage prop. It is effective in the presentation of Hayavadana. By gradually bringing down the curtain, the horse is exposed and concealed a few times. In the meantime, the "all-knowing spectator" has moved in and out of illusion and reality by virtue of half-curtain. The fact that it can reveal and hide even as the spectator is all eye makes the half-curtain the most visible symbol of the play's theme. Thus Karnad while using the folk strategy of half-curtain modernizes it by giving it a symbolic significance like Virginia Woolf's, perception of life as "a semi-transparent envelope." In a play dealing with complex states of minds arising out of confused relationship, the half-curtain comes in very handy.

Incidentally Rabindranath Tagore, the Nobel laureate—who was engaged in a lifelong experimentation with dramatic form and its evolution in the Indian theatrical tradition—arrived at the conviction that painted sceneries often impaired the theatrical effect of a play. He wrote:

> Poetic drama lays a claim on the reader's imagination; sceneries reduce that claim. The loss is the spectators'. Acting is a forceful, vivacious, dynamic matter. The scenery is just the opposite. Unlawfully entering into its dynamics it remains mute, inert and static. It narrows

> down the imaginative vision of the spectator by putting a fence around it as it were. The practice of putting a scenery in a place which should be better filled by imagination is a new feature introduced in this industrial age. In our country, in the traditional *jatras* there may not be enough room for the crowd of spectators, but there is no dearth of room for imagination, because it is not constricted by scenery. That is why in a production where I have a say I don't allow the childish act of frequent shifting of scenes, because a painted scene is on the one hand a mockery of the realistic truth and on the other, is inimical to the realization of the ideational truth.
>
> [Introduction. *Tapati, Rabindra Racanabali* (Collected Works of Tagore) Calcutta: Govt. of West Bengal, 1961, Vol. 6, 1033-34].*

Unlike other Indian plays *Hayavadana* is a play where Karnad uses the female chorus. It is a notable innovation of Karnad and is quite congruent with the subject of the play which has for one of its themes the woman question. Karnad might have got the idea of the female chorus from Eliot's *Murder in the Cathedral* or even from Euripides, but he puts it to a completely different use. In Euripides's *Medea,* the chorus of Corinthian women is in sympathy with Medea and in *Murder in the Cathedral* the chorus sings its suffering and helplessness as Thomas Beckett is going to be murdered while in *Hayavadana* the chorus ironically celebrates Padmini's desire and voluntary death by fire. The chorus in *Hayavadana* is not the voice of traditional wisdom as in Greek plays but only an externalization and objectification of the passionate feelings of Padmini and it merges with the protagonist as an integral component of the character.

Some other important folk devices are the use of mime and the use of painted curtain. The action of the play is often mimed,

* Translation from Rabindranath Tagore's original Bengali into English is by the author of the present article.

for example when the three characters proceed to Ujjain, a cart does not really appear on the stage. We are just told: "Kapila followed by Padmini and Devadatta enter miming cart ride. Kapila is driving the cart." The play in fact is replete with instances of miming. But what is significant is that even this simple act of miming the cart-driving assumes symbolic significance when looked at from the Freudian angle. In other words, Padmini's comments on the occasion lend a symbolic significance to the cart-driving: "How beautifully you drive the cart, Kapila! Your hands do not even move, but the oxen seem to know where to go" (95). The sexual overtone of the remark cannot be missed. This is further reinforced by what follows:

> What a terrible road. Nothing but stones and rocks—but one didn't feel a thing in the cart! You drove it so gently—almost made it float. I remember when Devadatta took me in a cart—that was soon after our marriage—the oxen took everything except the road. He only had to pull to the right, and off they would rush to the left. I have never laughed so much in my life. But of course he got very angry, so we had to go home straight (96).

Once we break the sealed metaphor it becomes conspicuous that Padmini is comparing her coital experience with Devadatta which was a failure and unsatisfactory with her experience with Kapila which was perfect and gave her a sense of fulfilment. Naturally Padmini celebrates the body of Kapila. As Kapila climbs a tree to collect the Fortunate Lady's flower to please Padmini we see Kapila through the eyes of Padmini:

> How he climbs—like an ape. Before I could even say 'yes,' he had taken off his shirt, pulled his *dhoti* up and swung up the branch. And what an ethereal shape! Such a broad back—like an ocean its muscles rippling across it—and that small feminine waist which looks so helpless (96).

This celebration of the body reminds one of Lawrence. It is not for nothing Karnad uses animal imagery ("like an ape") and Padmini looks upon Kapila as "a Celestial Being reborn as a hunter." In the *Aside* Padmini admits: "No woman could resist him" and this is immediately echoed by Devadatta in his *Aside*: "No woman could resist him" (96). Devadatta realizes how passionately Padmini loves Kapila: "I see these flames leaping up from those depths [...]. Look at those yellow, purple flames. Look how she is pouring her soul into his mould." Thus through Karnad's masterly treatment, the scene becomes charged with sexuality and modern sensibility.

The simple story of *Vetalpanchavimsati* enables Karnad to see in it the seed of story of search for completeness. She would like to have both a strong body and a strong mind in her husband. So her careless mixing of the heads is seen by Karnad as an instinctual solution to the problem of incompleteness. In a bid to have a complete husband, as it were, she puts Devadatta's head on the body of Kapila. But to bring home his point Karnad introduces a subplot—the story of Hayavadana—which is a pathetic story of search for identity and search for completeness. Hayavadana tells the Bhagavata:

> My mother was the Princess of Karnataka. She was a very beautiful girl. When she came of age, her father decided that she should choose her own husband. So princes of every kingdom of the world were invited—and they all came. From China, from Persia, from Africa. But she didn't like any one of them. The last one to come was the prince of Araby. My mother took one look at that handsome prince sitting on his great white stallion—and she fainted [...]. Her father at once decided that this was the man. All arrangements for the wedding were made. My mother woke up and do you know what she said? [...] She said she would only marry the horse! [...] Yes, she wouldn't listen to anyone [...]. No one could dissuade her. So ultimately she was married off to the white stallion. She lived with him for fifteen years. One morning she wakes up—and no horse! In its place stood a beautiful Celestial Being, a *gandharva*. Apparently this Celestial Being had been cursed by the god Kuvera to be born a horse for some act of misbehaviour. After fifteen

> years of human love he had become his original self again [...]. Released from his curse, he asked my mother to accompany him to his Heavenly Abode. But she wouldn't. She said she would come only if he became a horse again. So he cursed her [...]. He cursed her to become a horse herself. So my mother became a horse and ran away happily. My father went back to his Heavenly Abode. Only I—the child of their marriage—was left behind (79-80).

Now coming back to this brief story of Hayavadana. Karnad tells the story in the manner of a folk-tale where curse and transformation are quite common. But as Bhagavata says, "It's a sad story" and the Actor also confirms, "Very sad," and Hayavadana appeals to them: "You must help me to become a complete man," the story acquires a new dimension: existential anguish. The mother of Hayavadana, the Princess of Karnataka, might be happy with a horse—and this also has a strong sexual overtone—evident in the fact that after becoming a horse she ran away "happily"—but the story of Hayavadana is the story not only of an abandoned child but also of one whose identity is endangered. He is neither a horse nor a man, and he wants to be a complete man. Hayavadana says he tried everything to "accept his fate" and took interest in the social life of the nation, Civics, Politics, Patriotism, Nationalism, Internationalism, but everywhere he has been a misfit because he has no society. While Karnad satirizes the contemporary politics through a carnival-esque treatment of Hayavadana's various enterprises, he also does not miss the opportunity to express his atheism—another important modern sensibility—through this pathetic figure. When the Bhagavata tells Hayavadana that he should go to Benaras and "make a vow in front of the god there" Hayavadana rattles out names of various places sacred to different religions, where he had gone but in vain. His search for completeness took him to all kinds of saints as well but all this came to nothing. Thus through an ironic presentation of Hayavadana's enterprises Karnad demonstrates his rejection of gods and godmen and his avowed atheism. Karnad admits: "I was an atheist and am still one. But my atheism stemmed from resolute ideological stance. Sartre's atheism was very much in vogue then [...]. Relationship between God and men has been one of my preoccupations in my play" (*TL* 1995:128). The demystification of religious beliefs and practices—which must be seen as a reflection of modern sensibility is at its highest in *Hayavadana*. Lord Ganesha is presented as a symbol of incompleteness and imperfection. Hayavadana's authentic experiences of wasteful pilgrimage only reveal the sham and hypocrisy of religious ritual. Karnad's treatment of Kali is no better. In the first place when Padmini visits her temple she is just sleeping, and she wakes up only when Padmini's turn for suicide comes. The goddess puts all the three characters into great suffering on account of confused relationship and finally drives them to death. And when Hayavadana comes to her temple to pray for becoming complete man, she does not wait for Hayavadana to complete the sentence. "Make me complete man," and Hayavadana, ironically, becomes a complete horse.

> She said 'So be it' and disappeared even before I could say 'Make me a complete man.' I became a complete horse (36).

But that is not what he wanted. Unlike his mother he wanted to become a complete man and he became a complete horse on account of the capricious behaviour of the goddess. The sarcastic treatment of the divinities arising out of Karnad's atheism makes a significant departure from the classical and folk tradition of theatre and makes it eminently modern. The simple story of Betal becomes a rich complex story of modern sensibility in which the Lacanian notions of desire and lack, Freudian id, Sartrian existentialism and atheism, Brechtian expressionism and Strindbergian symbolism, Bakhtinian carnivalization and feminism and above all search for identity and completeness are all fused in a harmonious whole. The theatrical conventions of classical drama and folk drama, particularly Yakshagna, are ostensibly used, and they are made dramatically functional in projecting the fabric of Karnad's perception of modern existence. The form is traditional and the content is modern and Hayavadana is a play that remarkably reconciles tradition and the avant-garde as much in its structure as in its texture. In this connection, the very pertinent observations of Victor Turner are worth noting:

> Theatre is one of the many inheritors of that great multifaceted system of preindustrial ritual which embraces ideas and images of cosmos and chaos, interdigitates clowns and their foolery with gods and their solemnity, and uses all the sensory codes to produce symphonies in more than music: the intertwining of dance, body languages of many kinds, song, chant, architectural forms (temples, amphitheatres), incense burnt offerings, ritualized feasting and drinking, painting, body painting, body marking of many kinds, including circumcision and scarification, the application of lotions and drinking of potions, the enacting of mythic and heroic plots drawn from oral traditions (65).

NOTES

1. The mistake in the transposition of the heads of Devadatta and Kapila can be explained in terms of Freudian slip activated by id. In other words, the subconscious desire for Kapila's body makes Padmini put, albeit unconsciously, the head of Devadatta on Kapila's body. Furthermore, the 'mistake' also absolves her of the responsibility of transgressing the codified morality of her society.
2. Always in a state of lack, the Lacanian subject is engaged in a constant struggle for unity, completeness, fulfilment. The desire for recognition fuels the search for completeness and that precisely is one of the main themes, if not the central theme of *Hayavadana.*
3. In this connection Balwant Gargi writes in *Theatre in India* (New York, 1962):

   Among contemporary Western producers Bertolt Brecht borrowed much from Eastern theatrical traditions, used music, mime, stylization, and by mixing them with the vigorous realism of the West created his Epic Theatre, full of intensity, poetry, earthy speech and song, a theatre larger than life (235).

WORKS CITED

Dhanavel, P. *The Indian Imagination of Girish Karnad: Essays on Hayavadana.* New Delhi: Prestige Books, 2000.

Dodyia, J.S. (Ed.). *The Plays of Girish Karnad: Critical Perspectives.* New Delhi: Prestige Books, 1991. Cited as Dodyia.

Karnad, Girish. "Acrobating between the Traditional and the Modern." *Indian Literature,* March 1989: 85-89. Cited as *IL* 1989.

___. "Girish Karnad as the Playwright: A Discussion" by U.R. Anantha Murthy, Prasanna and Girish Karnad, *Indian Literature,* September-October 1995: 127-40. Cited as *IL* 1995.

——. Interview, "Performance, Meaning and the Materials of Modern Indian Theatre" by Aparna Dhanvadkar, *New Theatre Quarterly,* November 1995. Cited as *NTQ.*

___. Introduction. *Three Plays: Nag Mandala, Hayavadana, Tughlaq.* New Delhi: Oxford UP, 1995. All the references to *Hayavadana* are to this text.

Mann, Thomas. "The Transposed Heads." *Stories of a Lifetime,* Vol. 2, 214-87. London: Mercury Books, 1961.

Turner, Victor. "Are There Universals of Performance in Myth, Ritual and Drama?" *Modern Theories of Drama* (Ed. Brandt, George W.). Oxford: Clarendon Press, 1998.

Contributors

Dr Ashok Kumar Bachchan, Reader in English. L.N. Mithila University, Darbhanga, Bihar.

Dr Mallikarjun Patil, Lecturer in English, Gulbarga University, Gulbarga, Karnataka.

Dr Basavaraj Naikar, Professor and Chairman, Department of English, Karnataka University, Dharwad, Karnataka.

Dr Marie Fernandes, St Andrews College, Visiting Lecturer at University of Mumbai, Mumbai, Maharashtra.

Dr Usha Rani, Reader in English, Department of Evening Studies, Panjab University, Chandigarh (UT).

Dr Suman Jana, Reader in English, Vivekananda Mahavidyalaya, Burdwan, West Bengal.

Dr M.Q. Khan, Former Vice-Chancellor, Berhampore University and Professor of English, Ravenshaw College, Cuttack, Orissa.

Prof. Sobha Chattopadhyay, Professor and Head of the Department of English, Jadavpur University, Calcutta, West Bengal.

Dr Qamar Talat, Senior Assistant Professor of English, Government Arts and Science College, Durg, Chhattisgarh.

Suka Joshua, Department of English, Lady Doak College, Madurai, Tamil Nadu.

Dr N. Sharada Iyer, Reader and Head Department of English, Vasanta College for Women, Rajghat Fort, Varanasi, Uttar Pradesh.

Dr Santosh Chakrabarti, Guest Lecturer in English, Rabindra Bharati University, Kolkata, West Bengal.

Anurag Chauhan, Lecturer in English, Department of English, Guru Ghasidas University, Bilaspur, Madhya Pradesh.

Dr Mohit K. Ray, Professor of English, Dept. Burdwan University, Burdwan, West Bengal.